Washington Irving's Critique of American Culture

Washington Irving's Critique of American Culture

Sketching a Vision of World Citizenship

J. Woodrow McCree

LEXINGTON BOOKS
Lanham • Boulder • New York • London

Published by Lexington Books
An imprint of The Rowman & Littlefield Publishing Group, Inc.
4501 Forbes Boulevard, Suite 200, Lanham, Maryland 20706
www.rowman.com

6 Tinworth Street, London SE11 5AL, United Kingdom

Copyright © 2021 The Rowman & Littlefield Publishing Group, Inc.

All rights reserved. No part of this book may be reproduced in any form or by any electronic or mechanical means, including information storage and retrieval systems, without written permission from the publisher, except by a reviewer who may quote passages in a review.

British Library Cataloguing in Publication Information Available

Library of Congress Cataloging-in-Publication Data on File

ISBN 978-1-7936-1961-7 (cloth)
ISBN 978-1-7936-1963-1 (pbk)
ISBN 978-1-7936-1962-4 (electronic)

Contents

List of Illustrations		vii
Preface		ix
1	Style with Substance	1
2	Satire in the Name of World Citizenship	37
3	The Picturesque Aesthetic and Neoclassical/Romantic Boundary Crossing	63
4	American Ovid, American Virgil, American Claude, and Pumpkin Smasher	99
5	Irving's Critique of American Culture in "The Legend of Sleepy Hollow"	123
6	World Citizenship on Frontiers Near and Far	149
Bibliography		173
Index		181
About the Author		183

List of Illustrations

Cover: Thomas Cole, *The Mountain Ford*, 1846, Metropolitan Museum of Art.

Figure 1.1	Thomas Cole, *A Wild Scene*, 1831–1832, Baltimore Museum of Art.	11
Figure 2.1	William Sidney Mount, *Eel Spearing at Setauket*, 1845, Fenimore Art Museum.	51
Figure 3.1	Claude Lorrain, *Rest on the Flight into Egypt*, early 1640s, Cleveland Museum of Art.	74
Figure 3.2	Worthington Whittredge, *On the Cache de La Poudre River*, 1871, Amon Carter Museum.	77
Figure 3.3	Washington Allston, *Landscape with a Lake*, 1804, Boston Museum of Fine Arts.	87
Figure 4.1	Richard Wilson, *The Destruction of the Children of Niobe*, 1760, Yale Center for British Art.	101
Figure 5.1	Albert Pinkham Ryder, *The Race Track (Death on a Pale Horse)*, 1896, Cleveland Museum of Art.	133
Figure 5.2	Asher Durand, *Early Morning at Cold Spring*, 1850, Montclair Museum of Art.	141
Figure 5.3	Thomas Cole, *River in the Catskills*, 1843, Boston Museum of Fine Arts.	143
Figure 6.1	William Sidney Mount, *The Power of Music*, 1847, Cleveland Museum of Art.	154
Figure 6.2	George Caleb Bingham, *Fur Traders Descending the Missouri*, 1845, Metropolitan Museum of Art.	160
Figure 6.3	George Catlin, *Osage Warrior, Tal-Lee*, 1834, Smithsonian Institution.	167

Preface

In the spring of 2016, I took a trip to the Cleveland Museum of Art and was enthralled by the nineteenth-century American galleries. The combination of Thomas Cole's *Schroon Mountain* and Frederic Edwin Church's *Twilight in the Wilderness* was sufficient to realign my research and teaching interests, which had previously been oriented around ancient gnosticism, philosophy of religion, Hellenistic philosophy, and virtue ethics. As it turned out, my training in Hellenistic philosophy, initially necessary for understanding Christian gnosticism, was also relevant for understanding Irving. As a result of the fortuitous trip to Cleveland, I began research on Thomas Cole, the Hudson River School, and other American romantics such as Washington Allston. I was reading widely on Jeffersonian and Jacksonian era history, art, and literature to set them in a context. Initially, my study of Irving began as context for understanding Cole. However, because romantic art and literature were so intertwined in the United States and abroad, I realized that the romantic art of the period might also prove useful in setting Washington Irving in his own context. This is especially so because Irving had several close friendships with American artists while he was abroad, and he maintained those friendships when he returned to the United States.[1] When Irving was abroad, he built close friendships with the American romantic artist Washington Allston, American ex-patriot Charles Robert Leslie, Sir Walter Scott, the American painter Gilbert Stuart Newton, the Scottish artist David Wilkie, as well as the Irish poet Moore, who wrote the biography of Lord Byron. As Irving's biographer Stanley Williams has pointed out, Irving was himself very good at sketching, as he spent time with this group of artists from 1817 to 1819. They acknowledged his skill, and around the time he resolved to embrace a life of writing, he began to wonder if the art of sketching might be converted to a literary form by means of a verbal sketch of people and cultural landscapes.[2]

Thus was born the conception for *The Sketch Book of Geoffrey Crayon, Gent.*, now a full 200 years old.

I was initially interested in the study of Irving because passages in *A History of New York*, "Rip Van Winkle," and "The Legend of Sleepy Hollow" shared the deep distrust of rapid change in an industrializing mercantile society that was so deeply felt by Thomas Cole. However, as I proceeded in romantic studies, I found that much in Irving belonged as much to the eighteenth century as to the nineteenth. However, much of the scholarship on Irving has tendency to assume that this eighteenth-century background was more a matter of style than substance. Nothing could be further from the truth. The eighteen century was an age that, at its best, championed empathy, world citizenship, and the universality of the human condition. These are matters of substance and Washington Irving internalized them. I also found that many scholars tend to treat Irving in unnecessarily harsh ways, seeing him as little more than a plagiarizer and a "romantic light" who was for the most part adrift in a transatlantic identity crisis. While it is true that Irving was not a romantic in the same sense as Wordsworth or Coleridge, he had enough substance of his own in his unique fusion of eighteenth- and nineteenth-century ethics and aesthetics. Washington Irving fused the ethic of world citizenship with the love of picturesque travel and the love of diverse persons and cultures, including mixed identities. In more ways than one, Irving straddled the boundary line between classicizing and romanticizing modes. In an era of scholarship when liminality is studied and appreciated in so many ways, Irving's own unique capacity for crossing boundaries and forging a uniquely diplomatic identity should be more appreciated than it is. He supported the healing of the young Republic's relationship with England, he valued French and Spanish culture, and he advocated in his writings for a genuinely multicultural America with room for Dutch Americans, African Americans, Creoles, Native Americans, and mixed-raced persons. The one thing he did not want was a predominantly Anglo-Saxon Yankee civilization, and against this chauvinistic monoculture he launched a consistent critique and offered an alternative vision.

I will refer to several artworks from the period, or a couple which were influential upon it, such as paintings by Claude Lorraine or Richard Wilson. I will also discuss nineteenth-century American artists contemporary to Irving's body of work, such as Thomas Cole, William Sidney Mount, and George Caleb Bingham. When I do so, I am not claiming direct influence between writer and artist in either direction. Rather, I am seeing these works together as expressive of the tensions of an age, and, as such, they can shed light upon one another. The relationship is a matter of "affinity," not "influence," to use a phrase coined by Barbara Novak.[3] Sometimes similar images or themes emerge independently of one another as part of a large spirit of the age. Irving was first and foremost a student of human character, with all its dignity and foibles. His artistic friends in England tended overwhelmingly to paint scenes of human interest, such as pictures of merry old England, historical Spanish military heroes returning through the mountains, and often humorous scenes from Shakespeare or Don Quixote. Thus, it is not surprising that some of the most illuminating insights about Irving in his American context come from genre painters who were contemporary with Thomas Cole and Frederick Edwin Church.[4]

I have chosen Thomas Cole's *The Mountain Ford* as the cover for this book. It is a ruggedly picturesque landscape that borders on sublimity, with the kind of human interest that Irving tended to love in a painting. A very steep, protrusive mountain half-dome looms high in the middle background against a crisp, cloudless sky. To the right is a giant gnarly tree with sycamore-like blotchy bark on the massive trunk, twisting branches and large, prominent thick curved roots clinging to the riverside. A rider on a white horse comes to a ford in the mountain stream, and a few small boulders hint at a path across the potentially dangerous passage, whose white-capped ripples can be seen churning around the rocks. On the opposite side of the stream, a row of trees is much lower that the colossal tree behind the rider. There are several rocks and storm-broken dead branches that protrude over the edge of the river. The mountain ford and the pool of water are dark on such a crystal blue day, caught in the shadow of the massive mountain dome. The rocks and dead branches opposite the ford are reflected in the dark water. The horse starts back instinctively as horse and rider come to momentary pause—how best should one cross this stream? The painting is evocative of romantic psychic depths; there is no storm in the sky but there is a dark cloud in the river, or is it in the rider's heart? What is the true obstacle and how shall it be overcome? Perhaps the passage is death; perhaps it is an unresolved turmoil in the psyche of the rider or viewer.

I have chosen this painting to introduce a book on Irving's critique and vision of American culture, because Irving has a way of putting his thumb just on such points of hidden anxiety in American culture—the potentially dangerous or at least difficult crossings that we must all come to when we examine ourselves or our civilization. There is something troubling here. The horse must start back at the first encounter with the dark pool and the questionable footing ahead. Irving had a knack for poking into the heart of American anxieties, many of which revolved around issues of race and ethnicity. He was a vivid storyteller, and sometimes he used language we now consider racist. However, he was a person of immense empathy, and often his vivid language was intended to poke and lure us into an engagement with issues with which we still find not entirely comfortable; yet, he generally incorporated a very sympathetic portrait of so many people regarded as "other" in American civilization. "The less said, the better," he remarks at one telling, yet evasive, point in *A History of New York*. And yet Irving does say something that can speak to us still, not only about the restless nature of American culture, but about the highly textured human and natural landscape that renders the United States truly picturesque in the strongest sense of the word, with it celebration of immense diversity—mountain eminences, grand old trees, prairies, forests, openings that lead to wide vistas, and an almost endless array of non-Anglo-Saxon protagonists and sympathetically portrayed secondary characters.

Chapter 1 lays out the historiography of major trends in Irving scholarship since the 1930s, and it introduces the Cynic philosophers' concept of world citizenship that was so central to Washington Irving. Chapter 2 explores his early satire in the name of world citizenship, with attention to his critique of the abuse of Native Americans and Quakers, as well as his picture of African American communities in the Dutch period. Chapter 3 takes up the nature of picturesque art and travel, and the importance of his relationship with the American romantic Washington Allston. Chapter 4 follows up on the aesthetics with an exploration of Irving's success as an artist who provided historical continuity for American civilization as an American Ovid and Virgil; he was especially successful in creating a unique atmospheric sensibility for New York, just as the French artist Claude Lorraine created an enduring sense of Italian skies and light. I also note that in his atmospheric display he consistently subverted the category of the sublime in favor of a storied picturesque landscape. Chapter 5 takes up Irving's critique of American culture in "The Legend of Sleepy Hollow" and other stories by Diedrich Knickerbocker. In chapter 6, I explore his love of cultural and ecological diversity in the American West, a place where his philosophy of world citizenship surfaced quite clearly, and showed him to be essentially the same person who wrote *A History of New York*, though speaking in the mode of travel literature rather than burlesque history. For someone who has so frequently been described as adrift, aimless, and unstable, he had a remarkable number of consistencies across his literary career.

This study ranges from Irving's travel journals and letters from his European Tour in 1804 to the *History* of 1809 to *A Tour on the Prairie* of 1835, the last major nonhistorical work where he was clearly speaking in his own voice. *Astoria* continued his interest in the exploration of the American west. His beloved nephew Pierre Irving researched John Jacob Astor's documents and pulled them together into a workable pile, and Irving finished it, editing for both style and insight. It is still possible to recognize his voice in many passages, and I cite *Astoria* when it is clearly consistent with the voice proven to be his in more well-known writings. *The Adventures of Captain Bonneville*, however, was not truly written by Irving; it was merely polished, and it will not be used as a source of Irving's thought. He says in the introduction that the text is largely Captain Bonneville's, and I take him at his word.

As for editions, it is best, when possible, to use the text established in the Twayne series, The Complete Works of Washington Irving. This series will be used when possible, and it shall be designated CW after the first reference in the endnotes and bibliography. The one important exception is *A History of New York*, where the original 1809 version is found in the Library of America edition, and his substantial revisions are found in the Twayne edition of the 1848 authorized edition. Comparison of the two is quite illuminating. For understanding his earliest artistic self-conception, the 1809 version is more important. Most passages I cite are the same in both editions, but a couple are found in only one, and I point them out, as well as their significance. Interlibrary loan, where I live, was shut down for over six months due to the COVID virus, and I have had to make due with Library of America for *Bracebridge Hall* and *Tales of a Traveller, Astoria*, and *The Alhambra*.

I am especially grateful to scholars who have gone before me in an interdisciplinary mode, exploring the relationship between romantic art and literature, and appreciating Irving as a transatlantic figure, not as someone who failed to be adequately American. Such scholars include Donald Ringe, Joy Casson, Paul Giles, Andrew Hemingway, Allan Wallach,[5] and most recently H. Daniel Peck.[6] I am also grateful to Tracy Hoffman and the Irving Society for giving such a warm welcome to a new scholar at the 2019 conference in Boston, and to Professor Hoffman especially for providing very helpful insights regarding the first draft of the book. The paper that I presented at the ALA conference in Boston was offered in commemoration of the 200th anniversary of "The Legend of Sleepy Hollow." Hopefully, this monograph will contribute to a renewed appreciation of Irving's body of work after almost a hundred years of belittling by scholars who have found Irving overly sentimental and insufficiently engaged with the heart of human darkness that seemed so glaring to authors and critics after World War I initiated the modernist era. Irving did indeed explore the darkness of the human heart, but he poked at it playfully and diplomatically, and with a good humor that enabled people to laugh at their own folly rather than declare an insurmountable existential crisis.

Many thanks to the Librarians of State College of Florida Manatee-Sarasota, especially Theresa Ennis-Smith at Venice, and Caroline Zaput at Bradenton. I am grateful also to the administration of SCF for allowing me a sabbatical to finish the revision of this book and begin a work on Thomas Cole. Thanks also to SCF and USF English literature graduate and writing advisor Caleb Jordan for feedback along the way.

NOTES

1. In New York City, Knickerbocker writers and American artists often met for dinner and literary conversation in the Sketch Club, based on the precedent of the Bread and Cheese Club that James Fenimore Cooper founded. A typical topic in 1830 was "The Sublime" and it led to a clever joint composition. Irving was abroad when the Sketch Club was founded, and quickly went west when he returned to the United States in 1832. See James T. Callow, *Kindred Spirits: Knickerbocker Writers and American Artists, 1807–1855* (Durham: University of North Carolina Press, 1967), 11–29, 38–44.

2. Stanley T. Williams, *The Life of Washington Irving*, Vol. I (New York and London: Oxford University Press, 1935), 156–65.

3. Barbara Novak, *Nature and Culture: American Landscape and Painting, 1825–1875*, 3rd edition (Oxford and New York: Oxford University Press, 2007), 204–8.

4. Given Irving's reactions to artwork on his European tour and through his letters across his life, it is unlikely that Irving would have ever been interested in pure landscape; rather he was always drawn to works with a striking human component, whether comic, romantic, or religious.

5. Alan Wallach has been especially gracious and helpful in personal correspondence as I tried to sort out questions about the relation of Irving to Cole, a topic which will be explored more in a forthcoming work.

6. Dr. Peck is more an expert on Cooper than Irving, but he does interdisciplinary work comparing American art and literature, most recently with an excellent book on Thomas Cole's Catskill Creek paintings, discussed in chapter 5.

Chapter 1

Style with Substance

Washington Irving has the distinction of being the first American author widely read abroad, first with *A History of New York* in 1809, speaking in the persona of Diedrich Knickerbocker, and then with the 1819–1920 publication of *The Sketch Book of Geoffrey Crayon, Gent*. With Knickerbocker's *History*, he won the admiration of Sir Walter Scott,[1] and *The Sketch Book* won high praise from no less than Lord Byron himself.[2] With the complete publication of *The Sketch Book* to immediate praise on both sides of the Atlantic in 1820, the question posed by British critic Sydney Smith, "In the four quarters of the globe, who reads an American book?" was now preliminarily answered, though a heated debate about the virtues and vices of American literature and culture would continue in the British press into the 1850s.[3] Through his own lifetime and far into the nineteenth century, Irving was beloved to the citizens of the American Republic, both for his storytelling wit and for putting the United States on the literary world stage, though he also faced immediate and ongoing criticism for being too dependent on English models.[4] Emerson, with his emphasis on self-reliance, characteristically described Irving as one who "lacks nerve and dagger," and H.L. Menken dismissed him as an "Anglomaniac,"[5] an accusation that is without basis if one simply reads *The Alhambra* or *A Tour of the Prairies*. As Joy Casson summarizes the situation, "From the nineteenth century to the present, some of the most energetic and articulate critics of the arts have been passionately committed to the idea of American exceptionalism"; in view of this bias toward the uniquely American, "works of major American figures have often been dismissed as aesthetically inferior, imitative, and uninteresting."[6]

Despite criticism that began from 1820 onward, Irving was universally acclaimed as one of the finest living prose writers in English for over 30 years.[7] However, when it came time for American scholars to define what was American about American art and literature, Irving was especially seen to come up short.[8] As William Hedges has explained it,

> As the study of American literature apart from English literature became a respected discipline in the first half of this century, Irving's interest in Europe and the European past was used as a way of distinguishing him from writers alleged to be more truly "American."[9]

The question of American self-definition was, and is, a legitimate one.[10] However, scholarship in the 1980s–1990s raised acute awareness of colonial ideologies, and a broader tendency toward social analysis in emerging market economies, awareness of social class, the impacts of marginalization, and an interest in liminal states where boundary definition is blurred. These trends remain prominent across many disciplines.[11] It is clear that too much focus on the Americanness of American literature, especially when it results in the marginalization of those who do not fit into approved categories, is itself an expression of nationalism. Of course, with the new awareness of social status and its aesthetic boundary-markers, Irving's quasi-aristocratic gentility has not endeared him to critics in the social analysis schools of thought; the dismissiveness that initially arose from the perception he was not sufficiently American has been reinforced by the accurate perception of an aristocratic, or Federalist-Whig, sensibility in his work. The irony of the situation is that one of America's original literary boundary-crossers is now undervalued. My own perspective is that we need to move beyond facile categorizations of people such as Irving in the time of the early Republic, see him in the trans-Atlantic context that renders his work intelligible, and, in doing so, better appreciate the insights he had about American culture.[12]

Irving's work overall may be considered a "genial meeting ground"[13] between neoclassical and romantic modes of expression. Rudiger Safranski, in his portrait of German romanticism, demonstrates why the Enlightenment rationality could never be enough for an antiquarian such as Irving: "Reason in fact proved tyrannical in its tendency to seek a tabula rasa, to do away with traditions, attachments, customs, in short with the whole history in which people are enveloped."[14] The excesses of this so-called reason were illustrated most vividly in the iconoclasm of the French Revolution, a destruction which Irving abhorred.[15] The broader import of such a severance of the past, whether in the name of political liberty or science, is that it leaves you without a sense of grounded connection to the world. Is it this loss of connection that romanticism attempted to address, and that is why Irving had to be a romantic, even as he retained many qualities of Enlightenment thought seen in figures ranging from Joseph Addison and Alexander Pope to Oliver Goldsmith. Stanley Williams acknowledged that Irving was more than just an Enlightenment wit in the mold of the English eighteenth century; he also deeply engaged with Byron, Scott, and Moore both before and after he arrived in England a second time in 1815:

> Irving was already, it may be said, a superficial romantic, a lover of the grace and even splendor of old traditions and old ways. If he lacked the sweep of Scott and Byron, he was, nevertheless, nearer to their attitude than that of the eighteenth century "village school." When he arrived in England, he was a romantic in this restricted sense; and the restrictions were unhappily to persist, leaving him dead to the deeper impulses of Romanticism.[16]

The depth of Irving's lifelong friendship with Washington Allston suggests Irving's romanticism may not have been so shallow as Williams and others have supposed. Irving met Coleridge through Washington Allston, and he heard some of Coleridge's poems read over dinner in their circle of literary and artistic friends around 1818. Washington Allston and Samuel Taylor Coleridge were kindred spirits in creating a kind of grand Unitarian romantic theology. Irving was simply not interested in crafting a religious vision at this time, and it is perhaps unfair to say he was only a superficial romantic because he was not interested in their theological project. The themes of time and decay that Irving wrestled with in *The Sketch Book* were in fact the same as those of Shelley in "Ozymandias" and of Thomas Cole in his epic series of paintings, *The Course of Empire*.[17] In spite of Williams's exaggeration of Irving's shallowness, he was correct that Irving's writing was a fusion of themes and styles from the eighteenth and nineteenth centuries. Irving was a straddler of worlds, a hybrid figure, and this hybridity gave him an empathy for other people who were mixed or marginalized in one way or another.

TOO ENGLISH?

The claim that Irving was too English is helpfully addressed by Joy Casson. In a brief history of how Irving found himself as a writer between 1817 and 1820, Casson emphasizes the crisis entailed by the bankruptcy of the family import business in Liverpool in the aftermath of the War of 1812. Irving was shamed and shaken by the stigma of this loss, and he would not return to the United States until he could do so on his own terms as a self-supporting writer. He was not abandoning America at the first opportunity after the war; he was trying to find a way to return to New York without the shame of being a dependent even as his other friends from home moved on with successful careers and marriages.[18] A visit with Sir Walter Scott in 1817 helped him find an inner resolution to become a professional writer, and he discovered a kind of "citadel within."[19] Nevertheless, Irving recognized the need for literary models, even as he explored themes of mutability and fallen greatness in the English wanderings of Geoffrey Crayon in *The Sketch Book*. "As Irving emphasized again and again in his letters, he saw his period of literary apprenticeship in Europe as a prelude to an eventual homecoming."[20] Indeed, a kind of homecoming structure is found in three of Irving's works that are often deemed too European. The first installment of "sketches" that Irving sent to the publisher in 1819 began with the voyage to England and ended with "Rip Van Winkle: A Posthumous Writing of Diedrich Knickerbocker," the old Dutch scholar persona he had used in *A History of New York*. The final installment of *The Sketch Book* ended with "The Legend of Sleepy Hollow (Found among the Papers of the late Diedrich Knickerbocker)." Likewise, *Bracebridge Hall* ended with the two-part New York story of "Dolph Heyligen" and "The Storm Ship," and *Tales of a Traveller* ends with "The Money Diggers," a collection of Hells Gate and Long Island short stories also found in the papers of Diedrich Knickerbocker. While this pattern could be seen as a clever marketing device to appease an American audience that perhaps worried that he was forgetting them, Kasson's study suggests that such a pattern of voyage and return indicates a resolve on Irving's part to find his voice by engaging the greatest writers in England—as well as the German folktales recommended by Sir Walter Scott—and then turn back and address the American scene with an established voice. The purpose of my own work is to explore what Irving has to say about American culture. The length of his stay in Europe may imply some ambiguity about American culture, but Kasson is correct that there was a firm resolve and an intelligible strategy in his decision to stay abroad once he had resolved the bankruptcy of the family business.

Perhaps the best response to the claim that Irving was not really an adequately American voice—because he spent too much time abroad discussing English and Spanish places and characters—is found in an important study by Jeffrey Rubin-Dorsky. Rubin-Dorsky argues that Irving's long search for identity abroad was expressive of distinctly American anxiety in the early nineteenth century. In 1816, travel overseas was possible not only because of the end of the War of 1812, but also the nearly simultaneous end of the Napoleonic Wars. Many Americans jumped at the opportunity, but they did so with an excess of baggage. The people of this generation were acutely aware that they were the sons and daughters of the heroic founders of a classic era in American history. Despite expansive opportunities in a new Republic with lessened British interference in American life, there was a painful awareness that they might easily lose the community spirit of the founders. Indeed, this seemed to be happening as people turned to private, materialistic interest rather than the public good.[21] Irving expressed, in his

Journals and in *The Sketch Book*, a kind of "homelessness" that was characteristic of the age, which explains why his wistfully moody confessions were so popular. He was not the only one who felt it, and he expressed the temperament of a whole generation of Americans: "He belonged to no real place in time. . . . Only in the realm of imagination, the world of timelessness, could the pilgrim find the order and continuity, the wholeness and harmony, that had become his grail." Irving's stories such as "Rip Van Winkle" and "Sleepy Hollow" and even *The Alhambra* were popular with Americans not only because they hallowed American places with dreamy historic memories, but because he "essentially reenacted their doubts about identity and their fantasies about escape. In this respect he was a truly representative American author . . . Americans sought along with him not only a release from the oppressive realities of a materialistic society, but, as well, a source of continuity to replace the one that was fast becoming historically obsolete."[22]

Because Irving drew heavily on eighteenth-century modes of writing, it is widely supposed that he is nothing but a literary stylist, pleasantly superficial, but without substance.[23] Indeed, his favorite writer was Oliver Goldsmith, the most widely read author in the United States around 1800, along with Alexander Pope.[24] The most devastating and influential critique of Irving along these lines was that of Stanley T. Williams, who argued that Irving was "a 'superficial romantic' who 'loved scraps of culture' instead of 'erudition,'" and whose use of old folk traditions to vent his unstable, sentimental moods amounted to nothing more than "pilferings."[25] Williams, in his 1935 masterwork, branded Irving with a denunciation that would be repeated for almost a century, to the point of becoming a cliché among scholars who sometimes don't even bother to read Irving closely. Williams acknowledged the excellence of Irving's writing but relegated his skill to a matter of mere style rather than substance. Hawthorn, he notes, was "at one time enamored of" *The Sketch Book*, but "Emerson always thought Irving weak," and yet lesser writers continued to follow Geoffrey Crayon's example; "Unexpectedly its spirit appeared in quite alien books. It had in succeeding decades an inspirational strength at variance with its own frail substance, and in some minor ways this power is not yet vanished."[26] Williams also asserted that Irving was "a champion of" the concept of "literature" as mere "escape through sentiment,"[27] a point that Rubin-Dorsky explored more extensively. Apparently, in the aftermath of World War I, and in the middle of the Great Depression, the highest literary crime was to be a sentimentalist—an unforgivable sin which would obliterate all other accomplishments in the eyes of twentieth-century posterity. Only the darkness of Hawthorne, Poe, and Melville would suffice in the new era of modernism. Ralph Aderman summarizes Williams's assessment of Irving thus: He "was a gifted but unoriginal writer" who "recast the ideas of others into pleasing prose and well-turned periods . . . Irving then was a literary opportunist, not a serious writer."[28]

This inability to perceive the substance of Irving's literary achievement arises from a failure to understand the impact of John Locke's empiricism on eighteen-century English writers and early nineteenth-century American writers. Irving was, in fact, not merely a graceful stylist; he was a keen observer of human nature, the landscape, trees, flowers, and animal behavior, all of which he viewed with a classic eighteenth-century British empathy that found a congenial home in an era of romantic pathos on both sides of the Atlantic. John Locke's *Essay on Human Understanding* was published in 1690, but its impact stretched across the eighteenth century in England. In a nutshell, there was a new awareness that the contents of the mind arose from sensory input, not innate ideas. There was a particular focus on the sense impressions coming from the eyes, which were understood as a symbol of all the senses, and the preeminent tool of perception. Thus, a new emphasis on description emerged. Even in a writer such as Alexander Pope, who relied so heavily on witty heroic couplets, there was a new level of naturalist detail. One can see it especially in "Windsor Forest" and the descriptions of the gardens of Alcinous and the island of Calypso in his translation of *The Odyssey*.[29] The trend toward vivid naturalist description picked up midcentury with James Thomson's *The Seasons*, a long poem that most of our own contemporaries would now consider unreadable, but which was one of the most beloved texts in England and the United States for a century. The American colonies were slow to absorb Locke and other philosophers. They began to digest his thought in the late eighteenth century and in the 1830s Emerson was still wrestling the implications of his empiricism. As Donald Ringe has pointed out, the late American colonial period and early Republic, Locke's ideas were filtered to Americans the Scottish Common Sense school of philosophy led by Thomas Reid and others. The net result of this new emphasis on seeing was a flourish of extensive descriptive passages, and especially of expansive panoramic scenes, the type of prospects that were also appearing in landscape painting. Ringe describes this tendency toward lengthy vivid description as "the pictorial mode," due to its kinship with landscape art that was emerging as the same time.[30] Indeed, the old Renaissance idea that a painting could be an art like poetry found new life in the idea that a landscape could also be like a painting, and those vistas could be portrayed in both painting and literature. This new Locke-inspired empiricism was seen in the vivid descriptive sections of Irving's tales, the novels of James Fenimore Cooper, and of course the nature poetry of William Cullen Bryant.

Irving's accomplishment as a descriptive writer should not be underestimated. As Stanley Williams has pointed out, he was especially attentive in his description of fruit trees and blossoms, a feature of Irving's life that began in the garden of his childhood home on William Street in New York City, and which remained consistent throughout his lifetime: "The garden teemed with flowers, apricots, green-grapes and nectarines; to the end of his life Irving had a vivid way of describing blossoms and fruits."[31] Irving picked up this tendency to some extent from Joseph Addison's attentiveness to landscape details in *Remarks of Several Parts of Italy*, but Irving s observational and descriptive powers far surpassed that of Addison. A lovely sample is found in Irving's description of *Woolfert's Roost*, a passage that Williams rightly notes is really a description of Sunnyside. The house was

> full of nooks and crooks, and chambers of all sorts and sizes. It was buried among willows, elms, and cherry trees, and surrounded with roses and hollyhocks, with honeysuckle and sweetbriar clambering about every window. A brood of hereditary pigeons sunned themselves upon the roof; hereditary swallows and martins built about the eves and chimneys; and hereditary bees hummed about the flower-beds.[32]

Irving descriptive power regarding the trees and vines of America's eastern deciduous forest was, in fact, an essential component of the climactic scene in "The Legend of Sleepy Hollow," as Ichabod Crane was about to encounter the towering Headless Horseman:

> In the center of the road stood an enormous tulip tree, which towered like a giant above all the other trees of the neighborhood, and formed a kind of landmark. Its limbs were gnarled and fantastic, large enough to form trunks for ordinary trees, twisting down almost to the earth and rising again into the air.[33]
>
> As Ichabod approached this fearful tree, he began to whistle; he thought his whistle was answered: it was but a blast sweeping sharply through the dry branches. As he approached a little nearer, he thought he saw something white hanging in the midst of the tree: he paused and ceased whistling; but on looking more narrowly, perceived it was a place where the tree had been scathed by lightning, and the white wood laid bare. Suddenly he heard a groan—his teeth chattered, and his knees smote against the saddle: it was but the rubbing of one huge bough upon another, as they were swayed about by the breeze. He passed the tree in safety, but new perils lay before him.
>
> About two hundred yards from the tree, a small brook crossed the road, and ran into a marshy and thickly wooded glen, known by the name of Wiley's swamp.[34] A few rough logs, laid side by side, served for a bridge over this stream. On that side of the road where the brook entered the wood, a group of oaks and chestnuts, matted thick with wild grape vines, threw a cavernous gloom over it. To pass this bridge was the severest trial. It was at this spot that the unfortunate André was captured, and under the covert of those chestnuts and

vines were the sturdy yeoman concealed who surprised him. This has ever since been considered a haunted stream, and fearful are the feeling of the schoolboy who has to pass it alone at dark.[35]

As he approached the stream, his heart began to thump; he, however, summoned up all his resolution, gave his horse half a score of kicks in the ribs, and attempted to dash briskly across the bridge; but instead of starting forward, the perverse old animal made a lateral movement, and ran broadside against the fence. Ichabod, whose fears increased with the delay, jerked the reins on the other side, and kicked lustily with the contrary foot: it was all in vain; his steed started, it is true, but it was only to plunge to the opposite side of the road into a thicket of brambles and alder bushes.

In the dark shadow of the grove, on the margin of the brook, he beheld something huge, misshapen, black and towering. It stirred not, but seemed gathered up in the gloom, like some gigantic monster ready to spring upon the traveller.[36]

This passage is not a matter of mere style; there is superb naturalistic description of the setting—specific trees, bushes, a brook and a marsh—in a locale laced with history. There is also a vivid sense of Ichabod's awkwardness and panic. Even for those who are not as gullible or superstitious as the schoolmaster, the scene evokes a universal primordial fear, that of being stalked at night by something—one knows not what—that rustles unseen in the bushes not too far away.

Irving clearly had an extraordinary ability to establish a sense of atmosphere, and in the case of his Hudson River stories, this included a description of the distinctive changeableness of mid-Atlantic skies, alternating so rapidly between sunlight and storm, blue-skied clarity, and visible humidity. *Rip Van Winkle* opens with a tour de force of descriptive atmospherics:

Whoever has made a voyage up the Hudson must remember the Kaatskill mountains. They are a dismembered branch of the great Appalachian family, and are seen away to the west of the river swelling up to noble height and lording it over the surrounding country. Every change of season, every change of weather, indeed every hour of the day, produces some change in the magical hues and shapes of these mountains, and they are regarded by all the good wives far and near as perfect barometers. When the weather is fair and settled, they are clothed in blue and purple, and print their bold outlines on the clear evening sky; but sometimes, when the rest of the landscape is cloudless, they will gather a hood of grey vapours about their summits, which, in the last rays of the setting sun, will glow and light up like a crown of glory.[37]

Irving's descriptive skill in passages such as these are examples of the pictorial mode that arose in English and later American literature as John Locke's empiricist emphasis on seeing was absorbed in the general culture and the literature of the time.

Pushback on the Caricature of Irving

James Tuttleton was the most prominent twentieth-century scholar to challenge the now widely held view that Irving was all style and no substance: "The fact that Irving's best known stories strike us as inescapably the literature of the Catskills, yet in fact derive from folk legends and myths, points to a universality transcending time and place."[38] Tuttleton was frustrated with the heavily ideological readings of literature in the late 1980s and 1990s; he praised Irving for working, in *The Sketch Book*, with a "dominating theme that sets at naught all ideological posturing in literature: time, time's ruins, dilapidation, dust and decay, the mutability of all things, and oblivion."[39] Romantics, of course, took up these universal themes with acute attentiveness because the French Revolution, the Industrial Revolution, and the explanatory power of Newtonian physics together created an unprecedented sense of traumatic rupture with the past. "The Romantic vision is characterized by the painful and melancholic conviction that in modern reality something precious has been lost, at the level of both individuals and humanity at large; certain essential human values have been alienated."[40] Reflection on change was not only a universal theme, but a very pressing contemporary emergency.[41] Add to that America's rupture with Britain in two recent wars, and you have an acute need for continuity, as well as a longing for the sense of mystery in the cosmos that eighteenth-century science seemingly destroyed. Irving's use of folk materials was not "unoriginal"; it had a purpose of sustaining links with the past and reinforcing long-term shared values, even as a new identity was being forged.

VALUING THE PAST AND ASSESSING "PROGRESS"

In the early eighteenth century, Scottish philosophers David Hume, John Millar, and Adam Smith discussed the rise of commerce, the arts, and science. As summarized by John Brewer, the Enlightenment ideal that all people were fundamentally the same was expressed in the notion of stages of civilization; the development of society could be traced "from rude barbarism to modern civilization, from primitivism to modern commerce."[42] Different cultures were at different stages, but all were equal in that they could be assumed to go through the same stages. Each stage was a step in a common development, and even the primitive had some value as a foundation. This framework was, for many, a way of affirming the fundamental sameness of persons and cultures, while accounting for obvious differences; there was one humanity in different stages of development. While many authors working with this framework saw the peoples as lacking in refinement and needing correction by more advanced peoples, the "savage state" could also be understood as a state of sublime, wild grandeur, as in Joseph Addison's description of the Homeric stage of Greek civilization: "Reading the *Iliad* is like travelling through a Country, uninhabited, where Fancy is entertained with a thousand Savage Prospects of vast Desarts, wide uncultivated Marches, huge Forests, mis-shapen Rocks and Precipices."[43] Washington Irving would follow Addison in his descriptions of sublime moments in the American West, and the dignity of the wild Native American cultures.[44]

At the other end of the range of interpretive possibilities, the savage state could also be seen as a state of barbaric primitivism that warranted conquest and compulsory European acculturation in the name of "improvement."[45] The stages of civilization idea would be deployed in varying ways, and often it would be used to belittle Native Americans and rationalize their removal. However, this was not necessarily so, because the idea was fundamentally that humans are alike and civilizations that go through life stages. Children would, of course, be managed by adults, and so a widespread paternalism resulted, but a denial of anyone's humanity was not the intention of people like Hume who helped create the framework in his essay *Of Refinement in the Arts*. Hume's own ethic emphasized empathy, or fellow-feeling, as a basis for morality. His consistent emphasis was the human distaste for suffering, whether in ourselves or others.[46] If he reflected on the stages of development in human civilizations, he did not do so as a rationalization for inflicting suffering on less developed cultures. Irving would stand in the tradition of Addison and Hume as he understood this framework, and the distrust of so-called improvements that runs through so many of Irving's writings includes a distrust of those who would force Western civilization on the "savages."[47]

The American romantic artist Thomas Cole used the idea of stages of civilization subversively in his 1836 series *The Course of Empire*, for which *A Wild Scene* was a kind of first draft of *The Savage State* in the full series (see figure 1.1).

For Cole, the so-called apex of civilization—*The Consummation of Empire*—contained within it a greed and indulgence that carried the inevitable seeds of *Destruction* and *Desolation*.[48] The implication was that British and American empires would both fall like Rome as a natural outgrowth of overreach and overconsumption.[49] Washington Irving had a similar concern for the overreach and rapidity of change in the United States. Cole and Irving both challenged the notion that all was progress, that progress was inevitable, and both condemned the pace of "improvements" that were not truly an improvement.[50]

Figure 1.1 Thomas Cole, *A Wild Scene*, 1831–1832, Baltimore Museum of Art.

As the eighteenth century proceeded, there were "an unprecedented number of theatrical and musical performances, books and paintings" as manifestations of progress, and "forms of popular expression such as ballads and folktales, woodcuts and seasonal festivals" were marginalized. However, by the end of the century, "leading artists and intellectuals had become convinced that many forms of folk and popular expression needed to be rescued or preserved."[51] In this late eighteenth- and early nineteenth-century context, use of a folktale as the basis for storytelling was not an act of pilfering or plagiarism; it was an act of respect that preserved something of value that was being lost in the modern era. Celestina Savonius-Wroth has recently argued that Irving "was a participant in one of the earliest self-conscious revivals of folk traditions in the English-speaking world."[52] There was a sensibility in the earlier stages of civilization that needed to be retained. Perhaps it is best to let Irving address the accusation in his own words. In the last section of *Bracebridge Hall* (1821), Irving had been listening to other guests' tales, and was asked to share stories of his own. He offered a set of three related pieces by the late Diedrich Knickerbocker and added a footnote in the section called "The Historian" that immediately preceded "The Haunted House," "Dolph Heyligen," and "The Storm Ship":

> I find that the tale of Rip Van Winkle, given in the Sketch Book, has been discovered by diverse writers in magazines, to have been founded on a little

German tradition, and the matter has been revealed to the world as if were a foul instance of plagiarism brought to light. In a note which followed that tale I had alluded to the superstition on which it was founded, and I thought a mere allusion was sufficient, as the tradition was so notorious as to be inserted in almost every collection of German legends. I had seen it myself in three. I could hardly have hoped, in an age when every source of ghost and goblin story is ransacked, that the original of the tale would escape discovery. In fact, I had considered popular traditions of the kind as fair foundations for authors of fiction to build upon, and had made use of the one in question accordingly.[53]

When one considers how Irving used the story of Rip Wan Winkle to explore problems of modern identity, a sense of dislocation, and the rapid pace of change in contemporary society, it is clear he made the story his own.

There is also a general sense in more recent scholarship that Irving was honest about this process of borrowing, especially in *The Sketch Book* essay "The Art of Making Books," a playful little piece which emphasizes the collaborative nature of all bookmaking[54] and the naturalness of the process by which old works decay and are reborn in new life forms. In ancient atomist philosophy, all objects and organisms break down into their component parts, until only atoms remain, to be reconfigured into something else. Irving jests, perhaps seriously, that all great works are lost to decay, and that the new authors who utilize these component parts are, in fact, bringing new life to something that might otherwise be lost. The new organism build on the reconfigured atoms is a new creature, but one that enables the old fragments to go on living.[55]

Indeed, Irving's invocations of the past share features of the world's historic wisdom traditions as described by Huston Smith. These traditions assure us "that if we could see the whole picture, we would find it more integrated than we ordinarily suppose." However, "life gives us no view of the whole. We see only snatches here and there, and self-interest skews our perspective grotesquely." Meaning is found by being a part of a whole, a whole which we cannot perceive directly but only in "scraps" that hint of an unseen cosmic design. The world is better than it ordinarily seems, but "reality is steeped in ineluctable mystery; we are born in mystery; we live in mystery, and we die in mystery"; the universe may have an ultimately comic quality with a built-in resolution, but "things are more mysterious than they seem."[56] Irving's seemingly drifting and erratic use of various older materials, so displaced that you often cannot even tell when one story ends and another begins, is in fact a deliberate attempt to pull us into engagement with the fact that the world does not present us with tidy rational harmonies, but that a vision attained comes at the cost of irruptions and apparent irrationality in the process of a wider integration that does not quite arrive in this life.[57] Irving would provide visions of misty enchantment, moments of charm that would soften the disruptive quality of modern life, but his romantic mist was always momentary, and for all his geniality and occasional happy endings, there was often a lack of clear resolution of the tensions in his works.

The fact that the integration did not fully arrive in this life did not necessarily mean it would in the next. Irving was not clearly a religious person during the span of his fiction-writing career, though he did become Anglican later in life. He had had enough of his father's overbearing Presbyterianism, where every joy of life was treated as a sin.[58] What else he thought is difficult to know because he did not express his personal religion much in his public or private writings. Stanley Williams described him as "in faith, an unaggressive deist."[59] Irving did criticize the most extreme abuses of religion, such as Puritan witch trials, the persecution of Quakers, rationalizations for abusing Native Americans, and some Catholic superstitions, as well as the manipulation of gullible populations by church leadership. In the introduction to *Bracebridge Hall*, described himself as a nonintrusive Christian, a member of his civilization who accepted the basics of trust in God and tried to follow his religion's precepts, but who left dogma, explicit moralizing, and the conversion of souls to others.

Irving was perhaps slightly distrustful of the broader romantic movement as described by M.H. Abrams, where language and sensibilities from more traditional religious frameworks were retained by romantic poets, but given a new, more secular meaning. The religious content of the prior traditions was replaced by a more modern focus on the role of the imagination in creating meaning, even as traditional language was at times retained with all its evocative power; the new focus of these seeming theologians was the relationship of "subject and object, ego and non-ego, and the human mind or consciousness and its interactions with nature."[60] Irving did not engage in long meditative discourses on the nature of the creative self, as did Wordsworth,[61] and so he is sometimes seen as a "Romantic light"[62]; however, he seemed to share a kind of Byronic distrust of romantic quasi-theological discourse. On this matter, Irving seems more an eighteenth-century skeptic. Irving did not theorize extensively on the role of the imagination as creative inner light that functions as a source of quasi-religious illumination; rather, he used the power of imagination to create a sense of historical connection where that sense of continuity was lacking. Through his stories, he made the Hudson River valley, with its Dutch history, feel like a home with memories worth retaining. He succeeded in creating a kind of sacred, yet not quite religious, landscape along the Hudson River valley. He was a practitioner of the enchanted imaginative life, not its theoretician. His borrowing of older tales and fragments of many writers, in fact, shows his skepticism toward some romantic notions of an artist as an absolute creator. Irving knew that we stand on the shoulders of giants. Irving certainly shared the view that imagination was to supply some sense of meaning and continuity in the absence of historical connections, but whether imagination was an outright replacement for religion for him is hard so say. Also, imagination was highly valued in eighteenth-century England, and Irving may not have distinguished between neoclassical and romantic understandings of the term.

The tension between creativity and reworking of old materials in *The Sketch Book* is but one of many ways in which Irving occupied a "middle ground," what we might call a between-space with creative potential. Jochen Achilles, in one of the first studies to consider Irving in Transatlantic perspective, argues:

> The numerous English and a few American sketches of Washington Irving's *The Sketch Book* (1820) share a preoccupation with secluded settings which serve as scenes of a nearly universal, and therefore almost prelapsarian, harmonization of differences. They provide a middle ground between nature and culture, individual independence and social predetermination, the pleasure and reality principle, the *id* and the *superego*. Focusing centrifugal tendencies on the political as well as psychological planes, these Sleepy Hollows can be said to imaginatively evoke and tentatively construct identities with simultaneously signal their beleaguered status and potential obsolescence.... They can conveniently be considered both constructions and contestations of identity.[63]

Stability and instability are interdependent; Irving traveled between the poles of England and America, past and present, the eighteenth and nineteenth centuries. According to Achilles, the ultimate result of the creative tension in this hollow middle ground was ultimately an attempt "to guarantee a transatlantic ethical, political and ecological stability."[64] In other words, Irving's wanderings were not aimless, and he was not a passively wandering member of a lost generation. He was not truly adrift. Rather, he was active in identity construction and at the heart of this effort there was an ethic that had implications for humanity and a wider ecology. There was dislocation, but an attempt to heal the breach. There was substance behind the styles of his various personae.

James Tuttleton also challenged William's notion that Irving was an erratic drifter who could not focus. Though Irving does present himself in the revised edition of *Sketch Book* as one whose "varyings of mind" are as unstable as "a weather cock," Tuttleton suggests that this is but one of Irving's ever-shifting literary personas.[65] This hypothesis is at least plausible; Joy Casson points out, in a discussion of Irving's retrospective letter of 1823 to lost love Amelia Foster, "Irving could never write about himself without in some sense recasting himself as his own persona."[66] According to Tuttleton, Irving's lifelong accomplishments "make plain" that he "was also disciplined, self-controlled, in command of his talent, energetic in private life, and overtly political in his public life" as diplomatic appointee to England and Spain. His use of shifting personas and times periods is part of a larger pattern of dissociation that characterized Irving as a timeless writer who explored

> the imagination's capacity to penetrate to a truth about life that lies beyond the faculty of mundane thought and ordinary reality. . . . Something more than elegance of style lies at the heart of these, his two best stories. . . . These tales reflect a wizardry of style—like that of Shakespeare—taking the writer and his audience out of quotidian time into the world of pure imagination, where the rhythms of desire always find fulfillment, where our recurring need for freedom from the constraints of ordinary actuality finds a satisfying, if ambiguous, resolution.[67]

More recently, however, Andrew Hemingway has suggested that Irving's use of a "style ostensibly associated with English eighteenth-century literature" functioned as a method to shed light "on the contemporary world through the representation of anachronisms."[68] Whether one speaks of Irving's oscillation between different narrative personae, or Rip Van Winkle waking up a generation later after a long night's sleep, a common theme that ran through Irving's work was, in fact, that of dislocation and identity loss.[69] As Bryan Jay Wolf has pointed out, when Irving used folk material from a preindustrial order, the characters were ironically and "distinctively *modern*" (his emphasis): they are almost always marginal figures relative to the culture surrounding them, and they are "isolated from the recognized channels of productive activity within their societies."[70] Though this dislocation is bred of the broader international movement toward modernity and industrialization, it was also acutely American, for the United States had just made the most disruptive break with the past in the American Revolution.

In almost every way possible, Irving straddled boundary lines, a person in the middle, pulled in both directions. This is certainly true in the political realm that he found so distasteful because of extreme partisanship. He was born into a community of New York Federalist merchants and lawyers, but he chose a more pragmatic middle ground supporting New York Republicans such as the magnetic and trade-friendly Aaron Burr. Many in New York and the Middle states were dissatisfied being caught between a rigid Boston (and Hamiltonian) Federalism and an equally aggressive Virginia Republicanism.[71] Irving's brother Peter was a partisan of Burr, and he published on his behalf. Irving's broader circle of friends, including Governor Kemble, were sympathetic to Burr but were ultimately defined by pragmatism rather than ideology. Whenever a pragmatic middle path was possible, that was Irving's inclination. This adaptability enabled him to serve as a diplomat in England under Andrew Jackson, a diplomat to Spain under President Tyler—southern Whig who became president because William Henny Harrison died shortly after the 1840 election—and again under Democrat James Polk. A tendency to seek a pragmatic middle ground is also seen in Irving's choice to become Episcopalian in 1850. The Anglican tradition was itself a middle ground between Roman Catholicism and Protestantism, and the Episcopal Church, at that point in history, offered a way to value English traditions while being fully American.[72]

THE SUBSTANCE WITH THE STYLE

Irving, a child of the Enlightenment, offered a critique of all cultural bias and chauvinism, as was characteristic of the ancient Cynic philosophy which had been given new life in the eighteenth century through the study of the classics since the Renaissance, and—in particular—by Oliver Goldsmith's essay "Citizen of the World." Eighteenth-century English literature, especially in its influence on Irving, has often been understood as style over substance. However, empathy was a central value of the eighteenth century, going back to the influence of David Hume's emphasis on fellow-feeling as the basis for moral judgments, as well as a tendency, based on a reading of world literature from ancient Greece and ancient China, to try to transcend one's own cultural bias in favor of a non-egocentric perspective. Goldsmith made such a point writing in the persona of a Chinese scholar who was traveling through England. There was a comic element in this travel literature as cultural misunderstandings on both sides were explored, but the real goal was more substantial. People were being trained to look at their cultural practices from the standpoint of an outsider, and to transcend chauvinistic cultural bias:

> When I had just quit my native country, and crossed the Chinese wall, I thought every deviation from the customs and manners of China was a departing from nature. I smiled at the blue lips and red foreheads of the Tongusas. I could hardly contain when I saw the Daures dress their heads with horns. . . . But I soon perceived that the ridicule lay not in them but in me, and that I falsely condemned others for absurdity, because they happened to differ from my standard of perfection, which was founded in prejudice or partiality.[73]

The concern to distinguish between nature and culture, *physis* and *nomos*, was first raised within Western civilization with the travels of Herodotus into the Persian Empire, and it was explored further by the Cynics of the Hellenistic period. Possible responses were to recognize the validity of all cultures in a kind of cultural relativism (the Sophist option, a variant which emerged later as Skepticism), or to search for a simple, natural way of living by stripping away and seeing past all merely cultural values (the Cynic option).

Ancient Greek Cynics were not cynical as we understand the word; the initially pejorative term was based on the Greek word for dog, *Kuoon*. Cynics were doglike, or animalistic, in the eyes of their opponents because they tried to strip away all traces of human culture and taboo in favor of a truly natural, simple life, aware of a common relationship to all fellow humans and the cosmos itself. They eschewed money, power, and status in favor of a life of deliberate exile from any home polis.[74] Cynics were wanderers with a purpose, the attainment of absolute freedom, a fact that made them ideal prototypes for an American natural way of life, which Irving saw as admirably embodied in the fierce independence of Native Americans.[75] Diogenes of Sinope was the most famous of them, and he coined the phrase "citizen of the world," which Goldsmith then used. As Martha Nussbaum has explained, the moment Diogenes affirmed that he was a citizen of the world, and not simply one local polis

> might be said to inaugurate a long tradition of cosmopolitan political thought in the Western tradition. A Greek male refuses the invitation to define himself by lineage, city, social class, even free birth, even gender. He insists on defining himself in terms of a characteristic he shares with all other human beings, male and female, Greek and non-Greek, slave and free. And by calling himself not simply a dweller in the world but a citizen of the world, Diogenes suggests, as well, the possibility of a politics, or a moral approach to politics, that focuses on the humanity we share rather than the marks of local origin, status, class, and gender that divide us.[76]

Diogenes was revered through the entire Hellenistic period and was a cultural icon almost of the stature of Socrates, most famously immortalized in Diogenes Laertius' *The Lives of the Philosophers.*

Cynic philosophy, together with the Stoic idea of a spark of cosmic rationality shared equally by all, was in fact the foundation of the Enlightenment ideal of the equality of all persons:

> Cynic/Stoic cosmopolitanism urges us the recognize the equal, and unconditional, worth of all human beings, a worth grounded in moral choice-capacity ... rather than on traits that depend on fortuitous natural or social arrangements. The insight that politics ought to treat human being both as equal and as having a worth beyond price is one of the deepest and most influential insights of Western thought.[77]

Cynics and Stoics were admired and discussed through the eighteenth and nineteenth centuries, and the Cynic tendency to concise, witty retorts made them a natural favorite of writers such as Sterne, Goldsmith, and Irving.[78] The cosmopolitan ethical framework essentially replaced religion with rationality, both in ancient Greece and the European Enlightenment.[79]

In the Renaissance and the age of religious wars following the Reformation, however, the appropriation of Stoic and Cynic philosophies had a different function. It was a way for people of goodwill to find a thoughtful common ground with a trust in divine Providence and a journey toward a kind of philosophical and spiritual transcendence without getting into dogmatic fights over Protestant or Catholic points of controversy. It was a way to find a common ground and a shared humanity in spite of the issues that were tearing apart Western civilization.[80] The Stoic ideal put more emphasis on controlling the passions and personal reactions to any circumstance out of one's control, and doing one's duty as a citizen while trusting the cosmos to be good even when it did not appear so. The Cynic ideal lent itself more to the enjoyment of the simple pleasures of life, such as food and friendship, the rejection of materialism and social status as the primary sources of satisfaction in life, and the image of the philosophical wanderer that gave rise to artist images of travelers on the voyage of life. Irving the wanderer appreciated the Cynic ideals because of a greater sense of freedom and a capacity to enjoy life under any circumstance, and not merely suppress feelings as was often the case in the Stoic traditions. In the context of early nineteenth-century American Republic, the divisions were not so much Catholic or Protestant, but a rapidly diversifying Protestantism torn between Calvinism, Quakerism, Unitarianism, and the revivalisms of the Second Great Awakening, with rapid escalating dogmatism and sectarianism emerging just as national expansion west was reaching a frenzy pitch. It is not surprising that in such a context, a person of congenial and diplomatic temperament such as Irving would identify with Goldsmith's revival of Cynic cosmopolitanism, and that he would see that Cynic wanderer as the bearer of an ideal of American freedom. The choice to embrace this philosophy in public discourse does not in any way imply the abandonment of personal faith in a religious tradition. It simply means that such a person will be reticent to talk about their personal religion, if that person has a religious commitment, because religion is what people fight over.

The main problem with this Cynic/Stoic cosmopolitanism, according to Martha Nussbaum, is the ideal of absolute self-sufficiency; it is assumed that people need to simply stop being selfish and adopt a more rational perspective, and that they need no material base for flourishing; the reason the cosmopolitan ideal failed to create the ideal civilization it sought is that it did not take into account childhood development and the material basis of well-being that makes a caring community possible.[81]

Irving took for granted the Anglo-American literary culture's knowledge of Cynicism and Stoicism, and he alluded to these ancient schools frequently. From a very early date in his career, the "Letter from Mustapha" in *Salgamundi* III, February 13, 1807, Irving displayed a tendency to follow Goldsmith in a Cynic critique of one's own culture:

> The people of the United States have assured me that they themselves are the most enlightened nation under the sun, but thou knowest that the barbarians of the desert, who assemble at the summer solstice, to shoot their arrows at that glorious luminary, in order to extinguish his burning rays, make precisely the same boast;—which of them have the superior claim, I shall not attempt to decide.[82]

William Hedges characterizes *A History of New York*, written just two years later, as a critique of cultural ego-centrism directed at both old New Netherland and the contemporary United States: "the narrative exposes the emptiness of political and chauvinistic pretensions in the New Netherland that old Diedrich seeks to celebrate; by analogy; it 'ridicules . . . the high seriousness' of the 'republican myth-makers of post-Revolutionary America.' "[83]

When Irving wrote *Salgamundi* and the *History*, he was frustrated with the Jefferson administration whose trade embargo ruined his family business, and whose vision of a republic of equals seemingly encouraged a more general "mobocracy." For Irving, a moderate Federalist from a mercantile family, rule by the "sovereign people" was nothing but governance "by the tail of the ship."[84] His distrust in "the people" of the Jeffersonian age found expression in his comments on the abuse of Native Americans during the Jefferson administration, an abuse which was the culmination of a long history of colonial attitudes. For example, Irving noted in *A History of New York* that Native American life was precisely the kind of simple life—free of pretension—advocated by ancient philosophers, embodying the ancient character trait *atarachia*, the ability to remain undisturbed by ever-changing circumstance. If Native Americans had been ancient Greeks, they would be regarded as the wisest of philosophers; however, as they were not ancient Greeks, but people in the way of American "discovery," they were classified as "dumb beasts" who could be forcibly removed at convenience.[85] Cultural egocentrism was the main target of the ancient Cynics, and it was one of Irving's main targets. Only a Euro-centric chauvinist could praise Diogenes while dehumanizing Native Americans. A similar use of Cynic and Stoic cosmopolitan themes would appear again in Irving's 1835 publication *A Tour on the Prairies*, discussed in Chapter 6. That themes were used so consistently across such a wide range of writings indicates that Irving cosmopolitan values remained essentially unchanged from 1807 to 1835, with the exception that, by the time he returned to the United States in 1832 after a very long sojourn, he no longer feared "the people" as he did in his youth, and was willing to give Jacksonian democracy a chance. Irving would speak in many voices in many moods, and he would add to his classical cosmopolitanism as a wistful romantic sense that the world was subject to inevitable decay. However, William Hedge was incorrect when he claimed that Irving "found nowhere in his youth a set of beliefs or attitudes to which he could wholeheartedly commit himself."[86] Goldsmith and Diogenes had taught him to be a cosmopolitan citizen of the world who valued the world's rich diversity of people, customs, costumes, and terrain. He would never abandon that core moral value he learned in his youth, and in fact he would become more egalitarian as he aged.

Irving himself spent a life wandering like a Cynic, and he stated at the beginning of his first trip abroad, trying to soften the unhappy feeling about leaving his friends in New York, "I hope I shall in a little while become enough of *a Citizen of the World* to feel at home wherever I happen to be."[87] However, within a month he admitted to his brother William, "I am continually more and more sensible that I am not *Citizen of the World* enough to form a Traveler. One little spot of earth attracts my tenderest feelings."[88] Irving did become a long-term traveler, more cosmopolitan that even Jefferson or Franklin in embracing France, Italy, England, Germany, and Spain, and upon return to the United States, the lively mixture of peoples on the outer reaches of the American frontier. However, the confession to William was indicative of an abiding longing, the longing for a settled sense of home.

Irving's longing for the intimate and homey rather than the grandeur of the sublime is indicated in Geoffrey Crayon's disclaimer at the beginning of *The Sketchbook*:

> I fear I shall give equal disappointment with an unlucky landscape painter, who had travelled on the continent, but following the bent of his vagrant imagination, had sketched in nooks and corners and bye places. His sketch book was accordingly crowed with cottages, and landscapes, and obscure ruins; but he had neglected but he had neglected to paint St. Peter's or the Coliseum; the cascade of Terni or the Bay of Naples; and had not a single Glacier or Volcano in his whole collection.[89]

Like his persona Geoffrey Crayon, Irving was a lover of picturesque travel, but his travels were part of a long struggle to determine how to create a sense of rootedness in a very uprooted United States. He would have to go first to Europe and see how people in England and Spain created a sense of home before he could create his own back in New York.

When he was ready, in 1832, he did go home to America, and Sunnyside—the place of tenderest feeling he longed for in his letter to William—became a trend-setting American gothic home of the mid-nineteenth century, highlighted by Andrew Jackson Downing in his attempt to encourage Americans to cultivate beautiful homes and landscapes as a counterpoint to the crass utilitarianism of much American culture.[90] Irving was indeed a wandering citizen of the world, but he was also sensitive to particular nooks and crannies all around the world that exuded a particular sense of place. He felt too much the need for a home, and his self-chosen exile could thus only be temporary; indeed, one of his worst fears while he was abroad was expressed in a journal entry after he had visited the famed Protestant cemetery of Rome:

> Scarce a traveller resorts here but he reads the epitaph of a fellow countryman, who wandering in search of health had at length escaped from his load of miseries and infirmities. He drops the tear or heaves the heady sigh to his memory, for, when so far removed from his native shores he looks upon every fellow countryman as of the same family.[91]

At this stage of his life, it was seemingly easier to feel a sense of belonging in the fellowship of American travelers than in the United States itself, yet he retained an ambivalence in his seventeen-year sojourn, the love of travel combined with the fear of dying homeless. This ambivalence is part of a wider double-sidedness to Irving's being: he straddled the ideals of Enlightenment rationality, by which you could acknowledge the value of persons and cultures everywhere, and the romantic sensibility that pulled toward a specific place as an anchor of continuity. Indeed, for Irving, picturesque travel enabled a partial reconciliation of the two polarities, for its more thoughtful practitioners sought to assimilate diverse cultures to oneself—not just viewing them superficially—while simultaneously cultivating a sense of place. Though picturesque travel could be a mere indicator of social status, it had the potential to enhance in the traveler an abiding love of cultural diversity. In Irving's case, it did so.

Irving's Cynic concern to transcend cultural egocentrism—nationalistic chauvinism—was particularly relevant in an age of aggressive Anglo-Saxon American expansion, whenever it came at the expense of a diversely textured civilization. The Connecticut Yankee was the American character type that most radically undermined the kind of civilization Irving wanted to cultivate; they were aggressors spreading a monoculture, and there is nothing Irving disliked more than perpetual sameness. Any lover of the picturesque was trained "to look for a vantage point from which a scene would arrange itself into fore-, mid-, and backgrounds, but also to perceive such pictorial qualities of roughness, sudden variation, or broken tints."[92] However, Irving was a student of human character and colorful figures as well as pleasing scenery. You see his love of perpetual variety in his earliest travels through upstate New York to Montreal in 1803, where he rejoiced at the open sunny prospect of a bluff overlooking a river after the monotony of hours of unbroken forest along muddy roads, to his love of picaresque characters such as Antoine in *A Tour on the Prairies* in 1832. One sees the love of variety in his description of Charles Latrobe, one of his fellow travelers on the journey through the great plains west of the Arkansas River:

> Having rambled over many countries, he had become, to a certain degree, a citizen of the world, easily adapting himself to any change. He was a man of a thousand occupations; a botanist, a geologist, a hunter of beetles and butterflies, a musical amateur, a sketcher of no mean pretensions, in short, a complete virtuoso; added to which he was a very indefatigable, if not always a very successful, sportsman. Never had any man more irons in the fire, and, consequently, never was man more busy nor more cheerful.[93]

Commentators are often quick to assume Irving was a drifting, insecure wanderer, because he went through periods of seeming depression and unproductivity, and because his state of "inner unsettledness" resulted in seventeen years abroad.[94] Irving did describe himself as "unfitted for any periodically recurring task or any stipulated labor of body or mind." Those words were originally written in 1817 to explain to Sir Walter Scott why he did not want an editing job in Edinburgh—after having decided to be a professional writer, and they were repeated in the "Preface" of the revised edition of *The Sketch Book* in 1848, when he had settled into the life of a country gentleman, and was making occasional trips to New York for the theatre performances and research on George Washington at Astor's library.

It is often too quickly assumed—especially when people offer "psychologized" readings of his work—that carefree, work-shirking Rip Wan Winkle was really an alter ego for Irving.[95] Here in Irving's description of Latrobe from the 1832 trip west, we see something closer to a figure that he identified with, a citizen of the world who was well-traveled and perpetually busy. Latrobe—in Irving's estimation—was happy precisely because he had such a wide range of interests. He worked incessantly, but he did not always work on the same thing. Here lies a key to Irving's temperament, and his tendency to turn down mundane jobs, as well as his long-term refusal to marry. He simply did not want a job or a relationship where he was required to do the same thing every day; his love of perpetual variety was a stable character disposition, and it affected everything, including his vision of a diverse America. Indeed, Irving's life is a virtual embodiment of remarks by Joseph Addison:

> The Mind of Man naturally hates everything that looks like a restraint upon it, and is apt to fancy itself under a sort of Confinement, when the Sight is pent up in a narrow Compass, and shortened on every side by the Neighborhood of

Walls or Mountains. On the contrary, a spacious Horizon is an Image of Liberty, where the Eye has Room to range abroad, to expatriate on the Immensity of its Views, and to lose itself amidst the Variety of Objects that offer themselves to its observation. Such wide and undetermined Prospects are as pleasing to the Fancy as the Speculations of Eternity or Infinitude are to the Understanding.[96]

Irving followed Addison's recommended life of pleasure for a member of the mercantile class aspiring to a quasi-aristocratic way of life. Such a life plan took on a new urgency as American and English society became more dryly factual, mercantile, and rapidly industrializing; he had had enough of such drudgery sorting out the accounting for his brother Peter's failing business. The economic constraints marriage would have imposed on him would have limited his flexibility and the creativity whose coming and going he could not control.[97] The matter was acute in an American civilization so profoundly shaped by New England Puritanism, where the maxim was widely preached, "An hour's idleness is as bad as an hour's drunkenness."[98] Irving rejected the Puritan work ethic that allowed for no spontaneity or enjoyment of life; that is why he had a fascination with French traders since a trip to Montreal in early adulthood.[99]

French traders had a "joie de vivre" he found missing in the increasingly dominant Yankee mercantile industrial culture which was based on Puritan values:

No men are more submissive to their leaders and employers, more capable of enduring hardship, or more good-humoured under privations. Never are they so happy as when on long and rough expeditions, toiling up rivers or coasting lakes; encamping at night on the borders, gossiping around their fires, and bivouacking in the open air. They are dexterous boatmen, vigorous and adroit with the oar and paddle, and will row from morning until night without a murmur. The steersman often sings an old traditional French song, with some regular burden in which they all join, keeping time with their oars; if at any time they flag in spirits or relax in exertion, it is but necessary to strike up a song of the kind to put them all in fresh spirits and activity. The Canadian waters are vocal with these little French chansons, that have been echoes from mouth to mouth and transmitted from father to son, from the earliest days of the Colony, and it has a pleasing effect, in a still golden summer evening, to see a batteaux gliding across the bosom of a lake and dipping its oars to the cadence of these quant old ditties, or sweeping along, in full chorus on a bright sunny morning, down the transparent current of one of the Canada rivers.

But we are talking of things that are fast fading away! The march of mechanical inventions is driving everything poetical before it. The steamboats, which are fast dispelling the wildness and the romance of our lakes and rivers and aiding to subdue the world to commonplace, are proving as fatal to the race of Canadian voyagers as they have been to the boatmen of the Mississippi. Their glory is departed.[100]

Several scholars seem eager to see Irving as a failure in one way or another, and they use his diversity of interests and lack of consistent employment or literary productivity as evidence. For example, William Hedges asserted that "he never as a writer raised himself to a devoted singleness of purpose." I will argue that there is more unity than people often suppose in his works ranging from 1809 to 1835; nevertheless, one needs to understand Irving in his context. Both he and his fellow Knickerbocker James Paulding modelled their careers on the diversity of talents they saw in Oliver Goldsmith; the same words written of Paulding are as easily applied to Irving, if we merely add history and travel-writing: "He seems to have followed Goldsmith's example, making versatility—that is the writing of essays, novels, satires, poetry, plays—its most noticeable feature."[101] If versatility is one's self-conscious strategy, and one has an Addisonian commitment to maximum diversity of prospects, it seems unreasonable to criticize that person for not having a perfect singleness of purpose.

Furthermore, if one understands the love of variety characteristic of the picturesque aesthetic that developed in the decades after Addison, one again wonders why "singleness of purpose" would be required for success. The surprise of unexpected turns and vistas is at the very heart of this aesthetic.[102] Irving created an imagined history for New York when Americans were struggling with a lack of a sense of long-term cultural identity; he was the first American author to support himself fully through writing, he created several classic short stories of enduring value, and he wrote historical works on Columbus, the conquest of Granada, and the life of George Washington. He served as a diplomat in England and Spain, and one last time when he played a decisive role in determining the U.S.-Canada boundary line. He had many irons in the fire, and, despite the perpetual anxiety of needing to publish, he was, like Latrobe, happy to have those irons in the fire. He succeeded in avoiding the drudgery so characteristic of industrial and mercantile England and America, and he built a home that emphasized continuity with the past rather than the sense of harried dislocation so common to American civilization.

Irving's ideal was an America that was visually and ethnically "picturesque," that is, characterized by a high degree of cultural texture and variety that corresponds to the rich diversity of the landscape itself. Categories from aesthetic theory and practice—the beautiful, the sublime and particularly that of picturesque beauty—are crucial for understanding Irving's vision. When Irving painted a verbal picture of the United States using these categories, he was not simply imposing an aristocratic or upper-class "aesthetic imperialism" onto an alien landscape that he hoped Anglo-European Americans would soon possess.[103] Rather he was offering a vision of an America that finds an ultimate unity of composition while maintaining an astounding level of cultural diversity. Washington Irving was, in fact, the first great advocate of a truly multicultural America. This vision began with his championing of old Dutch American cultures that were being overwhelmed by English cultures in the form of Connecticut Yankees and extended into Long Island stories and his western writings as he found sympathy for African Americans, French traders, Native Americans, Creoles of both Spanish and French descent, and mixed-race persons. As part of his championing of diversity in America, he also had an acute sensitivity to nature; he saw not only with the eyes of a painter but the sensibility of naturalist who was simultaneously as observant as a landscape designer or amateur botanist, and as empathetic as a romantic poet.

Though Irving did not write any one essay on nature, sensitive descriptions of landscapes and animals are found scattered throughout his works. Irving was a citizen of the world for whom citizen shifted extended far beyond the human world. From his earliest journal entries to his trip out west in 1832, Irving showed an extraordinary attentiveness to trees in landscapes wild and cultivated; he showed a sensitivity to bees that have been displaced by the cutting of a honey tree, to a blind dog trying to find its way, to beavers and buffalos killed unnecessarily. His attention to such details in a pictorial mode is not just part of an aesthetic; it is part of an ethic. Thus, landscape imagery that seems merely aesthetic expresses the wider Cynic philosopher's commitment to be a citizen of the whole cosmos. To understand his love of variety and his picturesque ethic of world citizenship, it is necessary to study the art history and theory of the time, and how it could also be applied in the United States. Through these aesthetic categories that had for him an ethical meaning, we see a vision of what America should be, and an implicit critique of how it fails to live up to that ethic. For most practitioners of picturesque travel, there would be an upper-middle-class sense of cosmopolitanism, but not necessarily a full-blown ethic; however, for Irving the commitment to Oliver Goldsmith's version of ancient Cynic philosophy interacted in a unique way with picturesque art and travel and did in fact generate an ethic that was consistent over decades.

However, to understand Irving's critique of American culture, one must understand his diplomatic temperament. When he was young, he engaged in scathing satire in portions of *A History of New York*, and there would always be an element of satire and comic lampoon in his work, but the directness of his criticism of American colonists in early books of the *History*[104] would not be sustained. In the long run, he preferred, like a true gentleman, to say things more indirectly. He would sketch interesting characters without too much explicit moralizing, trying to put things in as positive a light as possible, while nevertheless giving the reader something to think about. His diplomatic skills were on display in the introduction to *Bracebridge Hall*, written at a time when the "Paper War" between England and the United States was raging at full force:

> Having been brought up, also, in the comparative simplicity of a republic, I am apt to be struck with even the ordinary circumstances incident to an aristocratical state of society. If, however, I should at any time amuse myself by pointing out some of the eccentricities, and some of the poetical characteristics of the latter, I would not be understood to be deciding on its political merits. My only aim is to paint characters and manners. I am no politician. There more I have considered the study of politics, the more I have found it full of perplexity; and I have contented myself, as I have in my religion, with the faith I was brought up in, regulating my own conduct by its precepts;[105] but leaving to abler heads the task of making converts. I shall continue on, therefore, in the course I have hitherto pursued; looking at things poetically, rather than politically, describing them as they are, rather than pretending to point out how they should be; and endeavoring to see the world in as pleasant a light as circumstances will permit.[106]

Irving was of course speaking in the persona of Geoffrey Crayon, Gent. I would suggest he does have some social commentary to express, with insights about England and the American Republic. However, he refused the tidy moralism of Yankees like Benjamin Franklin, and he eschewed electoral politics due to its excessive partisanship. Irving was in fact a very able politician of sorts as ambassador in London and Spain, representing U.S. interests graciously under Presidents Jackson, Tyler, and Polk. The claim he was not a politician has a bit of irony to it; we should trust remarks like that as much as we should trust him as he tells us, with a likely twinkle in his eye, that he is walking through a mansion with no hidden passages. However, he was a successful foreign minister because he was a genial one. He would engage in biting satire and raucous lampoonery in *A History of New York*. However, once he committed to a life of professional authorship in 1817, he would make his points in a playful, but more roundabout and diplomatic mode. The satire and comic exaggeration would continue, especially in the persona of Deidrich Knickerbocker, though they would always take a gentler form than that of the *History*.

NOTES

1. "Scott is one of those men of genius who delights in the genius of others, and he is not for having it all to himself. He has expressed the highest opinions of

Irving's productions, and there is perhaps not another man in this country whose good opinion is so valuable." Charles R. Leslie, "Letter to Miss Leslie," April 9, 1820, in *Autobiographical Recollections of the Late Charles Robert Leslie*, ed. Tom Taylor (Abermarle Street: John Murray, 1860, Scholar Select Reprint), 81–2.

2. Irving was connected to Lord Byron and Sir Walter Scott through the publisher John Murray. Murray introduced Byron to Scott in 1812, the same year he published *Childe Harold's Pilgrimage*. Murray also published writers such as Thomas Campbell, Thomas Moore, and Jane Austin. In 1817, Irving was introduced to Scott through a letter from Campbell. See Brian Jay Jones, *Washington Irving: An American Original* (New York: Arcade Publishing, 2008), 99, 150, 193.

3. Edinburgh Review 33 (January 1820), 79.

4. Larry J. Reynolds, *James Kirke Paulding*, Twayne's United States Authors Series 464 (Boston: Twayne Publishers, 1984), 10–1. James Kirk Paulding was a lifelong friend of Irving, but they differed on the issue of nationalist chauvinism. Irving rejected nationalism, seeking to be more of a citizen of the world in the spirit of Oliver Goldsmith, and sought reconciliation with England, which he regarded as an indispensable fount of identity for Americans. Irving's attempt to heal the postwar divide between England and the United States is most clearly seen in his 1819 *Sketch Book* essay "English Writers on America." Paulding's 1820 essay "The Wreck of Genius" seems at least partly aimed at Irving, who had published the first half of his most British-themed "sketches." Later, in 1835, Pauling would continue to articulate his agenda for American literature, that writers should free themselves of "English models" and "a habit of servile imitation."

5. Joy S. Kasson, *Artistic Voyagers: Europe and the American Imagination in the Works of Irving, Allston, Cole, Cooper, and Hawthorne*. Contributions in American Studies 60 (Westport, Connecticut: Greenwood Press, 1983), 37.

6. Kasson, 3.

7. Ralph Aderman, "Introduction" in *Critical Essays on Washington Irving*, ed. Ralph Alderman (Boston, G.K. Hall and Co., 1990), 2.

8. See the discussion or Stanley William's biography a few paragraphs below.

9. William Hedges, *Washington Irving: An American Study, 1802–1832* (Baltimore: Johns Hopkins Press, 1965), 2.

10. One of the first to address this issue of American identity was F.O. Matthiessen, who saw Emerson's ability to probe "to the origins of speech in order to find out the sources of its mysterious power" was the basis for the distinctly American literature that followed. In Emerson, language itself was reforged in the volcanic depths of the human spirit where "words become one with things." In Emerson, language itself was new again. *American Renaissance: Art and Expression in the Age of Emerson and Whitman* (London and New York: Oxford University Press, 1941), 30.

11. See, for example, Albert Boime, *The Art of Exclusion: Representing Blacks in the Nineteenth Century* (Washington and London: Smithsonian Institution Press, 1990); Angela Miller, *Empire of the Eye: Landscape Representation and American Cultural Politics, 1825–1875* (Ithaca and London: Cornell University Press, 1993). One early study in liminal figures was William Treuttner's *The Natural Man Observed: A Study of Catlin's Indian Gallery* (Washington, DC, 1979). George

Catlin was a Pennsylvania artist who aspired to the highest ideal of history painting as expounded by Sir Joshua Reynolds, but the United States was dominated by portrait painting, which was very competitive, and the lower status art form of landscape painting just beginning to emerge in the 1820s. Caitlin opted out and went west in 1830 to paint Native Americans before they disappeared. "As far as the critic was concerned, roaming the wilderness and painting Indians was a pursuit that placed the artist outside of traditional academic boundaries; therefore, he was not entitled to serious professional consideration." Treuttner, *The Natural Man Observed*, 14. Curiously, Caitlin went West and painted Osage and Creek peoples west of the Arkansas River within a year or so of Washington Irving's *Tour of the Prairies*.

12. The first major attempt in this century to situate Irving and other less-known figures in a context of fruitful boundary-crossing was Paul Giles, *Transatlantic Insurrections: British Culture and the Formation of American Culture* (Philadelphia: University of Pennsylvania Press, 2001), 142–63. More recently, a similar approach has been taken in Andrew Hemingway and Alan Wallach, eds. *Transatlantic Romanticism: British and American Art and Literature* (Amherst and Boston: University of Massachusetts Press, 2015), 1–25. Joy Casson's insightful book from 1983, cited above, was also in this category of interdisciplinary boundary-crossing.

13. The phrase is borrowed from Peter Antelyes, who described Irving's strategy in his Western writings as an integration of literature and the conception of the West as a marketplace. Antelyes's phrase is well chosen, and it captures a tendency toward compromise, a kind of straddling of polarities, that is characteristic of Irving more broadly. *Tales of Adventurous Enterprise: Washington Irving and the poetics of Western Expansion* (New York: Columbia University Press, 1990), xvi.

14. Rudiger Safranski, *Romanticism: A German Affair*, trans. Robert E. Goodwin (Evanston: Northwestern University Press, 2014), 16.

15. While touring the Cathedral of Bordeaux in 1804, he decried "the unhallowed hands of tasteless barbarians" that "have stripped the paintings from the walls, and torn the images of the saints from the niches in which they had retained peaceable possession for centuries." "Letter to Peter Irving," July 12, 1804, *Letters I*, 24.

16. Williams, Vol. 1, 178.

17. Irving has continually suffered at the hands of critics for not being someone else. He was not Wordsworth; he was not Coleridge; he was not Emerson; he was not Hawthorne, and he was certainly not Melville! For almost verbatim remarks along these lines, see Williams, Vol. I, 63. At one point Williams criticized Irving for playing the flute in his lodgings during his Grand Tour rather than writing Emersonian meditations on European civilization, an obvious symptom of shallowness and sentimentality. Irving was one who mistook "reverie ... for thought itself." See Williams, I, 27. Reverie was a central theme of the life, thought, and artwork of Washington Allston, so presumably Allston—America's greatest romantic painter before Thomas Cole—was hopelessly shallow as well. In the aftermath of World War I, sentiment and reverie were unforgivable sins among modernist standard-bearers.

18. One of his close friends, Henry Brevoort, had just married, and he had written shortly beforehand expressing a sorrowful feeling of being left behind. See Jones, *Washington Irving*, 142–3.

19. Kasson, 8–20.
20. Kasson, 37.
21. The impact of this generation gap between colonial fathers and early nineteenth-century children is discussed in *The Peale Family: Creation of a Legacy, 1770–1870*, ed. Lillian B. Miller (New York: Abbeville Press, 1996), 17–35, 135–49. Charles Wilson Peale, an Enlightenment patriarch, painter of the founders and the creator of the nation's first natural history museum, cast a long shadow with a heavy hand of controlling expectation in his children's lives. The paternal expectation was especially crushing for Raphaelle Peale, one of America's greatest still-life painters, but who died young at least partly as a result of an unresolvable struggle with his father's disapproval. The mercury and arsenic used for preserving natural history specimens in the museum seem to have had a long-term impact on Raphaelle's health, but the father excoriated him for a lack of self-control. Nicolai Cikovsky, *Raphaelle Peale Still Lifes* (Washington: National Gallery of Art, 1988), 116. The Quaker patriarch with a commitment to Enlightenment era scientific classification and rationality could be as harsh toward a child as the most severe Puritan of the colonial era.
22. Jeffrey Rubin-Dorsky, *Adrift in the Old World: The Psychological Pilgrimage of Washington Irving* (Chicago and London: University of Chicago Press, 1988), xiii–xviii.
23. For example, F.O. Matthiessen argues that "Franklyn and Irving had taken considerable pains to develop a style" but did not "pass beyond current models or usage." Only with Emerson did any American probe "the origins of speech," discover "the sources of its mysterious powers," and extend "the possibilities of expression" with a new and "enormous fertility of life" fitting to the potentiality of the expansive new republic. *American Renaissance*, 30.

Matthiessen followed Emerson in his desire for a nonderivative American literature, and shared Melville's view that Irving was nothing but an "appendix to Goldsmith," 187. Andrew Burstein, in his excellent biography of Irving, also seemed to see the eighteenth-century influence on Irving as a matter of style; however, Burstein did not imply, like the others, that it was style without content; Andrew Burstein, *The Original Knickerbocker: The Life of Washington Irving* (New York: Basic Books, 2007), 151.
24. Elsie Lee West, "Introduction," in Washington Irving, *Oliver Goldsmith: A Biography*, ed. Elsie Lee West. The Complete Works of Washington Irving, Volume XVII (Boston: Twayne Publishers, 1978), xv–xvi.
25. *The Life of Washington Irving* (New York and London: Oxford University Press, 1935), discussed in Burstein, *The Original Knickerbocker*, 335–6. Williams's biography is a tour de force of thorough scholarship and lucid, eloquent writing. He has learned to write gracefully, and how to mock someone, from Irving itself. The biography is a delight to read and it is full of rich biographical details and valuable insights; however, there runs through it a thread of contempt which surfaces over and over again in witty but condescending—and occasionally biting—remarks.
26. Williams, "Supplementary Studies," *Life*, Vol. II, 278. This passage is but one example of a refrain that runs through the meticulously researched biography.
27. Williams, Vol. II, 53.
28. Aderman, "Introduction," 17.

29. Peter Martin, *Pursuing Innocent Pleasures: The Gardening World of Alexander Pope* (Hamden: Archon Books, 1984), 3–6.

30. Donald A. Ringe, *The Pictorial Mode: Space and Time in the Art of Bryant, Irving and Cooper* (Lexington: The University of Kentucky Press, 1971), 1–8. See also chapter 1, "The New Epistemology," in Ernest Lee Tuveson, *The Imagination as a Means of Grace: Locke and the Aesthetics of Romanticism* (Berkeley and Los Angeles: University of California Press, 1960), 5–41.

31. Williams, Vol. I, 7.

32. Williams, Vol. II, 46.

33. For a discussion of great trees as America's antiquities in Washington Irving and Thomas Cole, see the second half of chapter 5.

34. By the time Irving wrote his revised edition, the use of the name Wiley would evoke a sense of impending disaster. In June 1826, the entire family of frontier settler Samuel Willey—a wife and five children—were buried alive in a massive avalanche in the White Mountains of New Hampshire after torrential rains. The incident was infamous, and aside from a few colonial war sites, provided a sense of hallowed history in the American wilderness. For proponents "of Archibald Allison's associationist philosophy, and other literary nationalists of the day, the Willey disaster provided the perfect opportunity for American writers to hallow their country's scenery with story and song as Scott and Burns had done in Scotland. . . . The avalanche had at last supplied Americans with ruins on a grand scale." The Willey Disaster site was visited by Nathanial Hawthorne in 1830, described in a letter to his mother, and alluded to in "The Ambitious Guest." The incident was commemorated in the painting, *The Crawford Notch of the White Mountains* by Thomas Cole in 1839. See John F. Sears, "The Making of an American Tourist Attraction: The Willey House in the White Mountains," in his *Sacred Places: American Tourist Attractions in the Nineteenth Century* (Oxford and New York: Oxford University Press, 1989), 72–8. Obviously, no such allusion was possible in the original 1820 version of "Sleepy Hollow"; nevertheless, the incident was famous, and for any reader after 1826, the reference to Wiley in a menacing setting would have been read as a portent of disaster. Irving would no doubt have been pleased with such an added, if unintended, layer of meaning to this climactic passage.

35. The major was arrested as part of Benedict Arnold's plot against West Point; three locals noticed something suspicious and found a note from Arnold in the major's boot. The United States did not have much history at that point; however, what little was available, Irving would utilize to create a sense of a storied landscape. In this case the story was so widely known, Irving could allude to it without providing details. There is a note of irony in the narrative: normally schoolboys were fearful of the spot; in this case, a gullible schoolmaster was even more spooked.

36. Washington Irving, *The Sketchbook of Geoffrey Crayon, Gent.*, ed. Hasked Springer (Boston: Twayne Publishers, 1978).

37. Washington Irving, *History, Tales and Sketches*, ed. James W. Tuttleton (New York: Literary Classics of the United States, Inc., 1983), 769.

38. James W. Tuttleton, "Style and Fame: Irving's *The Sketch Book*," in *A Fine Silver Thread: Essays on American Writing and Criticism* (Chicago: Ivan R. Dee, 1998), 13.

39. Tuttleton, "Style and Fame," 6.

40. Michael Levy and Robert Sayre, *Romanticism against the Tide of Modernity*, 63, cited in Hemingway, *Transatlantic Romanticism*, 7.

41. In *The Sketch Book*, the sentimental and wistfully melancholy ruminations on different characters in England seem to reflect significant personal meditation. He had faced the death of his first love Matilda Hoffman in 1809, the loss of the family business in 1816, and even more recently the death of his mother. A helpful and strongly autobiographical reading of these sentimental English episodes can be found in Joy Kasson, "Washington Irving: The Growth of a Romantic Writer," in *The Old and New World Romanticism of Washington Irving*, ed. Stanley Brown (Westport, Connecticut: Greenwood Press, 1986), 27–34. Because Irving seemed to be working out his personal losses and a crisis of identity in an indirect way, projecting his struggles onto Rosco and others, I would refer to these episodes as a kind of "refractory autobiography." Indeed, the tendency to almost never say anything directly is characteristic of Irving.

42. John Brewer, *The Pleasures of the Imagination: English Culture in the Eighteenth Century* (New York: Farrar, Straus and Gireaux, 1997), xix–xx.

43. *Spectator*, III:564, cited in Carole Fabricant, "The Aesthetics and Politics of Landscape in the Eighteenth Century," in *Studies in Eighteenth-Century British Art and Aesthetics*, ed. Ralph Cohen (Berkeley: University of California Press, 1985).

44. See Ch.4 for Irving's belief that the sublime was unsustainable. Many Americans stood in awe of Native Americans while assuming they were doomed.

45. See my discussion of Thomas Jefferson's agenda with Native Americans in chapter 2.

46. David Hume's ethic was part of his broader attempt to build a science of human nature modelled on Isaac Newton's physics. Based on observation of actual behavior (not prescriptions of how people ought to be), one could discover core principles of universal human nature. While Hume did indeed see egoism or self-interest as one operating principle in humans, in competition with moral sentiments, he saw the principle of benevolence as the heart of morality. Morality was for human primarily a matter of passion—we do not like to see people harmed and so we disapprove when harm is done. We approve or disapprove based on common human feelings that are observable in daily life across cultures. Fellow-feeling gives rise to benevolence, kindness, friendship, and the moral judgments that accompany them. Because human nature is as universal as the laws of physics that generated it, patterns of behavior are universal, both at the individual level and at the communal level. Thus, it is possible to understand another person anywhere in the world, and one can also observe the patterns that govern the rise and fall of nations. The confidence that one can charitably understand people of other cultures—a common feature of the eighteenth-century culture created by Hume and others, is at the heart of Irving's cosmopolitan experience. See David Hume, *An Enquiry Concerning the Principles of Morals*, ed. Tom L. Beauchamp. Oxford Philosophical Texts (Oxford and New York: Oxford University Press, 1998), 12–26.

47. See chapter 6.

48. A passage in David Hume's "Rise and Progress of the Arts and Science" lays out a sense of necessary fall built into the apex of a civilization that is curiously similar to Cole's own presentation: "When the arts and sciences come to perfection in any state, from that moment they naturally, or rather necessarily decline, or seldom or never revive in that nation, where they formally flourished." In David Hume, *More Works by David Hume* (London: Forgotten Books, 2008), 18. Alan Wallach has pointed out that a more likely source for the idea of an inevitable rise and fall of nations, with the luxury characteristic of a mercantile age as the crucial pivot in the turn toward a fall, is found in the widely read *Sketches of the History of Man* (1774) by Lord Kames. Cole is clear in his own note accompanying *Destruction* that the fall comes quickly in comparison to the gradual rise once the threshold of luxurious decadence is crossed. See Alan Wallach, *What's in a Name?* interpreting Thomas Cole's *Course of Empire* (Beecher Lecture: Thomas Cole National Historic Site, November 24, 2019), 6–8.

49. Recent scholarship has drawn attention to Cole's critique of the British Empire, but given that the framework implies all civilizations are fundamentally the same in their rise and fall, there is no reason to assert an American exceptionalism to the rule of history. As Tim Barringer points out in his discussion of *Destruction*, the Palace of Westminster in London, and a huge portion of Lower Manhattan had both recently burned, and these similar destructions were surely in the mind of the artist. Both empires are subject to the same law of history. See Elizabeth Mankin Kornhauser and Tim Barringer, eds. *Thomas Cole's Journey:Atlantic Crossings* (New York, Metropolitan Museum of Art), 210–15.

50. See chapter 5.

51. Brewer, *The Pleasures of the Imagination*, xx–xxi.

52. Celestina, Savonius-Wroth, "'In the Village Circle': Washington Irving and Transatlantic Folk Revivals," *Western Folklore* 79, no. 2 (Spring/Summer 2020), 180

53. Washington Irving, *Bracebridge Hall; Tales of A Traveller; The Alhambra* (New York, Literary Classics of the United States, Inc., 1991), 298–9.

54. Haskel Springer points out in the "Explanatory Notes" that references to Beaumont, Fletcher, and Jonson draw attention to the collaborative nature of writing, as Beaumont and Fletcher wrote plays together and Fletcher frequently worked together with Shakespeare and Ben Jonson. Washington Irving, *The Sketch Book of Geoffrey Crayon, Gent*, ed. Haskell Springer (Boston: Twayne Publishers, 1978), 311.

55. *The Sketch Book*, 63.

56. Huston Smith, *The World's Religions: Our Great Wisdom Traditions* (New York and San Francisco: HarperSanFranscisco, 1990), 388–9.

57. The tendency to allow one story to segue into another in *Bracebridge Hall* and *Tales of a Traveller* may also be partly based on the pattern of storytelling found in Ovid. See chapter 4 for a discussion of a relationship between Irving and Ovid.

58. "I was led to believe that somehow or other, everything that was pleasant was wicked," cited in Williams, Vol. I, 7.

59. Williams, Vol. I, 154.

60. M.H. Abrams, *Natural Supernaturalism: Tradition and Revolution in Romantic Literature* New York: W.W. Norton & Company, 1971), 13.

61. See "Preface to Lyrical Ballads (1800)" and *The Prelude, or Growth of a Poet's Mind*, in William Wordsworth, *The Prelude; Selected Poems and Sonnets*, ed. Carlos Baker (New York: Holt, Rinehart and Winston, Inc., 1954).

62. Commenting on a line in *Bracebridge Hall*, where Irving notes an affinity between all living things, William Hedges comments, "It looks like the drippings lapped up from the platter of a higher romanticism by a poor devil of an author." William L. Hedges, *Washington Irving: An American Study, 1802–1832* (Baltimore: John Hopkins Press, 1965), 126.

63. Jochen Achilles, "Besieged Sleepy Hollows in Transatlantic Perspective: Identity Construction and Contestation in Washington Irving's *The Sketch Book*," in *The Construction and Contestation of American Cultures and Identities in the Early National Period*, ed. Udo J. Hebel. American Studies Monograph Series 78 (Heidelberg: Universitätsverlag, 1999), 119.

64. Achilles, "Besieged Sleepy Hollows," 123–9.

65. Irving's self-description is revised from a letter he wrote to Sir Walter Scott in 1818, when he resolved to turn down an editing job in favor of a life as a professional writer. Nevertheless, Tuttleton is correct that Irving displayed intense discipline, even if it came in bursts. The self-presentation to Scott as an unfocused wanderer may well be a persona. Joy Casson suggested it is a persona similar to that of Geoffrey Crayon, and in its context speaking to Scott at a pivotal time in his life reflected increased resolve and self-confidence. In other words, the self-presentation as an unfocused wanderer may be playfully ironic and meant to gently excuse him from the job Scott had found for him. He was, in fact, more focused than ever before when he wrote the original letter.

66. Kasson, 29.

67. Tuttleton, "Style and Fame," 17.

68. Andrew Hemingway, "Introduction," in *Transatlantic Romanticism: British and American Literature, 1790–1860*, eds. Andrew Hemingway and Alan Wallach (Amherst and Boston: University of Massachusetts Press, 2015), 10.

69. Burstein discusses the dislocation of time and self as a major theme in both *A History of New York* and *The Sketchbook*, especially "Rip Van Winkle": "God knows . . . I'm not myself:—I'm somebody else—That's me yonder," 75, 127. See also Hedges, 137–42.

70. Bryan Jay Wolf, *Romantic Revision: Culture and Consciousness in Nineteenth-Century American Painting and Literature* (Chicago and London: University of Chicago Press, 1982), 109.

71. David O. Stuart, *American Emperor: Aaron Burr's Challenge to Jefferson's America* (New York: Simon and Schuster, 2011), 13–25.

72. At an earlier stage in his career, especially in the aftermath of the War of 1812 and then the "Paper War," becoming Episcopalian would have been but another reason for people to brand him as "too English."

73. Oliver Goldsmith, "Letter 3," *The Citizen of the World*, in *Oliver Goldsmith: The Vicar of Wakefield and Other Writings*, ed. Frederick W. Hilles. Modern Library (New York: Random House, 1955), 87.

74. Martha Nussbaum, "Citizens of the World," in *Cultivating Humanity: A Classical Defense of Reform in Liberal Education* (Cambridge: Harvard University Press, 1998).

75. See chapter 6.

76. Martha Nussbaum, *The Cosmopolitan Tradition: A Noble but Flawed Ideal* (Cambridge and London: The Belknap Press of Harvard University Press, 2019), 1.

77. Nussbaum, *Cosmopolitan Tradition*, 2.

78. "Someone having reproached him for going into dirty places, his reply was that the sun too visits cesspools without being defiled." Laurence Sterne, and Irving in his youthful scatological phase—reveling in the muck of early New York—would have appreciated such a passage. Diogenes Laertius, *Lives of the Eminent Philosophers*, Vol. II, trans. E.R. Hicks. Loeb Classics 185 (Cambridge and London: Harvard University Press, 1925, 2005), 65.

79. Nussbaum, *Cosmopolitan Tradition*, 214.

80. For an example of how neo-Stoic philosophical concepts shaped the art of the Flemish painter Jan Bruegel, see the important study, by Leopoldine Prosperetti, *Landscape and Philosophy in the Art of Jan Bruegel the Elder (1568–1625)* (London and New York: Routledge, Taylor and Francis Group, 2016; first printing by Ashgate 2009), 1–63. Jan Bruegel's family were Dutch Calvinists, but the whole region of the southern Netherlands was abruptly annexed to Spain and became Catholic at the snap of a finger. Rather than migrate to Germany or stay and face harsh social penalties, the family chose to raise Jan as Catholic. He was apparently sincere in his Catholic faith, and he certainly had better opportunities for artistic patronage as a Catholic. However, there were Protestants he knew and loved, and so he chose—like many people of goodwill—to find a pragmatic common ground. Surely this is the kind of pragmatic goodwill that Irving would approve of. The strategy is that, rather than fighting over religious dogma and focusing on what divides people, you work with religion-friendly philosophical frameworks that are neutral on the most controversial issues of the day. For Irving, it was the Cynic philosophy of world citizenship. However, focusing on such a framework does not imply that one has abandoned any religious belief. It simply means that a person talks less about religion and more about what people can agree on.

81. Nussbaum, *Cosmopolitan Tradition*, 212.

82. Washington Irving, *Salgamundi*, in *Irving: History, Tales, and Sketches: Letters of Jonathon Oldstyle, Gent.; Salgamundi; A History of New York; The Sketchbook of Geoffrey Crayon, Gent* (New York: Literary Classics of the United States, Inc., 1983), 81. Interlibrary loan has been down for over six months in Florida, and so sometimes I have to rely on Library of American rather than the preferred Twayne editions of the Complete Works of Washington Irving.

83. William Hedges, *"The Knickerbocker History* as Knickerbocker's 'History,'" in *The Old and New World Romanticism of Washington Irving*, ed. Stanley Brodwin (Westport, Connecticut: Greenwood Press, 1986), 161.

84. *Salgamundi*, 81.

85. Book I, Ch. 5, *A History of New York*, ed. Michael Black and Nancy Black. The Complete Works of Washington Irving VII (Boston: Twayne Publishers, 1984), 42.

86. Hedges, 3.

87. Letter to Alexander Beebee, July 22, 1804, in Washington Irving, *Letters: Volume I, 1802–1823*, ed. Ralph M. Aderman, Herbert L. Kleinfield, and Jenifer S. Banks. CW XXIII (Boston: Twayne Publishers, 1978), 38.

88. August 14, 1804, *Letters I*, 33.

89. Irving, *The* Sketchbook, 9–10.

90. Andrew Jackson Downing, *A Treatise on the Theory and Practice of Landscape Gardening* (New York: A.O. Moore & Co., 1859), 353–4.

91. April 4, 1805, *Journals I*, 280.

92. Michael Rosenthal, *Constable: The Painter and his Landscape* (New Haven and London: Yale University Press, 1983), 31.

93. Washington Irving, *A Tour on the Prairies*, ed. James Playstead Wood (New York: Pantheon Books, 1967), 5.

94. Hedges, 6–9.

95. Rubin-Dorsky, Adrift, 102; Burstein, *The Original Knickerbocker*, 128.

96. Joseph Addison, "The Pleasures of the Imagination," *Spectator* III: 540–1, cited in Fabricant, "The Aesthetics and Politics," 54–5.

97. Irving's overall relationship with women is helpfully discussed by Jennifer Banks, "Washington Irving, the Nineteenth-Century Bachelor," in *Critical Essays on Washington Irving*, ed. Ralph Aderman (Boston: G.K. Hall & Co., 1990), 253–65. Banks notes that women seemed to function as the voice of duty and responsibility, and in general he created an idealization that made them intimidating even as he revered them. . Banks notes that his long period abroad was due to his desire to be a cultural ambassador to Europe, as well as a desire to avoid routine jobs, not so much a desire to avoid marriage itself.

98. Samuel Eliot Morison, *The Oxford History of the American People* (New York, Oxford University Press, 1965), 73.

99. "Introduction," *Astoria, or Anecdotes of an Enterprise beyond the Rocking Mountains* in Washington Irving, *Three Western Narratives: A Tour on the Prairies; Astoria; The Adventures of Captain Bonneville*. Library of America 146 (New York: Literary Classics of the United States, Inc., 2004), 179.

100. *Astoria*, 213.

101. Reynolds, *James Kirke Paulding*, 4.

102. See chapter 3.

103. The general claim and precise phrase come from John Seelye in a private letter cited by Beth Lueck, *American Writer's and the Picturesque Tour* (New York and London: Garland Publishing, Inc., 1997), 96–7. My own thesis is deeply indebted to Beth Lueck's work on Irving and the picturesque. I will follow her on several points, but I dispute the notion that the aesthetic gaze is simply an imperialistic gaze.

104. See chapter 3.

105. This very mild acceptance of the mainstream religion of one's culture is consistent with the relativistic skepticism of Michel de Montaigne and the ancient Hellenistic philosopher Sextus Empiricus. See the discussion in chapter 2.

106. "The Author," in *Bracebridge Hall; Tales of a Traveller; The Alhambra* (New York: Literary Classics of the United States, Inc., 1991), 11.

Chapter 2

Satire in the Name of World Citizenship

Washington Irving embraced the philosophy of Oliver Goldsmith and aspired to be a citizen of the world. This meant tolerance and celebration of diverse peoples and customs, but it also involved a critique of religion when religious people of any creed displayed the chauvinism that undermined global civility. On the matters of religion, Irving was at least partly a child of the Enlightenment. Loretta Wyatt points out that across many years Irving "took scrupulous care to distance himself from the possibility of being supposed superstitious or credulous."[1] This is one of many areas of life where Irving maintained consistency from 1804 until 1848, when he joined the Episcopal Church after the death of his close friend John Jacob Astor. In the end, he chose the religion of his mother.[2]

From the biography by his nephew, Pierre Irving, we learn that he was not engaged at all with the stern Presbyterianism of his father.[3] Evidence of a consistent stance regarding at least the most extreme abuses of religion emerged in Irving's journals of his Grand Tour from 1804 to 1806. While he was especially concerned as a young man to show he was a rational and civilized traveler, and not a gullible one, this wary outlook toward religion did not really change over his body of work while he was writing fiction, travel narrative, and Spanish history. Calvinist religion, that of both New England Congregationalists and mid-Atlantic Presbyterians, demanded hard work and material prosperity, while denying the joy of life he would see in French traders. Religious commitment was not high in the post-Revolutionary American Republic until the Second Great Awakening began. Schooled by Oliver Goldsmith in classical cosmopolitan values, Irving "was immunized intellectually at an early age against most aspects of religion," and "he rejected church affiliation as an adult until long after his literary reputation was won."[4]

A typical remark on religion is found in his comments on a tourist site at Syracuse; the fountain of Arethusa was connected to a story by Ovid about the pursuit of the nymph by the hunter Alpheus. Arethusa was transformed by Diana into a fountain, and Alphaeus into a river. It was believed that they would mingle together so long as fountain and river flowed. "The ancients firmly believed that this fountain was conducted by subterranean canals under the sea quite (far) from Greece."[5] This very myth was alluded to in Samuel Taylor Coleridge's Kubla Khan, where "caverns measureless to man" in the depths of "a sunless sea" evoked a sense of primordial awe and a fount of sensuality. While for Coleridge the five-mile garden around this "romantic chasm" was "a savage place as holy and enchanted as e'er beneath a waning moon was haunted by woman wailing for her demon lover,"[6] Irving the young traveler simply wanted to assure his reader he was not duped by extravagant claims that a cup won in the Olympic Games at the fountain of Arethusa in Greece would emerge at the fountain of Arethusa in Syracuse: "They likewise pretended that the blood of victims sacrificed at the fountain in Greece stained the waters in Syracuse. *Priest-craft has been the same in all ages* and scruples at no falsehood or contrivance to support its impositions" (my emphasis).[7]

The fact that one does not want to be duped as a tourist does not imply a rejection of all aspects of religion. Nevertheless, the term "priestcraft" is significant because it formed a central theme in Anthony Ashley Cooper, Third Earl of Shaftebury's *Characteristic of Men, Manners, Opinions, Times*, a collection of essays pulled together for publication in 1711. This guide to manners was influential for all aspiring gentlemen throughout the eighteenth century and far into the nineteenth. When it was published, England was just emerging from an era of political turbulence and religious persecution in the aftermath of the Glorious Revolution of 1688. In the recent past, Catholics, Quakers, and other Protestant dissenters had all been legally proscribed or directly persecuted. Shaftesbury's response to government belligerence was that a civilized people should not persecute people for their religion, but that ludicrous religious beliefs and practices should be lampooned in a free press, so that not too many people succumb to the nonsense, a pattern that can be seen especially in Irving's mockery of New England witch trials. Shaftsbury had in mind various "enthusiasts," but also raised concern that Protestant clergy were beginning to function in the same way as Roman Catholic leadership. In Shaftesbury's history of "priest-craft," there was a long line of continuity in abusive manipulative behavior: "Ancient Egypt, infested with priests and superstitions, was the source of a pattern bequeathed first to the Hebrews, and then by long lines of filiation to later Rome and the Catholic Middle Ages," and then more recently Protestant leadership in England.[8] Irving's double criticism of Catholic superstition and Puritan power abuses follows Shaftesbury quite closely. Such priestcraft was all the same. Whether Irving read Shaftesbury's work directly, or whether he absorbed his ideals through polite conversation in a highly engaged social life with other aspiring gentlemen, the influence seems clear. Wit was valued and opponents were to be lampooned in a free press. Another way Irving followed Shaftesbury was "the harmonization of ethical and aesthetic experience."[9]

At Rome, Irving contrasted the greatness and rationality of classical civilization with the superstition that followed and "like a baneful blast has passed over the . . . Mistress of the World . . . sunk from her former greatness into a state of ignorance and poverty. . . . How have the mighty fallen!" "The people at large once manly, noble, and independent in their manners, now groveling servile, superstitious—cringing to their priests and tamely submitting to the most glaring impositions."[10] Such criticism of priests and ignorant lay people could have been written by any Protestant tourist, and here perhaps we see a fusion of Enlightenment skepticism with his disillusionment with his Presbyterian upbringing. At the very least, Irving was critical of vividly abusive extremes of Christianity in both Catholic and Protestant manifestations.

Irving's mockery of Cotton Mather in "The Legend of Sleepy Hollow" and by his criticism of the numerous witch trials in Massachusetts and Connecticut history in *A History of New York* were certainly a prominent part of his general characterization of New Englanders, but the critique of New England culture was presented because it so grotesquely violated the ideal of world citizenship. The burning of witches (and we might add, Quakers) is the most serious manifestation of Calvinist chauvinism:

> Finding, therefore that neither exhortation, nor sound reason, nor friendly entreaty had any avail on these hardened offenders, they resorted to the most urgent arguments of torture; and having thus absolutely wrung the truth from their lips—they condemn then to undergo the roasting due to their heinous crimes unto the heinous crimes they had confessed. Some even carried their perverseness so far as to expire under the torture, protesting their innocence to the last; but these were looked upon as thoroughly and absolutely possessed by the devil.[11]

The nonsense of the witch trials was exposed. First, there was the folly of assuming you could wring truth from people by torture. Second was the absurd policy of taking all emerging evidence—however contradictory—as proof of the guilty charge. If the person confessed, under duress, to being a witch, that person was executed; if someone maintained innocence to the end, this was taken as proof that the person was even more radically possessed by the devil and utterly recalcitrant in perversity. For Irving, as for Shaftesbury, the priestcraft that was "all the same" included Puritan leaders as well as Catholic.

When Irving went to the American West many years later, he would also describe some Native American beliefs as superstitious, such as the idea that thunder is caused by the gods' anger.[12] Henry Leavitt Ellsworth described an incident on the prairie in which Irving did not seem to him sufficiently respectful of the Bible. As they were settling into the camp one evening, Irving was reading a French Bible and joking around about "the curious things that took place" in the Old Testament stories, particularly on the issue of "courtship and marriage." Irving was probably getting a good laugh out of the story in Genesis 29 of how—through Uncle Laban's trickery—Jacob went into the wedding tent of Leah thinking it was Rachel, only to discover he had married and slept with the wrong person when he saw her face in the morning. This episode is surely a story Irving would have loved, but his lighthearted playfulness regarding a Bible story seemed irreverent to Ellsworth, and he thought Irving might better take heed to his eternal soul rather than sit so lightly upon life's depth.[13] Irving maintained a partially skeptical eye toward religion throughout his literary career, and his willingness to critique superstition or abuse of power was not limited to any one group. Being a citizen of the world meant being open to value persons and traditions from different cultures without chauvinism, but also a universal willingness to critique religious beliefs and practices everywhere based on universal moral principles.

Irving did, however, show some sensitivity to the aesthetic power of Roman Catholic worship. He wrote in a Christmas letter to his brother William:

There certainly is something very solemn & imposing in the ceremonies of the Roman church. Unwilling as we may be to acknowledge it—it must be confessed that the forms & ceremonies & situations & places have a powerful effect on our feeling in matters of religion. To enter a superb & solemnly constructed edifice

Whose ancient pillars rear their marble heads
To bear aloft its arched and ponderous roof—

Gives us a dignified idea of the being to whom it is erected. Its long and dimly lighted aisles and marbled chapels adorned with painting and statues pointing out some action or attribute of the Deity have an impressive appearance & the gloomy grandeur of the whole strikes us with reverence and respect.

"looking tranquility it strikes an awe!"

Then the service itself has such an air of pomp & sublimity that I always feel more filled with an exalted idea of the deity than at any other time—The Superb alters . . . the solemn movements . . . the full chant of the choir . . . the incense arising . . . has together an effect on my feelings irresistibly solemn.

Do not fear that I am turning Catholic—I only show you how easily the imagination of an indifferent spectator may be heated by form and shew. In matters of religion it is the most assailable part of the man—and were I attempting to introduce a new Doctrine my attempts should be chiefly directed against the imagination.[14]

As moved as he was by the awesome grandeur of some Catholic services, he noted these devices that appeal to the imagination can be used to touch people at their most vulnerable moments. The remark about a potential strategy for creating a new religion suggests that religions are human constructs. This is not to say that he did not necessarily believe in God; indeed he enjoyed the worship that evoked a proper sense of awe; however, specific religions with their particular doctrines were apparently human creations that, even when well-constructed— perhaps precisely because they were well-constructed—had the capacity to inspire people, for good or ill. It is of course possible that Irving was going out of his way to criticize Catholicism, simply to assure his more conservative Protestant brother he was not turning Catholic in all this enjoyment of Roman Catholic art. Nevertheless, the sensitivity that Irving showed here, and in his responses to a painting of the Virgin and Mary Magdalene by Guido Reni on his Grand Tour, was akin to the sensitivity of his response many years later to the *Christus Consolator* by Ari Schaeffer, a print of which triggered his conversion to Anglican Christianity. In spite of Irving's Enlightenment skepticism and joyless Presbyterian upbringing, there was a hint of religious sensitivity in the presence of great art that would eventually lead him to embrace Anglo-Catholicism.

Irving was also scathing in his criticism of the "ostentatious humility" by cardinals during Holy Week: It was "the most empty parade I ever saw" and "the most pompous farce imaginable." Presumably, it was the highly ritualized foot-washing on Maundy Thursday—a supposed act of servanthood on the part of leaders—that pushed the normally genial Irving over the edge into disgust. Seeing people in such elaborate finery pretending to be humble was too much for him to bear. It was not the artistry, but the hypocrisy, he loathed, as well as the tendency of those leaders to keep the common people in servitude to them. He criticized the common people as ignorant, but he was outraged when he saw them manipulated and abused. We have in one Holy Week service, two perversions of the ideal of humility: undignified groveling on the part of the people, and pretentious behavior on the part of priests who were supposed to be serving the people according to the command of Christ.

However, Irving did value Catholic and Anglican traditions as bearing valuable folk traditions that gave a sense of lively cultural flavor and historical continuity. In describing the costumes associated with the Feast of the Assumption in the French countryside near Montpelier, he noted, "This is a specimen of the liveliness and gaiety of heart that characterized this people before the revolution"; he went on to note that, in the heart of the town where Protestants were in control, such festivals are not allowed to continue.[15] In Irving's estimation, the spirit of the French Revolution and of Protestantism almost equally squelched the joy of life naturally found in traditional peoples. The Enlightenment skepticism in Irving was not simply a youthful stage of reaction. For example, When Irving spoke of the Spanish conquest of Granada in the late 1820s, the persona of Fray Antonio Agapida functioned as means of critiquing Catholic Spain;[16] Irving was consistent on the abuses of organized religion and the problem of superstition over the course of his most productive years, even as he acknowledged that the religion of the people could be the bearer of values worth preserving. Indeed, one wonders if his positive experience with Mediterranean common people in the south of France, and especially during his years in Spain, gradually helped him overcome his fear of the common person, and the fear that democracy was really mobocracy.

CULTURAL EGOCENTRISM 101

A pointed example of the Cynic-style critique of chauvinism endorsed by religion is found in the early chapters of *A History of New York*. In Book I, Chapter II, Irving lampooned speculation about the origins of the cosmos: "Of the creation of the world, we have a thousand contradictory accounts; and though a very satisfactory one is furnished by divine revelation, yet every philosopher feels himself in honor bound to furnish us with a better."[17] While this seeming support for the Bible would no doubt win a few initial approving nods from his readers, it quickly became as subversive of Puritan Christianity as it was the philosophy of the teaching of the Brahmins. In his whirlwind overview, Irving blurred together ancient myths, such as the recurring story of a boar or turtle who dove into the water to bring land to the surface—found in both Hindu and Mohawk tradition—with the speculations of ancient Hellenistic philosophers. His critique did not end with ancient mythology but extended to contemporary natural philosophers, who all too easily relied on the appearance of a comet as an explanatory device. "Here I cannot help noticing the kindness of Providence in supplying comets for the relief of bewildered philosophers"; such "modern sages" could "seize a comet by the beard, mount astride of its tail," and gallop away like a "Connecticut witch on her broomstick, 'to sweep the cobwebs out of the sky.'"[18]

Irving notes that the accounts of cosmic origin are so many and varied that he would just stick with the perfectly good one found in the revelation of the Judeo-Christian scriptures:

And now, having adduced several of the most prominent theories that occur to my recollection, I leave my judicious readers at full liberty to choose among them. They are all serious speculations of learned men—all differ essentially from each other—and all have the same title to belief . . .

For my own part, until the learned have come to an agreement among themselves, I shall content myself with the account handed down to us by Moses; in which I do but follow the example of our ingenious neighbors of Connecticut; who at their first settlement proclaimed, that the colony should be governed by the laws of God—until they had time to make better.[19]

While Irving, in his persona of Diedrich Knickerbocker, postures with a conservative stance that dispenses with foreign balderdash ancient and modern in favor of the comfortable homeland scriptures, his stance was in fact quite similar to that of the French skeptic Michel de Montaigne, who argued that because the evidence for all religions was equally bad, he would simply stick with Christianity, as a sociological guard against anarchy.[20] Skepticism provided the irony of a radical relativism whose practical implications are surprisingly conservative. In a world where no one has access to the truth, you just follow the evidence of the senses as best as you can, knowing they are imperfect, and follow your own culture's relativistic perspective out of convenience and a regard for social stability.[21] Such a view was found in the ancient skeptic Sextus Empiricus, revitalized by Montaigne during the Renaissance, and seemingly embraced by Irving.[22] However, with Irving there was an extra ironic edge; mere acceptance of the law of Moses as a matter of custom was the policy of the Connecticut divines, the people he was most inclined to criticize. Thus, even Irving's momentary Montaigne-like skepticism was undercut; should we just accept the customs of our culture because they are ours and we are comfortable with them? A Skeptic might say yes; a Cynic who was a world citizen would say no.

In this panoramic burlesque of global cosmogonies, Irving singled out "negro philosophers" as an example of acute cultural egocentrism; however, what seems at a first glance merely an appeal to racist attitudes of the period has, in fact, an ironic hook. The reader would be lured into a kind of condescension regarding other peoples' failings as their own greater chauvinism is about to be exposed: "The negro philosophers of Congo affirm that the world was made by the hands of angels, excepting their own country, which the Supreme being constructed himself, that it might be supremely excellent."[23] The idea here that God has shown particular favor to one ethnic group—Africans in the Congo—would to Irving's Anglo-American readers be seen as inherently ludicrous; however, it is nothing less than a critique of any conception of a chosen people, whether understood as the people of Israel or the Elect of Puritan theology or the Roman Catholic Church. Irving has tricked the reader into formally consenting to his cosmopolitan anti-chauvinism, luring them into the perspective with a hint of racist condescension that would have been accepted at the time. However, once the perspective was established, it would apply to all instances of chauvinism wherever they were found. The seemingly racist remark was, in fact, a trap, a hook luring people to a perspective that would ultimately transcend racism.

A similar point is driven home in Book I, Chapter V, where Irving mocked the idea that Native Americans needed to be converted to Christianity through an analogy with voyaging moon people who feel a need to convert earth savages to their heavenly religion. This analogy is part of a sustained satire of colonial American culture that runs through chapters IV–V. Chapter IV explored the question of the method of the peopling of the Americas. In the early nineteenth century, citizens of the new republic were fascinated to speculate about the origins of Native American peoples. One of the great struggles that American Protestants felt was that the New World was so far from the Middle East, the origins of Jewish and Christian scripture. They had great difficulty accepting that America was not part of the biblical story. A common way of relating North America to the Bible story was to suggest that perhaps Native Americas were descendants of Noah, or part of the ten lost tribes of Israel scattered by the Assyrian deportations of 721 BCE. In the 1830s, Joseph Smith, the founder of the Church of Latter-Day Saints, presented such an idea in *The Book of Mormon*. The Garden of Eden was in what is now Independence, Missouri, and Native Americans were descendants of lost tribes known as the Lamanites. Thus, American history and biblical history were not truly separate. Joseph Smith also denied the classical Augustinian and Protestant doctrine of original sin; God was too good to punish people for another person's sins; Humans still sinned as individuals, and were shown the way of life through revelation, but they were not characterized by all-pervasive depravity.[24]

The problem of Old World theology was acute for American Protestants. After the Revolutionary War, a new optimism emerged about humanity's place in a new Garden of Eden, and the old doctrine of utter human sinfulness did not seem to fit the sense of almost endless potential. At the same time, the Bible stories seemed so far away in time and place that people wondered if the Bible was even relevant to life on the American frontier. Joseph Smith daringly affirmed the United States was in fact the original Zion at the heart of God's plan. Emerson, on the other hand, responded to the problem by calling for a new relationship to the cosmos.[25] He recommended the abandonment of a Christianity that was clearly adapted to the Old World and no longer a living spirit: "Men have come to speak of the revelation as somewhat long ago given and done, as if God were dead," and when "the divine nature is attributed to one or two persons," it is "denied to all, and denied with fury."

Emerson wanted God to be present in all the cosmos, including America, and the only way for that to be true—as he saw it—was if God's presence were not concentrated, or incarnate, in one holy man who lived in Palestine 1,800 years ago.[26] Curiously, Emerson and Smith wrestled with the same problem, and came up with very different solutions, yet they shared the idea than humanity was full of a divine potential which normative Protestants, with their doctrine of human sinfulness, would deny. Washington Irving sided with both thinkers against classical Calvinism in the general sense of embracing a more optimistic view of human nature and the enjoyment of life.

Irving did not have the spirituality of a Transcendentalist like Emerson. In *A History of New York*, he simply had the rationality of an Enlightenment wit who would not put up with speculative nonsense, along with the imagination to make up a burlesque history of Dutch New York.[27] Irving thus lampooned the idea that the Native Americans' presence in the United States should be explained by recourse to biblical stories. He ridiculed Columbus, for example, for supposing that gold in Hispaniola must be the Gold of Ophir from Solomon's legendary mines.[28] The upshot of all the possible theories of how Native Americans got to America, including "by accident," is that the Americas have, in fact, been peopled, in at least "five hundred different ways"; indeed, the people of this country had a *variety of fathers*, which as it may not be thought very much to their credit by the common run of readers, the less we say on the subject the better. The question, therefore, I trust, is forever as rest."[29] Irving makes a playful remark hinting at profligate promiscuity in the peopling of America, but as elsewhere, his words form a kind of double entendre. As Michael West has pointed out, "Just as Irving was attracted to punning, so he gravitated toward narratives that turn on double meanings, often risqué ones, to the increasing discomfiture of readers."[30] In this case, the double entendre points beyond the sexual pun to a theme that runs through his life work; at the heart of the American experience are multiple ethnic and cultural traditions, not simple one Anglo-American civilization. In *A History of New York*, this theme would be addressed through the creation of an imaginative history of New Netherlands, with a corresponding idealization of those communities, in contrast to Anglo-American culture, in "The Legend of Sleepy Hollow" and "Dolph Heyliger." Irving would also show sympathy for a wide range of multiethnic characters in "The Money-Diggers" and *A Tour on the Prairie*. Advocacy for a pluralistic America, even more than any bawdy innuendo, would potentially bring "discomfiture" to American readers, and so Irving briskly moves on: The less said, the better. This habit of raising an issue and then quickly diverting to another topic is a pervasive strategy of Irving's cultural critique. Something will surface, and then it will plunge again into hidden depths, only to arise again from unconscious cultural anxieties at other moments.

The lighthearted playfulness of Book I, Chapter IV on the ancient people of America segued into a much more incisive satirical bite, for Irving now took up the colonial rationalization for the displacement of Native Americans. The first justification of the right of discovery, which assumed a territory "was totally uninhabited by man," was rendered ludicrous by the prior speculation on how Native Americans came to be there. If such energy was spent on explaining how they got there, then the lands were clearly already inhabited, and the right of discovery was nonsense. Since this argument failed, justification for displacement now depended on the barbarism of said inhabitants, the prime evidence of which is that "Nothing disturbs the tranquility of their souls," which are "equally insensible to disasters and prosperity. Though half naked, they are as contented as a monarch in his most splendid array. Fear makes no impression on them," and they are no respecter of persons. In short, they were uncivilized because they expressed "indifference to wealth" and other "objects of ambition with us—honour, fame, reputation, riches, posts," and other "distinctions." Such lack of concern proved that the aborigines must be "children in whom the development of reason is not completed."[31] However, as Irving pointed out, this indifference to material possessions and considerations of status was the defining feature of the most prominent Hellenistic philosophies, Stoicism, Epicureanism, and especially Cynicism. By the canons of Western philosophy and spirituality, such persons should be regarded as sages or saints, not barbarians ripe for plunder in the name of civilization.

Irving's critique of Euro-American colonial abuse of indigenous peoples struck at both religion and Enlightenment science at the end of chapter V, with the discussion of the conversion of earth savages to the doctrines of lunar religion. The possibility "that the inhabitants of the moon, by astonishing advancement in science" should arrive at "such a state of *perfectability*, as to control the elements and navigate the boundless realms of space" seems a little akin to Sir Francis Bacon's anticipation of submarines in *The Novum Organon*. The analogy between the disproportionate power of Native American canoes and Spanish ships crossing the Atlantic seems plausible enough. There could be people on another planet similarly disproportionate in scientific power, with the ability to navigate space. The technologically advanced race would regard us as savages, and our planet "nothing but a howling wilderness," the conception that Puritans especially had of the expansive American continent.[32] The problem in this scenario was not so much its plausibility, but the hubris of the technologically superior race in assuming it was approaching perfectibility, when in fact, an advance in science did not imply an advance in morality or spirituality: the advanced race was "possessed of superior knowledge in the art of extermination." The people of Euro-American civilization were obviously savages, because they lived with one wife, rather than the community of wives advocated by Plato, that denizen of a higher realm. These lunar philosophers had spiritual authority of a Papal bull by "the man in the moon himself," and, of course, whiteness and other Anglo-European features were clearly inferior to lunar pea green; thus, the colonists were "authorized and commanded to use every means to convert these infidel savages from the darkness of Christianity, and make them thorough and absolute lunatics." The miserable savages did not have the gratitude to see that the colonists had come "to improve" their "worthless planet."[33] Therefore, the colonists demolished

> our cities with moonstones; until having, by main force, converted us to the true faith, they shall graciously permit us to exist in the torrid deserts of Arabia, or the frozen regions of Lapland, there to enjoy the blessings of civilization and the charms of lunar philosophy, in much the same manner as the enlightened savages of this country are kindly suffered to inhabit the inhospitable forests of the north, or the impenetrable wildernesses of South America.[34]

The arguments Irving parodied go back to Germans and Swiss jurists on the laws of nations, and there is notable criticism of Spanish Catholic explorers,[35] but the incisiveness unleashed seems to be directed at the state of affairs in the United Stated at the end of the second Jefferson administration. The argument about the right of cultivation was used by Americans as widely ranging as Thomas Jefferson, New England Puritans, and Pennsylvania Quakers. All agreed that the blessing of such fertile farmland could not be wasted by allowing hunter-gatherers to roam indiscriminately; for northern Protestants, to do so would be an affront to the gracious provision of Providence. While the Quakers attempted to strike a balance between protecting Indian rights and forcing them to become cultivators of the land, the Puritans were more precise that the right to cultivation entailed the right to exterminate unproductive Native Americans.[36] Jefferson's view of Native Americans was more nuanced. He was concerned to rebut Buffon's claim that all the natural products of North America were but sickly variants on European ones. Jefferson countered that Native Americans were as strong, intelligent, and compassionate as Europeans; they were just at a different stage of civilization, and that their itinerant lifestyle led to poor nutrition and high infant mortality rates. When Indian women married whites and led a more settled existence, they had access to a more stable food supply, and gave birth to children as healthy as whites.[37] It was thus imperative to save the Native Americans from themselves by training them in the ways of settled agriculture. Jefferson also denied that Native American lands had been taken by conquest; he claimed that they always agreed to sell.[38]

Henry Adams summed up Jefferson's policy toward Native Americans best, attempting to protect their rights while ultimately removing them:

> President Jefferson earnestly urged the Indians to become industrious cultivators of the soil; but even for that reform one condition was indispensable. The Indians must be protected from contact with whites; and during the change in their mode of life, they must not be drugged, murdered or defrauded. Trespasses on Indian land and purchases of tribal territory must for a time cease, until the Indian tribes should all be adduced to adopt the new system. Even then the reform would be difficult, for Indian warriors thought death less irksome than daily labor; and men who did not fear death were not easily driven to toil.[39]
>
> There President Jefferson's philanthropy stopped. His greed for land equaled any settler on the border, and his humanity to the Indian suffered the suspicion of having among its motives the purpose of gaining Indian lands for the whites. Jefferson's policy in practice offered a reward for Indian extinction, since he not only claimed the territory of every extinct tribe on the doctrine of paramount sovereignty, but deliberately ordered his Indian agents to tempt the tribal chiefs into debt in order to oblige them to sell the tribal lands, which did not belong to them but to their tribes . . .
>
> Shocked as he would have been at such a method of obtaining the neighboring estate of any Virginia family, he not only suggested but vigorously carried out the system toward the Indians.[40]

Adams also pointed out that it was a widespread practice of Anglo-American settlers to go into Native American territories for hunting, but overhunt so severely that the indigenous tribes could no longer sustain themselves. Thus they "agreed" to sell and move on.[41]

Aggressive expansion into Native American territory by whatever method or rationalization possible was the one point of agreement between Jefferson and the New England Puritans who by Irving's time had become Yankees.[42] Indeed, a speech by Jefferson to a delegation of Kaskaskia Indians who wanted a friendly relationship with the United States sounded strangely akin to a Connecticut Yankee as presented by Irving: "You ask us to send schoolmasters to educate your sons and the sons of your people. We desire above all things to instruct you in whatever we know ourselves. We wish to learn you all our arts and to make you wise and wealthy. As soon as there is peace, we will be able to send you the best of school-masters."[43]

Irving's first edition of *A History of New York* lampooned many facets of the Jefferson presidency, such as his infamous indecisiveness in the face of immediate threats.[44] When Irving revised the *History* in 1848, he removed many of the criticisms of Jefferson, other dated political jokes, and a few items that were too bawdy. However, he left completely intact the satire regarding the need for religious conversion and the removal of Indians from their ancestral lands. By 1848, such a satire would function as an indictment of Indian Removal policy under Andrew Jackson and Martin Van Buren. The ever-pragmatic Irving, in fact, abandoned the Democratic Party and Van Buren in the 1840 election, and embraced the Whigs, who presented a more moderate vision of American expansion than the increasingly aggressive Democrats who were launching full-force into "Manifest Destiny." Though there were some personal factors involved in the decision to abandon Van Buren, Irving seems to have given up on the Democrats' policy on a wider scale, partly because of Van Buren's ineffectiveness in addressing the economic collapse of 1837, but perhaps also due to wider cultural concerns. Irving's original 1809 satirical remark that the moon people would remove barbaric Christians to unfertile expansive places like Lapland in fact anticipated the removal of Eastern American Indians to the seemingly unusable expanses of Oklahoma and beyond. By leaving the biting satire completely intact after Jackson and Van Buren had done exactly what he had predicted, Irving implicitly criticized the Indian Removal, the scale of which could only be imagined in satire in 1809, but which was now established historical fact by the time of Irving's 1848 authorized edition.

Now let us come back to the condescending remark Diedrich Knickerbocker had made about negro philosophers: "The negro philosophers of Congo affirm, that the world was made by the hands of angels, excepting their own country, which the Supreme being constructed himself, that it might be supremely excellent."[45] This chauvinistic claim—that they had been made directly by God, while the other people of the world were made by angels, that is, lesser beings—is what we may call culturally egocentric.[46] However, it was nothing in comparison with the chauvinism that Catholic and Protestant Christians, and Western cultures in general, had shown toward Native Americans. Here we see a pattern that occurs in Knickerbocker's discourse, and more widely in Irving. A condescending remark that we would regard as racist was in fact the laying of a trap. The reader would be lured into nodding in agreement, assuming the general biases of the age, but even as the reader joined Knickerbocker in racist condescension, their own culture's chauvinistic belief and behavior would be more radically exposed.

Knickerbocker's—and perhaps Irving's—view of African Americans is seen in the description of a black community of slaves at Communipaw across the Hudson River. The black people at Communipaw were known for hearty laughter, such that on a still summer evening you could hear them laughing together across the channel at the Battery at the southern tip of Manhattan.

> These negroes, in fact, like the monks of the dark ages, engross all knowledge of the place, and being infinitely more adventurous and knowing than their

masters, carry on all the foreign trade, making frequent voyages to town in canoes loaded with oysters, buttermilk and cabbages. They are great, astrologers, predicting the different changes of weather almost as accurately as an almanac—they are moreover, exquisite performers on three-stringed fiddles: in whistling they almost boast the far-famed power of Orpheus's lyre.[47]

The African Americans at Communipaw were not the community of cultural chauvinists the previous remark about negro philosophers might suggest. This community had the one thing Irving longed for and that Anglo-Saxon America lacked—a strong sense of place. There is a little teasing about the scale of "foreign trade" along the Jersey shore and American communities in general; however, this group was highly adapted to their environment, with skill in harvesting shellfish and producing and selling vegetables and milk. They were skilled on the water and they had uncannily good skills reading the weather. The remark about the almanac is ambiguous, since we cannot be sure how reliable he supposed an almanac to be. At the very least, they were as wise as anyone navigating the weather on the water can be. They were more skilled and industrious than their masters, and they also made the most of life even in their poverty, enjoying elaborate skills in whistling. The three-string fiddle refers to the fingers—a poor person's musical instrument; the mild jab at their poverty was in poor taste, though certainly normative for Irving's readership of aspiring merchants and potential gentlemen with Federalist leanings. There was perhaps, in the remark about the three-string fiddle, an allusion to an emerging rich tradition of African American fiddle playing, a tradition which would be featured in "The Legend of Sleepy Hollow" and documented by William Sidney Mount in Long Island.[48]

William Sidney Mount, like Irving, portrayed African Americans quite sympathetically, and with much less caricature than was typical at the time. The respect for people who were simply part of his community is seen most monumentally in his portrait of an African American country woman with river skills akin to those Irving described (see figure 2.1).

Mount's *Eel Spearing at Setauket* shows a solidly built black woman in a long dress leaning forward in a skiff, teaching an Anglo-American boy how to spear fish. She has the kind of strength, self-confidence, and practical skill that Irving described in the African Americans at Communipaw, and she is widely described as "a figure of unmitigated dignity." Albert Boime points out that Mount's mother had died when he was young, and he was all but raised by the household slave; the painting is likely a reminiscence of the care he received from her, conflated with another African American man who taught him eel fishing. As such it presents—first and foremost—a relationship, childhood memories, and a sense of being together in daily life experiences. Boime mentions that showing the African American man as

Satire in the Name of World Citizenship 51

Figure 2.1 William Sidney Mount, *Eel Spearing at Setauket*, 1845, Fenimore Art Museum.

such a strong figure may have been too threatening to Mount's audience.[49] However problematic the expectation on the slave woman to function as the boy's mother, and the fear of painting a strong African American male, this painting has an epic quality to it; it is almost as if the African American woman who raised him was a hero in the grand tradition of history painting, transferred to the realities of Long Island Sound.[50] The painting transcended the racial problems of the day, and showed a caring relationship—a moment in the life of a community where African Americans and Anglo-Americans learned to be together.

A similar picture of warm family memories is found in Irving's picture of family life in the golden age of New Amsterdam's first governor Wouter Van Tiller. When arriving at home, the family "always entered in at the gate, and most generally lived in the kitchen," which, if true, would mean that the slaves and the Dutch owners were always together in close quarters.

> The fireplaces were of a truly patriarchal magnitude, where the whole family, old and young, master and servant, black and white, nay even the cat and dog,

enjoyed a community of privilege, and each had a right to a corner. Here the old burgher would sit in silence, smoking his pipe . . . and the good vrouw on the opposite side would employ herself diligently in spinning. . . . The young folks would crowd around the hearth, listening with breathless attention to some old crone of a negro, who was the oracle of the family, and who, perched like a raven in a corner of the chimney, would croak forth for long winter afternoons a string about of incredible stories about New England witches—grisly ghosts, horses without heads—and hair-breathe escapes and bloody encounters among the Indians.[51]

This passage was in the 1809 version as well as the authorized version of 1848. His close friend Washington Allston, discussed in the next chapter, had a similar experience listening to African American storytellers as a child in Charleston.[52] Irving himself describes a similar experience listening to old French traders tell wondrous tales as a child, so there does seem to be some personal historical reminiscence behind this account. Both Irving and Allston were enthralled as children by "old crooners" with fantastical tales. One thing we may note about this passage is that Irving loved vivid detail, such as likening an old storyteller to a raven perched in the corner on the chimney croaking away. He no doubt learned the ability to capture attention with such lively imagery as he listened as a child to similar hair-raising stories.

Albert Boime, in his important work *The Art of Exclusion: Representing Blacks in the Nineteenth Century*, has pointed out that when Anglo-American artists portrayed African Americans they tend to project numerous fantasy conceptions upon them, such as African Americans being completely dependent on Anglo-European Americans for their well-being.[53] In this passage, we can see a widespread ruling class belief that slaves could be happy as a part of the family, and feel a sense of belonging. William Sidney Mount and Washington Irving both tended to avoid the most simplistic and offensive of caricatures of African Americans, and were thus somewhat progressive for their times; both portrayed a civilization where warm relationships between black and whites were possible. Of course, there was still a hierarchy of place within an overall "genial and humanizing" framework. One common stereotype of the time was that African Americans were simple and childlike and lived only in the present moment, grinning and making music.[54] A critic in the Boime school would see Irving's association of blacks with children as belittling; on this understanding, African Americans were perceived to get along with children because they were believed to be children. However, such a reading may be too one dimensional; first, it is not true in Irving's presentation that blacks were without past or future, only capable of enjoying the present moment—the stories they told were all about a sense of local place and history. As in Irving's description of the African American community at Communipaw, the African Americans had a sense of connection to the past that more mercantile Anglo-Saxons Americans of Irving's day lacked. Developing a sense of place through connection to the past was the primary goal of *A History of New York* and stories such as "The Legend of Sleepy Hollow." In the *History*, African Americans were oracles of historical connection; perhaps the children liked them, not because they were childlike, but because they gave the children a sense of wonder and history they could not get from their own more "matter of fact" mercantile families.

The entire chapter on the golden age of New Amsterdam was told with such flare and idealization that any reader can tell it was a fantasy of the way Irving wanted things to have been, not the way they were. The 1809 version of Book III, Chapter II emphasized the lack of financial ventures and a greater simplicity in the founding era:

> For the golden age, says Ovid, was totally destitute of gold, and for that very reason was called the golden age, that is, happy and fortunate.[55] . . . The genial days of Wouter Van Twiller, therefore may truly be called the golden age of our city. There were neither public commotions, nor private quarrels; neither parties, not sects, nor schisms; neither prosecutions, not trials, nor punishments; nor were there counsellors, attorneys, catch-poles or hangmen. Every man attended to what little business he was lucky enough to have, or neglect it if he pleased, without asking the opinion of his neighbor.—In those days, nobody meddled with concerns above his comprehension, not thrust his nose in other people's affairs.[56]

In the revised edition of 1848, Irving ended the description of the golden age with the anecdote that "in the sylvan days of New Amsterdam," St. Nicolas would fly across the treetops and rooftops every holiday afternoon, dropping presents down chimneys, "whereas in these degenerate days of brass and iron, he never shows us the light of his countenance, nor ever visits us, save one night in the year."[57]

Clearly the golden age—with its perfectly harmonized relationships—was a fantasy, and Irving made that as clear as possible. Irving's portrait of slave life in New Amsterdam was also a fantasy, and his willingness to remove the burning of Quakers from the list of Peter Stuyvesant's sins in later chapters (see discussion below) may indicate a similar willingness to overlook the difficult situation of slaves in Dutch New York. Nevertheless, as a fantasy, the picture of life in the golden age gives us access to Irving's values, and what he wanted for the present and future. He wanted an America where African Americans would have a permanent seat around the fireplace, and where their oracular spinning of fantastical yarns would be cherished, as he and Washington Allston clearly did. By the time Irving wrote the *History* in 1809, slavery was on its way out in New York and Long Island. Slavery would not be abolished there until 1827; however, it was not central to social life as it was in the South, and census records from 1800 and 1810 indicate that manumissions were on the rise and slavery in decline.[58] African Americans were on their way to becoming the ordinary working-class folk you see around town, a minority population that was valued for their skills in farming, fishing, domestic help, making music, and telling tales. This is the vision in Washington Irving's stories, a world where African Americans are ordinary people—to be accepted and appreciated.

A similar portrait of an enthralling African American storyteller is found in "The Haunted House," a reminiscence of the late Diedrich Knickerbocker used to introduce the haunted mansion stories "Dolph Heyligen" and "The Storm Ship" in *Bracebridge Hall* (1821). Knickerbocker, the farcical historian, was presumed alive but missing when *A History of New York* was published in 1809. One of his intrusive reminiscences about a walk along the Battery indicates that work was dated to 1804, a glorious October day before the wooden pilings were removed for fuel in a bitterly cold winter.[59] By the time "Rip Van Winkle" was published in 1819, the fictional Dutch historian who wrote the tale was "deceased." The reminiscence in "The Haunted House" dates to Knickerbocker's childhood, and so presumably prerevolutionary English colonial America where the old Dutch houses were falling into disrepair. However, the old African American Pompey was described as a freed slave. The pace of manumissions picked up dramatically after 1800, but it is at least historically plausible that there could be freed slaves around New York a generation earlier. Irving had to make the African Americans slaves in his ancient history of Dutch New York. When he portrayed more recent history, he began to show us freed slaves.

After describing the gabled Dutch house overgrown with weeds, Knickerbocker tells us,

> There was a gray-headed curmudgeon of a negro that lived hard by, who had a whole budget of them (ghost stories) to tell, many of which had happened to himself. I recollect many a time stopping by with my schoolmates, and getting him to relate some. The old crone lived in a hovel, in the midst of a small patch of potatoes, and Indian corn, which his master had given him on setting him free. He would come to us, with his hoe in hand, and as we sat perched, like a row of swallows on the rail of the fence, he would tell us such fearful stories, accompanied by the awful rollings of his white eyes, that we were almost afraid of our own footsteps as we returned home afterwards in the dark.

Knickerbocker noted that when Pompey died many years past, he was buried on that garden plot and forgotten. Others plowed the field and Knickerbocker found his skull on a stroll several years later. Gathering up what remains he could find, "I took care, however, to see the bones of my old friend once more buried in a place they were not likely to be disturbed."[60] While one could argue with Boime that you have here the stereotype of a gullible and superstitious African American who was best suited to the company of children, the abiding image here is the beloved memory of a revered childhood friend. Knickerbocker's final tribute to Pompey, besides becoming a storyteller himself, was to lovingly gather the bones for proper burial. Clearly, Irving was presenting a caring relationship that stretched across years, at least in memory. It may be pure fiction, or it may have been built on a real reminiscence—such as that of his friend Washington Allston—but this was the kind of world Washington Irving wanted to live in. There is nothing Irving loved more than a good storyteller, and he would consistently represent African Americans as among the best of them. The fact that he spent several years of his own life writing ghost stories indicates the admiration he felt for such African American traditions.

Irving's portrait of African American life early in *A History of New York* and his representation of fond memories of Old Pompey indicates that the snobbish remark about the "negro philosophers" in Book I does not represent his view adequately. The facile condemnation of another culture's foolishness back in Book I was, in fact, a trap. Early nineteenth-century readers were lured into momentary condescension as their own religious chauvinism was exposed through the satire of Book I; a warmer and truer picture reflecting Irving's intent was then offered in Books II–III to undermine racist expectations initially triggered. Even if Irving's presentation of relationships in the golden age was impossibly idealized, he presented the ideal because it represented an aspiration, an America where African Americans and Anglo-European Americans could enjoy one another's company, and where each felt a sense of belonging as they claimed their place around the hearth.

The whole of the *History*'s Book I was a whirlwind display of the Cynic philosophy of Diogenes and Oliver Goldsmith, and an absolute roast of religious and cultural chauvinism. It also lampooned the foolishness of all the world's more cosmological-oriented and highly speculative philosophers, especially those who like to spin creation myths or speculate where Native Americans came from. The skewering of these philosophers and antiquarians obsessed with origins is, of course, ironic, for Irving was about to offer his own creation account for New York. Book I was, in essence, an eighteenth-century satire, and Sir Walter Scott remarked that he felt like he had just read a work by Jonathan Swift.[61] After Book I, the real history of Dutch New York began, and the narrative voice changed somewhat. The lampoonery was still there, but the bite was, for the most part, gentler, or at least imbedded in a warmly atmospheric and playful narrative.

Knickerbocker would come closest to the scathing tone of his Book I critique of chauvinism in his critique of religious chauvinism in New England Puritans, and the grotesque inconsistency of burning Quakers in the name of Puritan freedom of speech and conscience. In Book III, Chapter VII, Knickerbocker described the Connecticut Yankees on the eastern frontier as "a horde of strange barbarians," language normally used within the culture of the time to describe Native Americans. When these Yankees were in England as Puritans, they dared "to think for themselves in matters of religion, exercising what they considered a natural and unextinguishable right—the liberty of conscience." Unfortunately, "liberty of conscience likewise implied *liberty of speech*," and these forefathers of the Yankees felt morally obligated to always say what they were thinking, a problem which has been rekindled with new vigor in our current age of the internet and social media. The perpetual expression of unfiltered free speech "put the country in a hubbub" and "aroused the pious indignation of the vigilant fathers of the church," so that the religious authorities were prodded to adopt a famous "Scripture text, and literally to 'heap live embers on their heads.' Nothing, however, could subdue that independence of tongue which has ever distinguished this singular race." They thus "embarked for the wilderness of America, to enjoy unmolested the inestimable right of talking."[62]

These Puritan ancestors were treated kindly by the bewildered aborigines of America, and they were ironically named *Yanokies*, which meant "silent men." Then the playfulness takes on a shaper bite:

> True it is, and my fidelity as a historian will not allow me to pass over the fact that having served a regular apprenticeship in the school of persecution, these ingenious people soon showed that they had become masters of the art. The great majority were of one particular mode of thinking in matters of religion; but to their great surprise and indignation, they found that divers Papists, Quakers and Anabaptists were Spring up among them, and all claiming to use the liberty of speech. This was at once pronounced a daring abuse of the liberty of conscience; which they now insisted was nothing more than the liberty to think as one pleased in the matters of religion—provided one thought right; for otherwise it would be giving a latitude to damnable heresies. Now as they, the majority, were convinced that they alone thought right, it consequently followed that whoever thought different from them, thought wrong—and whoever thought wrong, and obstinately persisted in not being convinced and converted, was a flagrant violator of the inestimable liberty of conscience, and a corrupt and an infectious member of the body politic, and deserved to be lopped off and cast into the fire. The consequence of which was a fiery persecution of diverse sects, and especially the Quakers.[63]

Knickerbocker—or perhaps it is simply Irving at this point—went on to point out that even though in the current day we no longer believe in torturing the body to save the soul, American political life was still vicious, with its use of libel, turning people out of office in extreme partisanship, and the practice of tarring and feathering. The practice of free speech in the late Jeffersonian era was of a kindred spirit with these more historic persecutions, and it was inconsistent with the ideal of "a *free country.*"[64]

Irving's overall picture of Puritan history is accurate enough. The Puritans were persecuted in England for their exercise of free speech and freedom of religion, and then they came to America and became the persecutors. As Martin Marty has put it, they came to America for their own religious freedom, but not for the principle of religious freedom: "These lovers of liberty essentially loved their *own* liberty."[65] The main thing Irving has neglected to tell us is that the historical Dutch governor Peter Stuyvesant was also extremely chauvinistic in matters of religion. He tried to prevent Jewish people from immigrating to New Amsterdam in 1654 after they were kicked out of the new Portuguese colony of Brazil. Governor Stuyvesant did so on the correct reasoning that he would also then be bound to let in Papists and Lutherans as well. His decision was overridden by the Dutch East Indies Company. New Netherlands became a place of religious tolerance despite Peter Stuyvesant, partly in pragmatic recognition of the need to accept able-bodied colonists, and partly in deference to the Netherlands' history of religious tolerance.[66]

Irving glossed over this inconvenient fact presumably because it did not fit his literary scheme of creating an ideal civilization in the dreamy memory of Dutch New York. All the persecution of heretics was left in the hands of New Englanders. Irving wanted to create a golden age in the Dutch colony, especially the reign of Wouter Van Twiller, a peacefully inept governor whom Andrew Burstein has likened to a Chinese Taoist sage, someone extremely wise who has the ability "to act without acting." The real Wouter Van Twiller was "militant, impulsive, and ultimately fired for alcoholism and fraud"; however, Irving needed to believe "that there is a better place to live than the present," and he believed he had the literary skill to take us there.[67] Burstein's reading of the Knickerbocker's first governor as a Taoist sage is in keeping with Goldsmith's presentation of a Chinese scholar in *A Citizen of the World.* The cosmopolitan Irving, in the spirit of his hero Goldsmith, would value ancient Chinese philosophy as much as ancient Greek or Christian wisdom. The chief glory of Wouter Van Twiller, according to Knickerbocker, was that in his whole reign, no one was punished,[68] an obvious rebuke to the Puritan regime of New England. The historian acknowledged that things were not as perfect with the next two governors, but he preferred to cast an aura of lovable bluster and ineffectuality. Attributing to Peter Stuyvesant the burning of Quakers would destroy that aura, and so Irving tidied history. Connecticut Yankees and their Puritan forbears, along with medieval and Renaissance Catholic leaders, were the prime exemplars of hypocrisy and intolerance.

In spite of Irving's historical inaccuracy regarding the first governor's gentleness, and the third governor's policies toward Quakers, Irving's critique of religious chauvinism and hypocrisy on the issue of freedom of conscience retains its power. Irving was a citizen of the world in the spirit of Goldsmith, but in the face of extreme hypocrisy and the abuse of Native Americans and Quakers, he would exercise that citizenship by protesting in the biting satirical mode of Jonathan Swift.

If these satires were all we had, we could simply say Washington Irving was an eighteenth-century wit and satirist in the tradition of Goldsmith and Swift who happened to write in the first decade of the nineteenth century. However, these clever and biting pages are an important but very small portion of *A History of New York* and Irving's body of work overall. To understand the narrative style of the rest of the *History*, indeed even to understand the description of New York City at the end of Wouter Van Twiller's reign in Book III, Chapter VI, we must understand the aesthetic theory that shaped the romantic age. Irving wrote in the style of an eighteenth-century wit at times, but he did much more as well. He was an aesthete in the picturesque tradition, with mastery of the discourse of the sublime and various forms of beauty; this feature runs consistently through a much larger portion of his work, from the *History* of 1809 all the way to *A Tour on the Prairie* in 1835. To aesthetics we now must turn if we are to understand Irving as a hybrid creature of the eighteenth and nineteenth centuries, a child of both the Enlightenment and the romantic age.

NOTES

1. Loretta Sharon Wyatt, "The Charm of a Golden Past: Iberia in the Writings of Washington Irving and Antonio Goncalves Dias," in Stanley Brodwin, ed. *The Old and New World Romanticism of Washington Irving* (Westport, Connecticut: Greenwood Press, 1986), 105.

2. Dupont's engraving of Ari Flescher's *Christus Consolator* was so moving to Irving when he discovered in a shop on Broadway in August 1848 that he ended his decades-long aloofness from Christian religious commitment. Pierre Irving, *The Life and Times of Washington Irving*, Vol. IV (London: Richard Bentley, 1864), 31–1. This response is similar to the reaction he had to Guido Reni's *Immaculate Conception* at Genoa (October 25, 1804) and especially Reni's *Magdalene* at Rome, with her "eyes cast up to heaven with and expression of languor—or grief—of devotion, rapture, & that gives an indescribable interest." April 1, 1805, *Journals and Notebooks, Volume I, 1803–1806*, ed. Nathalia Wright, CW (Madison: University of Wisconsin Press, 1969), 271. The *Magdalene* he saw in 1805 and the *Consolator* he saw in 1848 had a similar kind of pathos. Irving had a consistency in his response to art that spanned fifty years, and at last that sensitivity brought him home to his

mother's religion; he died in 1859 with *Christus Consolator* nearby, hung in his bedroom.

3. Burstein, *The Original Knickerbocker*, 8.

4. William Hedges, *Washington Irving: An American Study, 1802–1832* (Baltimore: Johns Hopkins Press, 1965), 33.

5. February 6, 1805, *Journals and Notebooks*, Vol. I, 191.

6. Samuel Taylor Coleridge, "Kubla Khan," in *Romantic Poetry: Ann Annotated Anthology*, ed. Michael O'Neill and Charles Mahoney (Oxford: Blackwell Publishing 2008), 186. Irving would come to love imagery such as persons wailing in the moonlight for a demon-lover around the time the poem was published in 1816. In fact, shortly after "Kubla Khan" was published, Washington Irving met Samuel Taylor Coleridge through their common artist friend Washington Allston. One wonders if meeting Coleridge and reading this poem may have pulled him toward a romantic sensibility.

7. *Journals*, 191.

8. "Introduction," Anthony Ashley Cooper, Third Earl of Shaftesbury, *Characteristics of Men, Manners, Opinions, Times*, ed. Lawrence E. Klein, Cambridge Texts in the History of Philosophy (Cambridge: University Press, 1999), xiii–xxi.

9. Klein, "Introduction," vii. The union of ethics and aesthetics in Irving is at the heart of my own thesis. See especially my discussion in chapters 1, 3, and 6.

10. April 3, 1805, *Journals*, I, 278.

11. Cited in Hedges, 76–7. William Hedges points out that Irving has made an historical error. The witches of New England were not burned, but hanged and pressed. Irving has conflated the witch trials of New England with those of Europe; aside from the method of execution, the picture of how these trial scenarios unfolded was accurate enough. The conflation of American and European witch trial is fitting enough to make Irving's broader point: Priestcraft, whether Puritan or Catholic, is all the same.

12. Irving, *Tour*, 103.

13. Henry Leavitt Ellsworth, *Washington Irving on the Prairie: Or a Narrative of a Tour in the Southwest in the Year 1832*, ed. Stanley T. Williams and Barbara D. Simison (New York: American Book Company, 1937), xiii, 72. The comic element of the Hebrew stories in Genesis and other portions of the Hebrew Bible has now been ably explored by Robert Alter in *The Art of Biblical Narrative* (New York: Basic books, 1981). Irving was able to appreciate this very real aspect of the biblical text, but most early nineteenth-century American Christians, even educated people such as Ellsworth, saw such enjoyment of the comic storytelling skill of the Hebrew narrators as sacrilegious.

14. "Letter to William Irving," December 25, 1804, *Letters: Volume I*, 138–9.

15. August 15, *Journals and Notebooks: Volume I, 1903–1806*, ed. Nathalia Wright. The Complete Works of Washington Irving (Madison: University of Wisconsin Press, 1969), 68.

16. John Frey, "Irving, Chateaubriand, and the Historical Romance of Granada," in *The Old and New World Romanticism of Washington Irving*, ed. Stanley Brodwin

(Westport, CT: Greenword Press, prepared under the auspices of Hofstra University, 1986), 94–5.

17. *History*, CW, 26.

18. *History*, CW, 30.

19. *History*, CW, 30–1.

20. See "Of custom, and not easily changing an accepted law," "Of the uncertainty of our judgement," and "Of prayers," in Michel de Montaigne, *The Complete Works: Essays, Travel Journal, Letters*, trans. Donald M. Frame. Everyman's Library (New York: Alfred A. Knopf, 1976), 93–108, 248–54, 278–87.

21. Samuel Enoch Stumpf and James Fieser, eds. *Philosophy: A Historical Survey with Essential Readings*, 9th ed. (New York: McGraw Hill, 2015), 111–2, 200–2.

22. Irving refers Montaigne in a passage from Goldsmith in *Oliver Goldsmith: A Biography*. Whether Irving read Montaigne directly, or absorbed his stance by way of Goldsmith is unclear, but they share the same outlook. See CW, Vol. XVII, 71.

23. *History*, CW, 28. Mircea Eliade has since demonstrated that many cultures claim that their homeland is the *axis mundi*, the center pole around which the world revolves. While such claims may well instance extreme chauvinism at times, they may also serve metaphorically as a way to find the spiritual center of the cosmos by being grounded in local traditions. The search for the center is part of the age-old spiritual quest to see the cosmos as an ultimate unity—and oneself as capable of sharing in that unity—and not simply as chauvinism. Most people would rather be "centered" than fragmented or lost. To lose the center is the fate of the modern in William Butler Yeats *The Second Coming*, spinning "round and round in a widening gyre," where "the falcon can no longer hear the falconer."

24. Danny L. Jorgenson, "The Latter-day Saint (Mormon) Religion in America and the World," in *World Religions in America*, 4th edition, ed. Jacob Neusner (Louisville: Westminster John Knox Press, 2009), 235–43.

25. Ralph Waldo Emerson, "Nature," in *Emerson: Essays and Lectures*, ed. Joel Porte. Library of America (New York: Literary Classics of the United States, Inc., 1983), 7.

26. Emerson, "Divinity School Address," 79–81.

27. Irving would convert to the Episcopal Church in 1848, in response to the death of John Jacob Astor and the discovery of an engraving of the painting *Christus Consolator* by Ary Shaffer in a German bookshop on Broadway, according to Pierre Irving. *The Life and Letters of Washington Irving*, Volume IV (London: Richard Bentley, 1864), 31. The pathos of this painting was similar to the emotion expressed in paintings of *The Assumption of the Virgin* by Guido Reni—"an expression of languor—of grief—of devotion"—that so moved Irving on his Grand Tour; see Journal entry for April 1, 1805, *Journals I*, 271. It would seem Irving had a consistent sensibility toward a few special pieces of religious art, a sensibility that would eventually trigger his conversion to Anglo-Catholicism.

28. *History*, CW, 36. Irving would have been delighted to know, if he did not by the end of his study on Columbus, that Columbus had taken a Hebrew scholar on the journey to the West Indies, and upon arriving in Hispaniola, he realized he had need of a botanist instead. See Carolyn Fry, *The Plant Hunters: The Adventures of the*

World Greatest Botanical Explorers (Chicago and London: University of Chicago Press, 2013), 10–11.

29. *History*, Book I, Ch. IV, CW, 40.

30. Michael West, *Transcendental Wordplay: America's Romantic Punsters and the Search for the Language of Nature* (Athens: Ohio University Press, 2000), 291–6.

31. *History*, Book I, Ch. V, CW, 42.

32. In 1662, Michael Wigglesworth described areas outside Puritan settlements "nothing but/ A waste and howling wilderness, / Where none inhabited/ But hellish fiends, and brutish men/ that Devils worshipped." See Hans Huth, *Nature and the American: Three Centuries of Changing* Attitudes (Berkeley: University of California Press, 1957), 5–7. Irving would satirize this Puritan viewpoint, in "The Devil and Tom Walker."

33. *History*, Book I, Ch. V, CW, 47–9.

34. *History*, Book I, Ch. V, CW, 50.

35. "Explanatory Notes," *History*, 314–5.

36. Barbara Alice Mann, *George Washington's War on Native America.* Native America: Yesterday and Today (Westport and London: Praeger, 2005), 53–55; 199, note 26.

37. Thomas Jefferson, *Notes on the State of Virginia*, in *Thomas Jefferson: Writings*, ed. Merrill D. Peterson, Library of America 17 (New York: Literary Classics of the United States, Inc., 1984, 2011), 184–6.

38. Jefferson, *Notes*, 221.

39. The resistance to the drudgery of daily labor might be one reason Irving sympathized with the Native Americans in the face of the all-consuming Puritan and Quaker work ethic, with its pervasive insistence on self-disciple and utilitarian productivity.

40. Henry Adams, *The History of the United States of America During the Administrations of James Madison.* Library of America (New York: Literary Classics of the United States, Inc., 1986), 348–9.

41. Adams, *The History of the United States*, 343–6.

42. For this process, see Richard L. Bushman, *From Puritan to Yankee: Character and Social Order in Connecticut, 1690–1765.* Cambridge and London: Harvard University Press, 1967.

43. Cited in Anthony J.C. Wallace, *Jefferson and the Indians: The Tragic Fate of the First Americans* (Cambridge and London: Belknap Press, 1999), 73.

44. Burstein, *The Original Knickerbocker*, 76–81.

45. *History*, Book I, Ch. I, 393.

46. The notion that higher elements of the universe had been made by God—the chief craftsman himself, and lower elements were made by assisting lower gods is found in Plato's *Timaeus* 68e–70a. The passage includes a claim that as the beginning, before God started to create, nothing had any proportion except "by accident" (69b), a phrase Irving lampooned when talking about the peopling of America.

47. *History*, Book II, Ch. II, CW, 61.

48. Deborah J. Johnson, *William Sidney Mount: Painter of American Life* (New York: American Federation of the Arts, 1998), 60–2.

49. Boime, *The Art of Exclusion*, 95–8.

50. In the original 1809 *A History of New York*, Irving transferred Virgil's epic story *The Aeneid* to the shores of the Hudson. The Dutch wandering by sea from Communipaw to Oyster Island, to Gibbet Island, through Buttermilk Channel and Hellgate is likened to the storm-tossed wandering of Aeneas as he tries to fulfill his destiny of founding Rome. Both Irving and Mount were transposing epic modes of art into the simple American context of the Hudson River, the East River and Long Island Sound. Book II, Ch. III, Library of America, 444.

51. *History*, Book III, Ch. III, CW, 104.

52. William Dunlap, *The History of the Rise and Progress of the Arts of Design in the United States*, Vol. II (New York: George P. Scott and Co., 1834), 153.

53. Boime, *The Art of Exclusion*, 18.

54. Boime, *The Art of Exclusion*, 90–2.

55. In the Revised Edition of 1848, many of the allusions to Ovid and Virgil were removed. The original 1809 version was made for educated gentlemen who would have enjoyed being bombarded by constant allusion to the classics in a burlesque; the ability to catch the allusions and chuckle was an indicator of status. The 1848 version was revised for a more widely democratic audience who would not have understood or enjoyed so many allusions. Nevertheless, the task of being an American Virgil or Ovid was central to the original vision of *A History of New York*, as will be discussed in chapter 4.

56. *History*, Book II, Chapter II, , 474.

57. *History*, Book III, Chapter II, CW, 100–1. The contrast between the sylvan age, and the iron age is but one of many environmental threads that run through Irving's life work. The golden age was known for its great trees, as seen in the description of Wouter Van Twiller puffing his pipe beneath a great sycamore tree in History, Book III, Ch. II, CW, 99.

58. Johnson, *William Sidney Mount*, 97–9.

59. *History*, Book III, Ch. V, "A Delectable Walk," 488. In the 1848 version the walk retained the date but removed the reference to the burning of pilings is in Book III, Ch. VI, due to the addition of an episode about the patroon Killian Van Rennselaer as Ch.V.

60. *Bracebridge Hall*, 302.

61. Jones, *Washington Irving*, 99.

62. *History*, Book III, Ch. VII, CW, 117.

63. *History*, 118.

64. *History*, 119.

65. Martin Marty, "Protestant Christianity in the World and In America," in *World Religions in America*, 4th edition, ed. Jacob Neusner (Louisville: Westminster John Knox Press, 2009), 36.

66. Jonathan D. Sarna, *American Judaism: A History* (New Haven and London: Yale University Press, 2004), 1–9.

67. Burstein, *The Original Knickerbocker*, 75–7.

68. *History*, Book III, Ch. I, CW, 94.

Chapter 3

The Picturesque Aesthetic and Neoclassical/Romantic Boundary Crossing

> You see, I am once more venturing my *life & fortunes* on the "vasty deep" speeding away to Sicily, that Island of Fable and Romance. Accustomed to our *honest* American hills and dales where *stubborn fact* prevails and checks the imagination in its wanderings, you may conceive with what enthusiasm I haste to those "poetic fields" where fiction has shed its charms over every scene.[1]—
> New Year's Day Letter, 1805

In Washington Irving we find a unique fusion of a Cynic philosopher's commitment to world citizenship, complete with its rejection of chauvinistic cultural biases, and the picturesque aesthetic that revels in the diversity of landscapes human and natural, artistic and ecological, especially when they are rich in poetical associations. To understand the pictorial qualities of Irving's vivid description in all his stories and in many of his travel essays from 1819 to 1935, we need to understand the aesthetic that was interacting with his sense of cosmopolitan world citizenship. The aesthetic discourse of the sublime, the beautiful, and the picturesque may seem tangential to Irving's critique and vision of American society; however, it is not, because this aesthetic and the accompanying pictorial sensibility that Irving developed in narrative form is the very means by which he created the sense of place to central to his own vision, and so central to understanding his critique of American culture.

This chapter turns often to journals and letters from his Grand Tour of 1804–1806, because they are so foundational for his identity formation. There are parallels from those early writing with passages ranging all the way to *A Tour on the Prairie* and *Astoria*. Another reason for exploring his Grand Tour is that it was formative in terms of his core relationships with American artists abroad; these artists were very influential on his pictorial sensibility and his particular type of "moody atmospherics." His friendship with Washington Allston, which began in Rome in 1805, especially shaped his sensibility as a romantic. In his relationship with both art and artists we see the kind of hybridity that characterizes his work. Another goal of this excursion through the aesthetic landscape of the early nineteenth century is to show a widely-ranging consistency across many works. For someone who is frequently seen as an immature man-child, unstable and adrift, he had a remarkable number of stable tendencies from 1805 to 1835. These consistencies constituted an underlying unity that transcended the diverse personae, genres, and styles that he utilized.

For many practitioners of picturesque travel, such an aesthetic would have been simply a sign of refinement and social standing, a superficial cosmopolitanism that indicated someone was in the educated upper classes rather than the common mob who were supposedly unable to appreciate beauty. When Irving was on his Grand Tour, he displayed such attitudes from time to time, lamenting, for example, that Italian commoners were not able to appreciate the glories of the ruins about them.[2] However, he was trained in the ways of cosmopolitan travel by no lesser figures than Laurence Sterne, Joseph Addison, Oliver Goldsmith, and Ann Radcliffe, whose novel *The Italian* he carried with him.[3] As noted in the introduction, Oliver Goldsmith's essay "The Citizen of the World" had a particularly great impact on him, and in Irving's hands the ideals of picturesque variety, and empathy for all humans whatever their culture, became a full-blown ethic that was consistent across his literary career. This fusion of ethic and aesthetic is the result of a productive tension at a kind of borderland, the transition from Enlightenment neoclassicism toomanticism. The Cynic cosmopolitan ethic comes from his eighteenth-century reading as a young man. However, to understand the fusion of a philosophically grounded ethic with a widespread aesthetic in the eighteenth and nineteenth centuries, we must first understand a bit about that aesthetic. As it turns out, that aesthetic itself straddles the eighteenth and nineteenth centuries. In this realm there is no tidy demarcation between neoclassical and romantic, but rather overlapping polarities on a continuum.

There is not as clear a demarcation for the emergence of romanticism in the realm of aesthetics, for trends that are recognizably romantic, or proto-romantic, go back to the mid-eighteenth century and, in the realm of landscaping, even earlier. Somewhat ironically, the emergence of romanticism was made possible by the empiricism of John Locke, just as much of the romantic sensitivity to suffering and the valuing of individual experience was made possible by the eighteenth-century empiricist David's Hume's ethic of empathy. Locke argued against the existence of innate ideas and insisted that all our ideas come from sense experience. Because the content of our minds was determined by what went into them, it became more important to pay attention to what was put into our minds. For educational reformers such as William Godwin, this meant greater attentiveness to the environment of childhood formation. In the wider realm of life's enjoyment, it became more important to surround oneself with beauty. Thus, in a response to Locke's empiricism, as well as Newton's physics—with its sense of harmony pervading the whole universe—it became necessary to pay more attention to the beauty of nature and imitate it in vividly naturalistic poetry, such as that of James Thomson's *The Seasons*. It was also appropriate to imitate nature's beauty in the creation of gardens less formal than those of the seventeenth century and more suitable for reflection. Thus, from 1720 onward, we see not only the creation of semi-wild classicizing landscapes, but the appearance of hermitages and grottos where the soul could retreat to an admittedly aristocratic "Sleepy Hollow" that was modeled on the rural retreats of Cicero, Horace, and Virgil.[4] The eighteen-century imagination tended to depend on the stimulation of the mind through sensory input; the romantic concept of imagination emphasized more the role of the imagination as itself a creator; however, the boundary between the two is not entirely clear, for those English Enlightenment poets, artists, and gardeners who supposedly conceived the mind as a merely passive receiver were, in fact, actively arranging all that sensory input to generate a more richly enjoyable experience full of historical associations and poetically evocative memory.

For Washington Irving, the picturesque landscape had a kind of beauty that was a middle category between beautiful, gentle rolling open fields and smooth green lawns found on many English country estates and the more grand, terrifying sublime of dangerous cliffs and chasms found in the Alps and Wales.[5] The picturesque was a middle ground of texture and variety, more diverse and more visually interesting than smoothly undulating pastoral beauty, but less intimidating than the sublime grandeur of a precarious precipice. For Irving, the picturesque was emblematic of a beautiful and stable civilization. Most often picturesque art, as Irving understood it, would contain a mixture of wild and civilized as a form of variety: "What was sought and admired in America was the varied prospect, the mixture of wild and improved nature which gave the promise of progress and bore the trace of civilization."[6]

Edmund Burke's 1757 treatise *An Inquiring into the Origin of Our Ideas of the Beautiful and the Sublime* provided the standard definition of the sublime and the beautiful that was the springboard for further elaboration or reaction in the late eighteenth and nineteenth centuries. For Burke, emotional response was the heart of our aesthetic judgments about the world, just as emotional response was at the heart of moral judgments for Hume. The terms "sublime" and "beautiful" were, for Burke, mutually exclusive categories. The sublime had to do with a sense of danger and being overwhelmed by vastness and immensity,[7] while the beautiful was more smooth and gentle, triggering the kind of emotional security found in the traditional English countryside with its open rolling fields, or in the bosom of a wife in a situation of domestic happiness. The sublime was a powerful emotional response related to astonishment in the face of things that were in one way or another menacing or precarious, to the point that "the motions" of the soul "are suspended with some degree of horror": "No passion so effectively robs the mind of all its powers of acting and reasoning as *fear*."[8] The emotion of sublime response to danger involved a kind of exhilarated halt in the face of something threating, an awe that really constituted an altered state of consciousness. The sublime was generated by a fruitful tension, almost a paradox, for there was both danger and the enjoyment of it. These two coexisting opposites triggered a kind of mental expansion (or breakdown) in the process of being stretched by fear, awe, and stunned enjoyment. A classic example of a sublime landscape is found in a passage from Irving's *Astoria*:

> In the after part of the day, they came to another scene surpassing in savage grandeur those already described. They had been travelling for some distance through a pass of the mountains keeping parallel with the river as it roared along, out of sight, through a deep ravine. Sometimes their devious path approached the margin of cliffs below which the river foamed, and boiled and whirled among the masses of rock that has fallen into its channel. As they crept cautiously on, leading their solitary packhorse along these giddy heights, they all at once came to where the river thundered down a succession of precipices, throwing up clouds of spray, and making a prodigious din and uproar. The travellers remained for a time gazing with mingled awe and delight at this furious cataract, to which Mr. Stuart gave, from the colour of the impending rocks, the name of "The fiery narrows."[9]

Burke's had pointed out that "terror is a passion which always produced delight when it does not press too closely"; This aspect of sublime enjoyment is clear in this scene by Irving; one can only enjoy such a scene from a relatively safe vantage point—it will not be delightful if the viewer supposes she is about to topple into the magnificent chasm. The problem with the experience of the sublime is that is it not sustainable; it is akin to a spiritual mountaintop high from which one must always come down. A person can pass through a chasm in the Alps on a stormy night, and even find it exhilarating, but one cannot stay there.

The formal category of picturesque beauty was developed in the later eighteenth century partly because people found Burke's definition of beauty too narrow. The beautiful, for Burke, related more to so-called feminine qualities, such as the smooth and supple curves of a woman's body, or similar qualities found in the gentle landscape of a country estate; these qualities evoked feelings of tenderness, love, and a sense of security, what you might call domestic sensibilities.[10] This prototypical love was not, for Burke, merely a matter of sexual feeling, however. It was the love that one feels with a trusted dog,[11] or at a pub with friends.[12] The kinds of things that evoke warmth and tenderness for Burke are as follows: smoothness, gracefulness, relative smallness, timidity, gradual variation in gentle undulations, soft colors, and delicacy. In the confines of his overly rigid framework, small orange or almond trees blooming in spring, with delicate colors and tender new growth are beautiful; towering oaks or elms—however gracefully cascading their branches may be—are not.[13] This bifurcation of beautiful and sublime in Burke anticipated the increased emphasis on feminine domesticity that emerged during the Industrial Revolution as small-scale family cottage industries failed, men went off to work in factories or morality-free large-scale trade empires, and the woman at home became the bearer of values in a more restricted domestic sphere that was intended as a safe space from the more crudely utilitarian world.[14]

Burke's example of delicate almond blossoms in spring undermines his claim that mere physical features and a sense of stable well-being are central to the idea of the beautiful. Everyone who goes to see cherry blossoms in spring knows they are graceful, elegant, delicate, and will soon give way to green fruit and foliage in the normative stages of life. There is a wistful quality to the savoring of delicate spring beauty, because of the heightened awareness it will not be there long.[15] The very example Burke uses as a prototypical beauty illustrates that ideas, not just physical properties, contribute to the sense of longing for the beautiful; we long for such delicate elegance to remain, but we know it will not. There is some sense of security in the image of the passing blossom, in that it gives way to summer and autumn fruit. Thus, there is a sense of well-being in the anticipation of fruit, even as one wishes the blossoms could stay longer. In other words, there is meaning in nature's cycles and its provision for human well-being. In this example alone we can see why Burke's discussion of beauty gave rise to associationism as an alternative.

Though Burke did tie the sublime and the beautiful to emotional response, he was widely seen as too simplistic. Sense impressions would give rise to feelings of being overwhelmed or of security and welling-being. Associationists from Archibald Alison to Washington Irving to Thomas Cole knew that humans were more than automatons reacting with feelings of awe or coziness to sensory stimuli. They insisted that the real sense of beauty in things came from a more complex set of associations, childhood memories, and a storied history that gave meaning to a culture. Ultimately, aesthetic taste came from the complex operations of mind, not a mere appropriation of the external date of the senses; poetry and art had a kind of rich "suggestiveness," not mere representational capacities in a merely empirical mode.[16] From the time of Addison's travels and earlier, Italy was regarded as a sacred landscape because of associations with Homer, Virgil, and Horace. Likewise, For Irving, Scotland was rendered beautiful by the associated poetry of Robert Burns and the tales of Walter Scott: As Irving explained in *Abbotsford*, Irving memoir of his visit to Sir Walter Scott's home, "It seems to him (Scott) as if the country had grown more beautiful because Burns had written his bonnie little songs about it."[17]

Burke's theory of beauty was challenged by William Gilpin, who insisted that Burke had also placed too much emphasis on smoothness and smallness; for example, Burke had stated, "Take any beautiful object, and give it a broken and rugged surface; and, however well-formed it may be in other respects, it pleases no longer."[18] Burke's explanation of the basis for a distinction between beautiful and sublime and was also corrected by associationist theorists such as Lord Jeffery and Archibald Allison,[19] who saw his theory of how physical attributes create an emotional impact as too crassly materialistic. Beauty was found in scenes that trigger an association with great ideas, such as the passing of time and relation to the creator, the cycles of life, and pleasant memories of childhood well-being. Burke had indeed said that beauty and sublimity, and especially the feelings of love and well-being, were determined by "the quality of bodies."[20] Such an affirmation rendered Burke not only an empiricist, but a materialist. Alison's disciples, such as the painter Thomas Cole, shuddered at the thought that beauty could be reduced to mere materialistic sensuality: After citing Alison on the view that some artists were abandoning true art to "merely please the eye": "Take away from the paining that which affects the imagination, and speaks to the feeling, and the remainder is merely for sensual gratification."[21] In the face of what they saw as a purely superficial and materialist understanding of beauty, Burke's opponents insisted that it was the emotional associations with personal experience, history, and poetry that generated aesthetic response, not merely the physical qualities of immensity, obscurity, or smoothly gentle undulation.

Unfortunately, Burke's words about the displeasing nature of rough, broken textures were spoken as a great age of British archeological discovery was about to unfold, and people of taste had long been importing archeological and statuary fragments to major British institutions, installing ancient statues or simulating ruins on their estates. As early as 1620, in the reign of King James I, antiquarians and art experts such as Robert Cotton and Lord Arundel were importing statuary and fragmentary inscriptions to their English estates. Similar art patrons had used old Roman statuary as fountains in gardens. Under Lord Arundel, "For the first time in England, busts and statues came to be thought of as part of a garden aesthetic."[22] As English collectors brought an array of items from Italy, a full 200 years before Burke's treatise, Burke's question of smooth versus rough and broken was discussed at length. Many people, understandably, had a preference for the smooth and unbroken elegance of smooth marbles and graceful classical poise, such as found in the Adonis of Arudel's collection, and there would always be restoration work done to bring back this effect. However, Burke's claim that smooth is beautiful and broken fragments were displeasing could not be sustained even then, though some collectors shared the view. For Arundel and his librarian Francis Junius, fragments were understood as more intellectually stimulating because they required more interpretation. Connoisseurs of art were not entirely trusted in an age when a Puritanism played a large role in English culture, just as they continued to play a large cultural role in American early nineteenth-century culture. The art lover must not be seen as a mere sensualist; antiquity was to be valued for more than the mere pleasure of the eye; smoothly graceful nudes might be indulged in as a purely sensual pleasure, but scultural and architectural fragments were associated with ancient sites and the active intellectual task of reconstructing cultural memory. There needed to be an intellectual and moral edification to the task of art and architectural history. Arundel was at pains to explain that he was a moralist with values that would improve civilization, and not merely a hedonist. At stake was the very Renaissance concept of the artist, where intellectual, moral, and spiritual elevation was at the heart of artistic identity, and not mere imitation of surfaces, however natural they might be.[23]

The same dynamic essentially replayed itself in the later eighteenth-century English reaction to Burke's definition of beauty. Burke's empiricism reduced beauty to a simplistic emotional response to sensory stimuli; the Renaissance concept of the artist as an intellectual on par with poets and scholars was no longer necessary. An artist could, in principle, simply create emotional reactions almost automatically through the presentation of stimuli; if you want fear or awe, just paint a path through a dark towering canyon. Such an implication was understood and soundly rejected by Alison and Cole; Irving was less afraid of worldly pleasures than Thomas Cole, due to his rejection of Calvinism and his embrace of French joie de vivre, but even Irving would not want to be regarded as a mere sensualist—his emotional responses were responses to the history of a place and the sense of home they provided, and an outgrowth of his empathy for people who had experienced loss with time and change.

By the eighteenth century, the experience of ruins was even more widespread. Indeed, English travelers on the Grand Tour made a point to the see the Grotto of Egeria the Nymph outside Rome from at least 1700; Egeria was an oracle at whose fountain of civilizing wisdom flowed forth in ancient pre-Roman times, and the grotto, like its many imitations, was known for rough texture of stone formed into a crudely naturalistic cave. Alexander Pope, for example, was unable to travel due to health issues, and one friend brought him a fragment of Egeria's grotto itself. Since Pope could not travel, he built his own extensive grotto at Twickenham in 1725, and his designed landscape had a shell temple where the gods were to appear at a hilltop clearing surrounded by woods.[24] Pope and a friend also built a new set of medieval ruins set at the edge of woodlands around 1720; there was an invocation of the English medieval past and not just classical Italian imagery. Notably, these classicizing shell structures and simulated medieval ruins had a rough and broken texture, and yet they were part of an elegantly beautiful yet textured landscape. Pope's naturalistic landscapes—a balanced union of nature and artifice—were the paragon of texture and variety; they were widely visited and very influential.[25] Irving himself visited the Grotto of Egeria in 1805: "This was the favorite retreat of Numa Pompilius to enjoy the coolness of the grotto and the delightful groves by which it was surrounded—The water is pure and limpid—The grotto highly picturesque."[26] The grotto was beautiful in picturesque mode, textured and full of historical association. Burke's unnecessarily rigid bifurcation between smooth beauty and displeasing roughness was irrelevant to almost anyone who traveled.

In such a context, Burke's claim that a rough and broken texture could not be beautiful was contrary to the experience of the English who made the Grand Tour, contrary to emerging trends in naturalist landscaping from 1720 onward, and it was practically an affront to national pride in British archeology, which was very prominent from 1764 onward through the collecting of Sir William Hamilton in Italy. Hamilton was the British Envoy to Sicily based in Naples, just as the Herculaneum was being excavated; he also represented the Royal Society in geological exploration of Mt. Vesuvius. Hamilton's first major collection of antiquities was acquired by the British Museum in 1770, and in fact the impact was so great that the museum shifted from a focus on manuscripts to archeological remains.[27] An aesthetic theory that insisted that an Apollo or Venus with a broken arm could not be beautiful because it was not fully smooth could not survive the rise of interest in Italian archeology; indeed, the English love of Italian grottos had doomed Burke's theory of beauty even before he uttered it, and a defense of the physical and moral beauty of roughly broken fragments had been made by Arundel's librarian Junius 200 years before Burke. It is hard to imagine a more rigid and less useful theory of beauty.

Gilpin's theory of picturesque beauty was offered in defense of architectural fragments and wild Welsh landscapes, emphasizing rough, broken textures and increased variety in an ultimately harmonious beautiful composition. Picturesque compositions could also be grand as well as intimate, opening the door for the appreciation of spectacular mountains that, under Burke's theory, could not be beautiful.[28] Gilpin insisted that Burke's definition of beauty was too limiting and not borne out by experience.[29] Crumbling rocks, such as found on craggy mountainsides or grand architectural ruins covers in moss, were beautiful as component parts of a variegated but integrated vista. Picturesque beauty was a kind of beauty characterized by this higher degree of texture.

Crumbling stone was more conducive than perfectly smooth marble to association with lofty ideas of humanity's temporary place in the cosmos, as seen in Thomas Cole's meditation on Rome during his own Grand Tour in May 1832:

> I would select the Colosseum as the object that affected me most. It is stupendous, yet beautiful in its destruction. From the broad arena within, it arises around you, arch above arch, broken and desolate, and mantled in many parts with lurustinus, the acanthus, and numerous other plants and flowers, exquisite both for their color and fragrance. It looks more like a work of nature than of man; for the regularity of art is lost, in a great measure in dilapidation, and the luxuriant herbage, clinging to its ruins as if to "mouth its distress," completes the illusion. Crag rises over crag, green and breezy summits mount into the sky. To walk beneath its crumbling walls, to climb its shattered steps, to wander through its long arched passages, to tread in the footsteps of Rome's ancient kings, to muse upon its unbroken height, is to lapse into sad, though not unpleasing meditation.[30]

Irving had a similarly nostalgic response to the ruins of the Roman Amphitheatre at Bordeaux, walking it at night as Cole visited the Colosseum by moonlight: "as I passed under the dark arches of the Grand Entrance, I have almost expected to see an old Roman stalking amid the gloom."[31] Cole's meditation as he contemplated the crumbling Colosseum had more emphasis on physical texture and new plant growth, and less on imagining individual people; however, it was nevertheless similar to the wistful ruminations of Geoffrey Crayon touring Westminster Abbey and other historic sites in *The Sketch Book*, brooding upon the mutability of all things. For both, it was the association with history that triggered a response, not merely the physical features of a place.

Irving clearly stood in this associationist tradition, by temperament and literary training, if not by reading treatises on taste. First, an early version of associationism was found in the writings of Alexander Pope, a writer with whom Irving was very familiar. "Windsor Forest," written in 1704, begins with a citation from Virgil's *Eclogues*, and finds the landscape enchanted by the memory of poets who have passed on: "I seem thro' consecrated walks to rove;/ I hear soft music die along the grove:/ Led by the sound, I roam from shade to shade,/ By godlike poets venerable made."[32] In early eighteenth-century England, there was a revival of interest in Virgil's pastoral works and Pliny's writing on Italian villas, and this interest was reflected not only in the poetry of the age, but in naturalistic landscaping that was populated by classical gods and temples; associations with the golden age of classical Latin literature were newly appreciated in England's own revitalized Augustan age.[33] Furthermore, Irving had associationist inclinations even as a child in New York: "I was always fond of visiting new scenes and observing strange characters and manners. . . . As I grew into boyhood . . . my holyday afternoons were spent in rambles about the surrounding country. I made myself familiar with all the places famous in history or fable."[34]

Alison's *Essays on the Nature and Principles of Taste* were published in 1790, reissued in 1811, and were extremely influential in the United States; there is evidence of discussion of associationist principles in the American periodical *Port Folio* from 1809 onward.[35] Even though Irving probably did not read Alison, he likely would have heard such discussion in his Burrite circle of friends, for Aaron Burr was a patron of artists such as John Vanderlyn, whom Irving met in Paris in 1805; Irving also would have picked up Alison's associationist ideals from the circle of American artists abroad he associated with from 1805 onward. Regardless of whether Irving ever directly studied or discussed the critique of Burke by the leading guides of taste in the late eighteenth century, by the time Irving toured Europe in 1804, Gilpin's ideas regarding the picturesque were in the air. Brigitte Bailey has suggested that even if Irving did not read Gilpin directly, he would have "absorbed" the aesthetic

> from the fiction and tourist writing he read before or during his tour: Ann Radcliffe's *The Mysteries of Udolpho* (1794) and *The Italian* (1797), or Patrick Brydone's *Tour Through Sicily and Malta* (1773). Brydone, according to Batten, helped to shift travel descriptions from "blueprints" to "rough sketches like those of Claude Lorrain."[36]

By the time Irving published *The Sketch Book* (1819–1820) and *Bracebridge Hall* (1822), the associationist aesthetic of Alison and the picturesque aesthetic of Gilpin were taken for granted by English and American travelers, and for Irving these associations and sense of texture extended to the plants in a landscape, not just storied castle ruins:

> Having been born and brought up in a new country, yet educated from infancy in the literature of an old one, my mind was filled with historical and poetical associations, connected with places, and manners, and customs of Europe, but which could rarely be applied to my own country. . . . England is as classic

ground to an American as Italy is to an Englishman, and old London teems with as much historical association as mighty Rome . . .

I cannot describe the mute but deep-felt enthusiasm with which I have contemplated a vast monastic ruin, like Tintern Abbey, buried in the bosom of a quiet valley, and shut up from the world, as though it existed merely for itself; or a warrior pile, like Conway Castle, standing in stern loneliness on its rocky height, a mere hollow yet threatening phantom of departed power. They spread a grand. and melancholy, and, to me, an unusual charm over the landscape; I for the first time beheld signs of national old age, and empire's decay, and proofs of the transient and perishing glories of art, amidst the ever-springing and reviving fertility of nature . . .

I thought I could never be so sated with the sweetness and the freshness of a country so completely carpeted with verdure, where every air breathed of the balmy pasture, and the honeysuckled hedge. I was continually coming upon some little document of poetry in the blossomed hawthorn, the daisy, the cowslip, the primrose, or some simple object that has received a supernatural value from the muse. The first time I heard the song of the nightingale, I was intoxicated more by the delicious crowd of remembered associations than by the melody of its notes; and I shall never forget the thrill of ecstasy with which I first saw the lark rise, almost from beneath my feet, and wing its musical flight up into the morning sky.[37]

In addition to Irving's clearly associationist inclinations, we also see in this passage a few prominent features that characterize his writing. First, Irving reveled in vivid juxtapositions. "Old age, and empire's decay" are poised together in one moment with the "ever-springing and reviving fertility of nature." Second, it is the literary "muse" that casts a "supernatural" aura upon a scene; poetic association is almost a substitute for religion in rendering the world a meaningful place. Without the poetry of a storied history, there is no enchantment, and yet nature itself is part of the storied history of renewal.[38] Finally, Irving also had an acute attentiveness to natural scenery and specific plants. His works are peppered with frequent descriptions of specific trees and wildflowers. He had the sensibility of a naturalist, and his eye for these plants would eventually be channeled into the landscaping projects of a gentleman farmer, as well as enriching his essays with an affirmation of the value of individual living beings.

For afficionados of picturesque travel in the early nineteenth century, the associationist aesthetic also made more sense than Burke's rigid dichotomy between the beautiful and the sublime, for Burke's theory contradicted the experience of beauty found in the most popular landscape painter in England. The French artist Claude Lorrain had spent his career in Italy in the mid-seventeenth century, and many of his works were almost immediately brought to English estates after his death: "British collectors acquired so many works by Claude that it is no exaggeration to say that nearly all of his paintings, drawings, and—to a lesser extent—prints have been in British collections at one time or another, or are still there today."[39] Lorraine became the prototype practitioner of early picturesque landscape. Specializing in "boulders, trees, and ruins—Claude was interested in creating a sense of spatiality and

Figure 3.1 Claude Lorrain, *Rest on the Flight into Egypt*, early 1640s, Cleveland Museum of Art.

concentrated entirely on the middle distance and background. . . . His chief themes were Arcadian landscapes with reclining or dancing peasants on the one hand, and maritime views on the other."[40] Lorrain's compositions contained lush, mature framing trees or classical ruins, the architecture often seen in crisp delineation in golden late afternoon sunlight, and occasionally crumbling in the shadows; Claude typically provided a middle ground with a smooth body of water with distant mountains or a city on a hillside in the background under a serene sere Italian sky. In figure 3.1, *Rest on the Flight into Egypt*, we see a unity in diversity as the eye is led from a foreground path with travelers to the distance by an aqueduct that leads the eye to the distant mountains.

Claudian scenes were classicizing and pastoral, giving a sense of a stable world order spanning a couple thousand years, yet often with some indication of decay, such as ancient sculpture strewn on the ground as it was found along the Tiber River in the mid-seventeenth century.[41] Claude's elegant paintings, offering stable symmetry and order, with just a hint of decay, provided the earliest definition of picturesque beauty. In the early eighteenth century, when so many English upper-class persons were importing Claude Lorrain paintings to their estates at home, a landscape was picturesque if it looked like a picture by Claude.[42]

By the time Gilpin developed his theory of picturesque, he described Claude's paintings as beautiful rather than picturesque, because they had the classicizing stability, and not quite the level of movement and variety of texture he intended. Nevertheless, a Claude such as *Rest on the Flight to Egypt* has quite a bit of movement in it, as the eye zigzags as a traveler's from the foreground, across the lake by way of an aqueduct and into the distant mountains. It is not surprising that an educated traveler such as Irving, who was highly interested in art but who did not study these treatises closely,[43] would not grasp that these scenes were now regarded as beautiful, but not picturesque.

By the end of the eighteenth century in England, due to the influence of Gilpin and prints after Salvator Rosa, Joseph Mallord William Turner, and Paul Sandby, it was possible to see dramatic wild scenes in Wales with bold chiaroscuro as picturesque. The turning point was the 1745 Scottish Jacobite Rebellion, after which British surveyors and topographical artists were sent out to document the territory and bring improved roads and other amenities to Scotland. Paul Sandby, who documented Scottish landscapes, was one of the first British landscape artists not dependent on European painting for his compositional emphasis.[44] Over time, due to the images of these wild northern regions brought back by Sandby and others, there was a turn toward the more dramatic in the conception of the picturesque. There was a new level of emphasis on "movement, surprise, asymmetry, variation," and "difference." Tim Barringer and Jennifer Raab emphasize that this new dramatic picturesque was the antithesis of the older, gentler Claudian picturesque.[45]

Such a distinction, however, was lost on Washington Irving; he loved heightened variation in keeping with the spirit of his age, while speaking of the picturesque in Claudian terms. Irving himself tended to seek a high degree of variety in his travels and in the human characters he was so skilled at observing and describing; however, he does not seem to have been particularly attracted to the complexly wild, rugged, and dramatic picturesque in the style of Sandby, and later the pure wilderness scenes of the American painter of the Catskills, Thomas Cole.[46] Irving wanted a human component in art that was lacking in dramatic wilderness vistas beyond human history and association. When Irving did speak of wild grandeur, he described it as sublime, not picturesque. Irving reveled in human and natural variety, but he described that highly varied picturesque in terms of an earlier eighteenth-century definition that was more associated with civilization. Irving was steeped in the writing of Alexander Pope, Joseph Addison, Oliver Goldsmith, and Ann Radcliffe. It was from these authors, not the late nineteenth-century aesthetic theorists, that he would draw his vocabulary. Pope, for example, saw the picturesque as an elegantly naturalistic and varied background for a mythological or historical commemorative site. For Irving, as for Pope, the picturesque would be tied to human artistic, poetic, and historical or religious associations. It was not conceivable to Irving that an utterly wild mountain scene—whether done by Paul Sandby or Thomas Cole—could be picturesque, unless it evoked memories of painters such as Claude, had some historical association, or appeared like a park. When Irving spoke of the picturesque, he was fusing the language and aspirations of these literary writers into his own experience, not making fine distinctions in picturesque theory based on the leading theories of the day, even though he would have known, vaguely, of those theories.

One point that would be important for Irving, as well as American landscape painters such as Thomas Cole and Asher Durand, was that Claude's formula for beauty included lush mature towering trees. Burke's claim that beauty was found only in small delicate things such as new growth on small olive trees in the spring ran into an opposing consensus. Everyone of taste in England, and soon enough American travelers as well, knew that Claude's lush, towering trees along the frame, or just off center, were beautiful. For example, Thomas Cole, who often followed Claude's compositional formula in his more pastoral paintings, described towering elms with elegantly cascading branches as "the paragon of beauty."[47] Claude's tall, lush trees, combined with architectural elements and Italian peasants, also provided the storied association with pastoral poets such as Virgil, Horace, and Ovid so meaningful to Irving.

For Irving, this kind of gentle Claudian picturesque would be found as far west as the Arkansas River, albeit without the historical associations. The role ascribed by Thomas Cole to tall, graceful elms would be played by towering cottonwoods and sycamores in his painterly description of streamside trees breaking up the expanse of prairie:

> The broad sandy shore where we landed, was intersected by innumerable tracks of elk, deer, bears, raccoons, turkeys, and waterfowl. The river scenery at this place was beautifully diversified, presenting long, shining reaches, borders by willows and cottonwood trees, rich bottoms bordered by cottonwood trees; rich bottoms and lofty forests; among which towered enormous plane-trees, and the distance was closed in by high embowered promontories. The foliage had a yellow autumnal tint, which gave to the sunny landscape the golden tone of one of the landscapes of Claude Lorraine.[48]

Irving frequently expressed a feeling of sheltered well-being when arriving at a grove of oaks or cottonwood after a long stretch in the open air.

Figure 3.2 shows a somewhat intimate view approaching a grove of cottonwoods. At times on his trip out west, the closest thing Irving could find to moss-covered ruins were "the remains of an old Indian encampment on the banks of a fine stream, with the moss-grown skulls of deer lying here and

Figure 3.2 Worthington Whittredge, *On the Cache de La Poudre River*, 1871, Amon Carter Museum. *Source*: Worthington Whittredge, *On the Cache de La Poudre River*, 1871, Oil on canvas, Amon Carter Museum of American Art, Fort Worth, Texas, 1975.4.

there about it."[49] However, the cluster of trees along a river, forming a kind of grassy savannah, provided the feeling of being in a park, the element of civilization that best merges the natural with human artifice:

> After resuming our march, we came in sight of the Arkansas. It presented a broad and rapid stream, bordered by a breach of fine sand, overgrown with willows and cottonwood trees. Beyond the river, the eye wandered over a beautiful champaign country, of flowering plains and sloping uplands, diversified by groves and clumps of trees and long screens of woodlands; the whole wearing the aspect of a complete, and even ornamental cultivation, instead of native wilderness.[50]

Irving first encountered Claude Lorrain paintings on his European Tour of 1804–1806,[51] and they would impact his perception of the landscape even thirty years later as he wrote *A Tour on the Prairies*. He certainly saw works by Lorrain at the Palais Pamphili in Rome, which had "a superb gallery of paintings particularly landscapes . . . by the inimitable Claude Lorraine particularly two large ones which are counted as two of his best productions."[52] Three weeks earlier, Irving had described the Bay of Naples in Claudian terms:

> The sky was clear and transparent with two or three floating clouds tinged with those rich colours which are so much admired in the paintings of Lorrain. The horizon was glowing with the parting rays. Over the whole view—The Bay—The city the islands—was diffused the most Luxurient tinges—everything was softened—enriched & heightened and blended into a harmony with the rest—forming a prospect as lovely as I ever beheld.[53]

In this passage, we see the beginning of a lifelong pattern, a use of Claude as a lens through which to interpret new experiences, from Italy to the Arkansas River, and also a desire to soften the harsh realities of life into something more livable through the casting of an atmospheric veil, "endeavoring to see the world in as pleasant a light as circumstances will permit."[54]

The use of the European artistic lens as an interpretive aid has sometimes been understood as a means to impose an imperialist, or magisterial gaze, in which one is claiming a prospect as territory, especially when there is an elevated perspective and a wide vista.[55] This claim is overstated or at least deployed too one dimensionally, though for Irving it is certainly true that he envisions the emergence, if not necessarily the imposition, of a civilization across America. John Conron points out that the picturesque aesthetic had "a remarkable adaptability to nineteenth-century American culture's clangor and jangle of contrary tendencies. While it comes to serve the status quo, the picturesque is also appropriated by Transcendentalists to articulate a mystical view of the world, and by urbanists and feminists."[56] There was no one ideological usage of the picturesque aesthetic that was always in play, and Irving forged his own unique usage embracing the love of diversity that extended to human cultures and living creatures in nature.

We must also remember that the U.S. frontier was an unknown territory; since the earliest days of philosophy, humans have wrestled to understand the unknown by analogy with the known.[57] When Meriwether Lewis came to the Great Falls of the Missouri River on his journey to the west, looking toward the downward incline that would ultimately lead to the Pacific, he ruminated that he needed Salvator Rosa with him to adequately capture what he was seeing.[58] Salvator Rosa was known for wild mountains with gnarly, stormswept trees. There is, to some extent, a "magisterial gaze" here; Lewis and Clark were exploring land recently purchased from Napoleon for the United States. However, it is reductionist to assume there was no other dimension to an experience of this sort. Lewis was a thoughtful person conversant with the discourse of the sublime.[59] When Americans experienced the raw wildness of the frontier, seeing it as a Rosa painting helped them understand what they were seeing. The unknown is always rendered known by the known. Scholars who see nothing but the land grab that was Manifest Destiny in these experiences are failing to see something at the heart of exploration. There was an overwhelming wonder, mystery, and outright danger that was exhilarating but almost too much to cope with. Familiar artistic categories rendered the vast new landscape intelligible, navigable, meaningful, and thus emotionally survivable.

Irving too would use European landscape painting as an interpretive aid to understanding what he was seeing. However, instead of Rosa, he generally saw the beauty and stability of Claude. This was part of a broader pattern with Irving. Irving incorporated the sublime into several vivid descriptions, but they were relatively brief interludes that formed a greater, and more balanced, picture. For example, he described a sublimely panoramic view of the city of Rome. In April 1805, Irving visited the Pantheon and St. Peter's Basilica, where he saw the chamber of Raphael and the Sistine Chapel of Michelangelo, both of whom were widely regarded as the most sublime of artists, and then he climbed to the exterior top of the dome for a prospect:

> Mounted up into the cupola of the church and from thence into the ball—which is large enough to contain twenty men. Went outside and climbed up an iron ladder that goes over part of the steeple & the outside of the ball and is affixed to the cross. The latter is very large & of bronze. The height is fearful and tremendous, and I clung to the cross as firmly as the strictest Catholic as a slip

would precipitate me to an immense distance from hence- the view was superb. I was as if on a point and could command an uninterrupted view on every side, no object intervening to accept it. The city laid below me like a map and I could trace both the ancient and modern parts—The winding of the Tiber, the bridges, the churches, temples, walls, ampitheatre & The Campania, the ampitheatre of hills that surround it, the Appenines to the left and the Mediterranean to the right. After contemplating this sublime view for some time, I descended from my hazardous situation into the church.[60]

The hills and mountains around the city might be classified as picturesque in themselves, but the sense of immense chasm beneath him and the unusually high vantage point for an all-encompassing vista, combined with the precariousness of his perch, together render this a sublime composition.

Donald Ringe has pointed out that Irving described a similar sweeping panorama in his description of the Tower of Comares in *The Alhambra*.[61] Irving described a more vastly stark sublime at the beginning of *The Alhambra*, as he journeyed across southern Spain in May 1829: "It is a stern, melancholy country, with rugged mountains, and long sweeping pained destitute of trees, indescribably silent and lonesome, partaking of the savage and solitary character of Africa. What adds to the silences and loneliness is the absence of singing birds," yet "the vulture and the eagle are seen wheeling about the mountain cliffs, and soaring over the plains, and groups of shy buzzards stalk about the heaths."[62]

There are several similar descriptions of stark, treeless expanses in *Astoria*, where the traders sponsored by John Jacob Astor in 1810 were far beyond civilization in virtually unknown territory, and they were at risk of starving. One wonders if perhaps Irving's experience of the stark sublime in the south of Spain stimulated his interest in the American west; it provides at least a partial explanation of why he so quickly went west when he returned to the United States in 1832.[63] He certainly carried the memory of his recent time in Spain with him:

> Here one of the characteristic scenes of the Far West broke upon us. An immense extent of grassy, undulating, or as it is dimly termed, rolling country, with here and there a clump of trees, dimly seen in the distance like a ship at sea; the landscape deriving sublimity from its vastness and simplicity. To the southwest, on the summit of a hill, was a singular crest of broken rocks, resembling a ruined fortress. It reminded me of the ruin of some Moorish castle, crowning a height in the midst of a lonely Spanish landscape.[64]

The group touring the prairies teased Irving for being a romantic dreamer who saw castles on the horizon, and named it "Irving's Castle"; however, he had just been in the south of Spain three years earlier, and the terrains were, in fact, quite similar.

Donald Ringe has called this feature of Irving's writing the "pictorial mode." Irving described the scene as if he were writing a painting, a pattern he would maintain throughout his career in moments of richly vivid description. The core concept went back to the time of Alexander Pope and his fellow landscaper gentle-friends along the Thames, who as noted earlier, were transforming Locke's empiricism of the eye into poetry and landscape art. Pope had explicitly stated that a garden landscape "was like a picture hung up"; painting was as intellectual and gentlemanly as poetry, and now landscaping was a kind of art that imitated painting in its graceful Claudian harmonies.[65]

While there are sublime moments found in Irving's journals and published writing, Natalia Wright points out that an overwhelming number of descriptions are written in a picturesque mode. I would add, what is true of his journals is true of all his writing through 1836. Despite many variations of narrative voice, degrees of satire, and shifts between fiction and romantically ruminating essays, Irving had a consistency. Indeed, the variation of personae and narrative styles was all part of a picturesque aesthetic, with its "single criteria of diversity or variety."[66] We must ask, why he was so consistent? Was he simply addicted to picturesque travel, perpetually unable to resist the next interesting turn on the highway, even in his choice of narrative voices? Though Irving did love picturesque variety to an almost astounding degree, there is something bigger at stake than his personal need for visual and intellectual stimulation. A civilization—for Irving—could not be based on the sublime, and Irving was interested in what kind of civilization America was going to become; a civilization could have the sublime as a component, as part of a vigorously textured variety, but there must be a more all-encompassing element of stability; one cannot live perpetually at the edge of a chasm whose rocks are about to crumble beneath you.

In fact, Anglo-European Americans and recent immigrants in the Eastern United States and Middle West often felt they were living at the edge of a precipice, so rapid was the change that was overwhelming them. That many Americans felt that way in the first half of the nineteenth century is evidenced by the popularity of Thomas Cole's *Voyage of Life*, whose third part *Manhood* shows a man praying in a boat on a stormy river with jagged rocks, as the boat is about to be sucked into a whirlpool of rapids. Anyone who is interested in the forging of a civilization with some semblance of stability, would incline toward some variant on the pastoral or the picturesque. For Irving, and for Cole in his Arcadia paintings, Claude offered stability in an age of turbulence and perpetual change. To see the American West as a Claude painting is to suggest, or at least hope, that the beauty found there would be as enduring as Italian mountains and skies, and that a civilization would emerge where beauty could exist with a sense of community well-being and continuity with the ages, in a culture full of meaningfully storied poetic associations.

THE BEGINNING OF IRVING'S ART

A journal entry from Irving's European tour indicates both his early pictorial sensibility, and a possible hint at his attitude toward religion as a child of the Enlightenment leaning into the romantic era. His Christmas eve journal entry was copied into a Christmas day letter to his brother William during his youthful Grand Tour of Europe in 1804, as he was on a ship departing Genoa:

> In a little time the sun emerged in full splendor from the ocean—his beams diffused a blaze of refulgence through the clouds of indescribable richness—the curly tops of the waves seemed tipp'd with gold and the snowy summits of Corsica and the opposite shore of Italy brightened with reflection of his rays. . . . Had those happy days continued when the Deities made themselves visible to man and now and then paid him a sociable visit—we might perhaps have been entertained by the *raree shew* of Neptune and Ampithrite and all their gay train of Nereids and Dolphins—Such a morning would have been the very time for them to take a *drive* round their dominions and examine that all was safe after late Stormy Weather. But those days of romance are over—The Gods are tired of us heavy mortals and no longer admit us to their intimacy. In these dull *matter of fact* times our only consolation is to wander about the haunts they once frequented and endeavor to make up by imagination the want of the reality. There is a poetic charm that diffuses itself into our ideas (if I may so express myself) in contemplating this classic part of the world. Our imagination becomes tinctured with romance and we . . . can scarcely behold objects in their true light from the fiction and illusions that envelopes them. Tis like beholding a delightful landscape from an eminence on a beautiful sunset. A delicious mistiness is spread over the scene.[67]

Here we see the descriptive ability and wistful charm that would eventually make Irving a successful writer, and here we also get a first glimpse of the imaginative air—the mistiness—he would cast over the old Dutch villages of the Hudson River.

Much of the detail was likely inspired by Pope's translations of *The Iliad* and especially *The Odyssey*. Yet, there is a different, more wistful tone than one finds in Pope. Pope was all cosmic optimism. The discoveries of Newton had shown the world intelligible and harmonious, and the application of Locke's empiricism led to a new ability to describe the world in detail, as well as an awareness of the need to surround oneself with beauty through great landscaping and architecture projects. The mind was shaped by what went into it, and so Pope and other made sure that beautiful images went into the mind through the senses. By the end of the eighteenth century, romantics such as Wordsworth and Blake saw Newtonian physics and especially the optics studies so important to Locke as demystifying and desacralizing the world. For such romantics, eighteenth-century science had ruined the experience of the rainbow, and its value must be recovered by the power of imagination and feeling.[68] Something had changed between the age of Pope and the age of Irving. Alexander Pope created semi-naturalistic harmonious landscapes where the gods were to manifest at a hilltop shell temple, almost as if it were a *Star Trek* transporter pad for beaming down to earth.[69] Irving on the other hand was wistfully aware that the old gods were no longer with us. England and the American republic had become a "dull, matter of fact" world. The breakthroughs of the seventeenth century had not led to the restoration of the human spirit, but to a utilitarian word of mercantile calculation and natural discoveries assessed for the sake of pragmatic application, not a sense of wonder. Irving realized there was a cost to the Enlightenment demythologization of ancient religious worldviews—the loss of enchantment. The elegiac tone is reminiscent of Virgil's pastoral poetry and especially Ovid, who wrung a wistful sense of loss out of almost every elegant story. The influence of these elegiac writers in the eighteenth century indicates how blurred the line sometimes was between neoclassical and romantic. The pastoral nostalgia of Virgil and Horace, and especially the wistful and sometimes catastrophic stories of Ovid would segue into romanticism.

   We should also note how like a painting Irving's description is. The shimmering water of Irving's sunrise fantasy evokes the sensibility of a marine painting by Claude Lorrain. The mythological aspect of the reverie is akin to the kind of scene that would be painted by Nicolas Poussin, the great classicizing landscape painter who portrayed the era when river gods and nymphs did still visit us. It is as if Irving has somehow fused the two in a shimmering, joyful—and yet elegiac—image. The description may share the classical sensibility of Claude and Poussin simply due to common sources because Irving read Virgil, Horace, and Ovid, but Irving was making direct reference to works by both Poussin and "the inimitable Lorrain" in his journals by early April.[70] Claude especially had been collected by English aristocrats since 1700, and substantial collections were available to respectable visitors by 1800, and Poussin paintings were more available in Paris. It is unclear whether Irving would have seen any Claude or Poussin landscapes before he arrived in Rome in late March 1805, as he had not yet been to England; he went to Paris after his stay in Italy. Most likely he had heard them described in English travel literature, and then finally saw them in Rome, though it is possible he saw some in the south of France between Bordeaux and Genoa.[71]

Given Irving's own tendency to pictorial description, is it no surprise that he immediately became close friends with the American romantic painter Washington Allston the moment they met in late March 1805. Irving was traveling with Joseph Cavell, an American from the South he had met in Naples. Once they arrived in Rome on March 27, they heard three other Americans were in Rome, one of whom was Washington Allston, and had dinner with the group on March 30.[72] He became friends with Washington Allston very quickly, later describing himself as "completely captivated" by Allston's "intellect and refinement."[73] On April 3, he spent the day with Allston touring the Borghese Palace and other sites, and so began a long series of relationships with artists, which would resume when he moved to England in 1815. In a letter from 1815, giving travel advice to a friend, Irving mentions that he and Cavell eventually found a room near the Spanish Steps, living with the artist Caracciolo, a landscape painter who was also known for engraving the works of Claude Lorraine.[74] If Irving did not know Claude's art directly before he arrived in Rome, he was certainly made aware of their skill and their importance through days and evenings spend with Allston and Caracciolo.

Washington Irving and Washington Allston were kindred spirits. Andrew Hemingway describes them as sharing an aristocratic, conservative romanticism:

> If Romanticism is best understood, as Lowy and Sayre have argued, "as essentially a reaction against the way of life in capitalist societies," it was one that proved adaptable to a range of political proclivities. The political tenor of American Romanticism was overwhelmingly "conservative." . . . That is, it was infused with a sense of loss for an imaginary ancient regime of stability and organic wholeness. This should not be taken to imply a desire to return to the manners of the pre-Revolutionary French court or the politics of absolutism, but rather something more mythical: an idealized world of chivalry, paternalism, and noblesse oblige grounded in a secure order of ranks, if not in the actual social relations of feudalism. It . . . was closer to Burkean conservatism in the assumption that while commerce might bring benefits, the leveling forces of capitalism needed to be constrained by traditional social and political institutions and forms of deference associated with them. The outlooks of Allston, Cole, Cooper, and Irving all can be seen to match this ideal type.[75]

The paintings of Claude Lorraine and Nicolas Poussin were attractive to artists in this conservativeromantic mode because they radiated a sense of a stable classical order of "balance and calm" that "was far more than a pleasing display of the beauty of nature. . . . To achieve balance, rhythm and overall harmony inevitably meant to depart from the natural model and replace it with an 'ideal' invention."[76] The romantic artists inspired by Claude and Poussin could never simply paint "after nature"—in the sense of merely making a copy of what they saw. Their goal was not to make the scene look as realistic as possible; rather artists like Washington Allston saw themselves as painting after nature in the sense of painting out of an engagement with the deep spirit of nature, not simply the surface appearance; there was a kind of projection of self into nature, not as an imposition, but because they felt their own imagination was engaging and expressing the living heart of nature, a nature that was greater than themselves, but which they could find by seeing into the world with eyes of reverie. William Gerdts and Theodore Stebbins describe Allston's early works inspired by Claude, Poussin, and Rosa as "landscapes of the mind, constructed from memory diffused through imagination—memory of his experience with places and with works of art"[77] For such romantics, imagination and idealization were paths to truth.

The two weeks with Washington Allston wandering Rome's sites made such an impression that Irving momentarily considered joining Allston in a career as a painter.[78] They saw Michelangelo's Moses at the Vatican together, and after a tour of the Borghese Palace, they visited the studio of the sculptor Canova, whose "group of Cupid and Psyche . . . surpasses any group I have ever seen for sweetness of workmanship and expression."[79] One thing the two had in common was a childhood love of ghost stories and outrageous adventure. Allston was enthralled by a beloved old African American storyteller on the family plantation in Charleston. After making preliminary efforts in mud sculpture,

> these delights would sometimes give way to a stronger love for the wild and marvelous. I delighted in being terrified by the tales of witches and hags, which the negroes used to tell me; I well remember with how much pleasure I recalled these feelings on my return to Carolina; especially on revisiting a gigantic wild grapevine in the woods, which had been the favorite swing for one of these witches.[80]

William Gerdts points out that Allston inclined to a "personal associationism more than any other American painter of his time."[81]

Washington Irving was similarly enraptured adventure stories told by French traders as a young man. During trips to Canada "long years since" he had met

> Hardy fur traders from the interior posts; men who had past years remote from civilized society, among distant and savage tribes, and who had wonders to

recount of their wide and wild peregrinations, their hunting exploits, their perilous adventures and hair-breadth escapes from the Indians. I was at an age when imagination lends it coloring to everything, and the stories of these Sinbads of the wilderness made the life of a trapper and trader perfect romance to me.[82]

Clearly, Irving and Allston had similar temperaments, and memory suffused these special moments with a numinous glow. It is no wonder they immediately became intimate friends. One can imagine the two budding romantics sharing such memories as they wandered the historic sites of Rome and gathered for dinner in the evenings with their circle of friends. In the long run, the conversations with Allston about ghost stories and the transformative power of memory, begun in 1805 and resumed when he returned to England ten years later, may be what tipped Irving away from eighteenth-century satire and burlesque to romantic stories of gnarly trees on the path in the moonlight as characters such as Ichabod Crane and Wolfert Webber launched themselves into seemingly haunted nights looking for not quite accessible riches.

The combination of Claude Lorrain and Nicolas Poussin paintings available in Rome seems to have had an immediate impact on Allston's artistic vision. Just as Poussin painted river gods and nymphs, so Washington Allston also painted "Diana and Her Nymphs in the Chase" in 1805, of which "Landscape with a Lake" of 1804 seems an early version. It was painted just a few months after Irving left Rome, and it seems to be almost a preparatory study, but one so strong that it stands on its own (see figure 3.3):

> The *Landscape with a Lake* is an important picture, too often ignored because of the magnum opus that succeeded it . . . the picture evinces a clarity of form and spatial recession, a geometric structure and a balanced monumentality of the impressive trees and mountain formations very different from any of Allston's earliest work. The picture is a truly classical landscape, not in subject but in formal aesthetic—in its simplicity, symmetry, and formal harmony.[83]

Irving, the eighteenth-century satirist with romanticizing tendencies has found an intimate who could also fuse the classical and romantic. After Irving left Rome, Allston spent about six months with Samuel Taylor Coleridge, building another romantic" lifelong friendship. Allston would introduce Irving to Coleridge when they finally all met again in England around 1817.[84]

Allston's own landscape paintings of Italy, such as *Italian Landscape* of 1805, has the compositional format, with peasants in simple cloaks in the foreground, towering trees dominating the middle ground on the sides and in the center, and the same style of clouds as several of Poussin's major landscapes, such as *Landscape with a Man Pursued by a Snake* and *Landscape with Travellers Resting*.[85] Allston's richly vibrant skies ultimately have the

Figure 3.3 Washington Allston, *Landscape with a Lake*, 1804, Boston Museum of Fine Arts. *Source*: Photograph © 2021 Museum of Fine Arts, Boston.

influence of Titian, and Allston was in fact known as the American Titian, but there was likely some mediating influence by Poussin as well in his dreamily classicizing presentation of landscape. Around 1815, the same time that Washington Irving returned to England after almost ten years in America, Allston began using the same Poussin-like clouds in paintings of women in dreamy reverie, such as an intimate embrace in *The Sisters of 1816* to *The Spanish Girl in Reverie* of 1831, to the other-worldly *Evening Hymn* of 1835.[86] These Allston women are enveloped in the very kind of enchanted mistiness of mood that Irving would shortly transfer to the little villages of the Hudson, and Irving's years in Spain and publication of *The Alhambra* may have influenced Allston's choice of the Spanish girl as a subject matter in 1831.

THE ART OF LANDSCAPING

Another realm in which we find Irving straddling neoclassical and romantic worldviews is in his love of picturesque landscaping. Irving spent the last twenty or so years of his life as a gentleman farmer, managing Sunnyside as he alternated between life on the estate and research at John Jacob Astor's library in New York City. Interestingly, Irving seems to have been attracted to this aristocratic country ideal as a tentative life plan as early as 1805, just before he met Allston. When he was in Palermo in February, he was introduced

> to the family of Prince Belmonte. He is a man of the first rate abilities & enjoys the particular confidence of the King. He will not accept any place in government but bends his <mind> chief thoughts to the improvement of his estate. He is very engaging in person and elegant in his manners.[87]

This description of the prince is virtually a description of Irving's life from 1832 onward. He dined with President Jackson upon his return to the United States, was in the confidence of Martin Van Buren, managed Sunnyside after he moved to the estate in 1836, and he met with President Millard Fillmore for public festivities. He served as a diplomat twice more, but he turned down as many government posts as he accepted over the course of his life; he noted that the positions he did take were ones where the key component for success was the pouring of wine; one should not press Irving's self-deprecating humor too literally, for he was a highly skilled diplomat who helped settle trade disputes with England and negotiated the Canada-U.S. border through his strategic charm and wine-pouring abilities.[88] Apparently, Prince Belmonte made an impression on Irving more significant than his brief, approving Grand Tour journal entry would indicate; it is as if he tucked away this image as an ideal life plan and lived it out almost exactly.

Estate management was a strong interest and priority for Irving, as it had been for Sir Walter Scott. Throughout Irving's writing we see not only an ability to paint a landscape with words, but also a high degree of knowledge of the trees that were a part of his real and imagined landscapes.[89] He spoke highly of commanding romantic vistas at the country estate of James Kirk Paulding.[90] He managed Sunnyside with an eye to picturesque composition, transplanting and cutting dense patches of trees so as to create distant vistas: "I have opened beautiful views, and have given room for the air to circulate. The season is now in all its beauty; the trees in full leaf, but the leaves fresh and tender; the honeysuckles are in flower, and I think I never saw the place look so well."[91] In one of Irving's first surviving journal entries, from a trip through upstate New York to Montreal in 1803, we see a distaste for being completely enclosed by woods, and the pleasure of coming to an opening with a vista.[92] For someone who has been perpetually accused of being aimless, unstable, and adrift, Irving had an extraordinary number of consistencies across long stretches of time, in matters large and small.

The picturesque has generally been understood as characteristic of romanticism; however, in the arena of landscaping there is no clear demarcation between periods. A love of semi-wild gardens was characteristic of English neoclassicism. According to Walter Nathan, "England had taken the lead with a new conception of beauty in nature. Pope, Addison, and Horace Walpole had all ridiculed the French idea of embellished nature; the formal garden gave way to the 'picturesque' English type of landscape architecture, which, together with the revival of the Gothic style, spread like wildfire through Europe and the United States."[93] In his 1709 essay "The Moralist," Anthony Cooper, the Earl of Shaftesbury, argued for luxuriantly wild variety against Italian and French formality:

> O Glorious Nature! Supremely fair and sovereignly good! All-loving and All-Lovely, All Divine! . . . I shall no longer resist the Passion growing in me for Things of a *natural* kind. . . . Even the rude *Rocks*, the mossy *Caverns*, the irregular unwrought *Grottos*, and broken *Falls* of Waters, with all the horrid Graces of *Wilderness* itself, as representing NATURE more, will be more engaging, and appear with a Magnificence beyond the formal Mockery of Princely Gardens.[94]

Addison made such appeals as early as 1710. Pope himself had stated, "All gardening is landscape painting. Just like a landscape hung up."[95] In 1728, Pope's landscaper Batty Langley argued to the newly enthroned King George II,

> Since the pleasure of a garden depends on the variety of its parts . . . we should well consider of its dispositions, so as to have a continued series of harmonious objects, that will present new and delightful scenes to our view at every step we take. . . . Nor is there anything more shocking than a stiff regular garden, where . . . the same is repeated in all the parts, so that we are tired rather than being further entertained with something new as expected.[96]

Sarah Rutherford of the National Trust of England has stated, "The English Landscape Garden is arguable the greatest contribution Britain has made to the visual arts worldwide."[97]

On large English estates, there was what you might call an Arcadian picturesque, with elegant clumps of trees, punctuating smooth lawns in with gently winding paths overlooking artificially created ponds; frequently, there were large stretches of woods and not simply clusters of towering oaks, elms, and lindens. This type of large-scale landscaping was practiced most famously by Capability Brown from 1740 onward. Brown incorporated Hogarth's idea of "The Line of Beauty" discussed in the 1853 treatise *Analysis of Beauty*; gentle curves rather than straight lines became the norm in the landscaping of great estates.[98] Some have called these landscapes beautiful (as opposed to sublime or picturesque), and they were intended to evoke memories of the paintings of Claude Lorraine. Sometimes the lawns were very large and smooth with little variety; for example, the estate Croome in Worcestershire had a vast lawn with a great cedar of Lebanon towering in the distance.[99] Claude paintings, in fact, often had more diversity and movement in them than some of Brown's landscapes; the attempt to make a landscape look like a Claude painting was successful only as a very loose approximation on vast estates; smaller estates such as those of Alexander Pope and Richard Boyle, Earl of Burlington, along the Thames near London would actually fulfill the Claudian ideal more successfully.[100] From 1713 onward when Pope first saw Burlington's landscape at Chiswick, this circle of friends, aided by the designer William Kent, would transform the semirural Richmond-Twickenham section of the Thames into the idealized Italianate landscape known well in England through the paintings of Claude Lorrain and Gaspar Poussin. There was a combination of Palladian revival classicizing architecture with gently flowing wooded landscapes punctuated with open park-like spaces. This more informal landscaping came to represent the ideals of freedom, simplicity, and naturalness as proper for a nation based on the ideal of liberty, in contrast to the values of an autocratic monarchy expressed in the more formal gardens of Versailles.[101]

As the century proceeded, there was an increased desire for greater variety with an increasingly wild effect. More bushes, wildflowers, stones, and statues were added as well as more winding watercourses. The vast smooth lawns of Capability Brown were difficult to maintain, and the fully picturesque landscape—on Gilpin's definition—came into vogue. However, the two modes were practiced over a long period even if the highly textured, even rugged, diversity was more popular later in the century. Irving commented in 1852 that a landowner in upstate New York was trying to maintain the earlier form of gentle and smooth landscape in the tradition of the earlier English landscaping; the forest had been thinned too extensively and left only isolated clumps of trees, giving the feel of an English park.[102]

The influence of the highly varied semi-wild English garden throughout the eighteenth century is seen in Marie Antoinette's Petit Trianon. This park within a park was given to the French Queen by Louis XVI in 1774. She chose to cultivate it as an Anglo-Chinese garden full of twists, turns, and hidden nooks, incomplete and deliberate contrast to the highly geometric main formal gardens at Versailles. In response to the extreme classicism of Louis's design, as well as his rigid control of court life, the wild English-style garden became for the queen a kind of personal haven,[103] just as Sunnyside would be a haven for Washington Irving. The kind of landscape garden often described as romantic was actually prominent in England throughout the eighteenth century, praised by Addison and Pope, and was influencing other cultures by the 1770s. A similar exportation of English landscaping occurred in Naples in 1785, when Sir William Hamilton convinced Queen Maria Carolina, the sister of Marie Antoinette, to establish an informal English garden at the Caserta villa overlooking Mt. Vesuvius.[104]

Irving certainly valued the picturesquely textured landscape mode, but it had been advocated by Irving's neoclassical literary heroes long before Gilpin's aesthetic theory, and Irving categorized rugged landscapes as sublime, following the older model. The boundary line between classicism and romanticism was, in this case, quite fluid. John Dixon Hunt, in a classic study of poetry, painting, and landscape, has pointed out a consistent relationship between romantic writers and eighteenth-century writers in their relationship to naturalistic landscaping:

> Attitudes to landscape underwent much change and revision during the last third of the eighteenth century. I am concerned to show how they originated in the Augustan age, shaped by its distinctive habits of mind. . . . It is no accident that in 1794, Wordsworth offered to provide essays "upon poetry, and upon the arts of painting and gardening" for a new review; for his linking of the same arts that Horace Walpole had celebrated testifies to Wordsworth's own education in looking at natural scenery. The Romantic poet's confidence that "Laying out grounds, as it is called, may be considered a liberal art, in some sort like poetry and painting; and its object, like that of all the liberal arts is, or ought to be, to move the affections under the control of good sense" was also an eighteen century conviction.[105]

Washington Irving lived at this blurred boundary line between the classical eighteenth century and the romantic age; his life was in so many ways expressive of doubleness and hybridity. The creative tension inherent in all these dualities that also contained continuities would be fruitful for his creation of a highly personal artistic mode. He would launch himself forth as an American Ovid, an American Virgil, and an American Claude for the romantic era.

NOTES

1. Letter to Andrew Quoz (James Paulding), January 1, 1805, *Letters*, I, 167.
2. March 25, 1805, *Journals*, I, 257.
3. Williams, Vol. I, 52, and 392, Ch. III, note 33. See also William Hedges, *Washington Irving: An American Study, 1802–1832* (Baltimore: Johns Hopkins Press, 1965), 36–40. Irving carried Anne Radcliffe's *The Italian* and Patrick Brydone's *A Tour Through Sicily and Malta*, which followed Homer and Virgil closely.
4. John Dixon Hunt, *The Figure in the Landscape: Poetry, Painting, and Gardening during the Eighteenth Century* (Baltimore and London: Johns Hopkins University Press, 1976), xi–xii, 1–5.

5. The French Revolution and the Napoleonic Wars made travel on the continent unsafe for periods, and so the English began to travel more extensively in Britain.

6. Edward J. Nygren, "From View to Vision," in *Views and Visions: American Landscape before 1830*, ed. Edward J. Nygren (Washington, DC: Corcoran Gallery of Art, 1986), 37.

7. Edmund Burke, *On the Sublime and the Beautiful*, Part I, Section VII, in Harvard Classics 24 (New York: P. f. Colliers and Son, 1909), 36.

8. Burke, Part II, Section I–II, 51.

9. *Astoria*, Chapter XLVIII, in Washington Irving, *Three Western Narratives: A Tour on the Prairies; Astoria; The adventures of Captain* Bonneville, ed. James P. Ronda (New York: Literary Classics of the United States, Inc., 2004), 523.

10. Burke, Part III. Section XV, 98.

11. Burke, Part III. Section XIII, 97.

12. Burke, Part III. Section X, 94.

13. Burke, Part III, Section XVI, 99. The opening line of Virgil's *Georgics* described elms used as trellises for grape vines as part of a lovely fertile countryside: "What makes the crops rejoice, Maecenas, under what stars/ to plow and marry the vines to their arbor of elms . . ." see *Virgil's Georgics: A New Verse Translation*, trans. Janet Lembke (New Haven and London: Yale University Press, 2005), 3. Burke's claim that an elm tree cannot be beautiful shows him oblivious to the Latin pastoral tradition that dominated English education, as well as the Claudian tradition of art popular in England from 1700. Such a claim illustrates the problems that arise when a rigidly rationalist dichotomy is imposed on experience.

14. For a helpful description of the impact of the Industrial Revolution on small-scale cottage industries and family farms, and its impact on male-female relationships, see the Introduction to Treuttner and Wallach, 3–13.

15. See Robert Frost: "Nature's first green is gold/ The hardest hue to hold/ Her early leaf's a flower/ But only so an hour."

16. Ringe, *The Pictorial Mode*, 3–15.

17. Washington Irving, *The Crayon Miscellany*, ed. Dahlia Kirby Terrell, CW XXIII (Boston: Twayne Publishers, 1979), 133.

18. Part III, Section XIV, 97.

19. Lord Jeffery, "Essay on Beauty," Preface to Archibold Alison, *Essays on the Nature and Principles of Taste*, 5th edition (London: Alexander Murray, 1871), 29.

20. Burke, Part III, Section I, 77.

21. "Notes on Art," December 12, 1829, in Louis Legrand Noble, *The Life and Works of Thomas Cole*, 3rd Edition (New York: Sheldon, Blakeman, and Company, 1859), 116. Cole's consistent fear of being mere sensual was ground partly in his Calvinist upbringing in England and the influence of Puritan, Quaker, and Unitarian ideals of self-control over sensual passions in the early Republic. However, Cole's anxiety was also grounded in historic-artistic discourse. In the seventeenth century, there was a debate "which purported to oppose reason and emotion with the relative authority of line and contour versus color in art. Rubens became the ideal of the devotees of the latter, while Poussin was promoted by the former." For those who

celebrated the classicizing control and balance of Poussin, the energetic brushwork and vibrant use of color of Rubens and his followers was seen to lack skill in drawing and was also regarded as excessively sensual. Likewise, in the eighteenth century, Joshua Reynolds made a distinction between the Grand Style of Michelangelo, Raphael, and the Caracci, "which was characterized by intellect and dignity of expression" and the Ornamental Style of Venetians and Flemish artists, "which only pleased the senses with bravura technique, ravishing mixed colors, and virtuosity." See Peter C. Sutton, *The Age of Rubens* (Boston: Museum of Fine Arts, 1993), 87–89. Cole's remarks were directed at Turner—who in his more modernist paintings seemed to make a merely superficial splash of brushwork and color. Clearly, Cole was on the side of Poussin and the Grand Style artists, insisting on defined forms, excellent drawing, and intellect as essential to the artistic task rather than mere explosions of color and loose brushwork. Cole's remarks cited here were not directed at Burke's theory of beauty directly, but they indicate why Alison, Cole, and other associationists could never accept Burke's materialist account of psychological response in the experience of the sublime and the beautiful. Materialism and crass sensuality in any theory or any work of art were unacceptable.

22. David Howarth, *Lord Arundel and His Circle* (New Haven and London: Yale University Press, 1985), 63.

23. Howarth, *Lord Arundel*, 79–84.

24. Susan Weber, *William Kent: Designing Georgian England* (New Haven and London: Yale University Press, 2014), 366–7.

25. Mavis Batey, *Alexander Pope: The Poet and the Landscape* (London, Barn Elms Publishing, 1999), 53–8.

26. April 4, 1805, *Journals*, I, 281–2. Irving was attentive to the fact the grotto has been misidentified, for it had a hulking male torso of a river god, not the nymph Egeria. The true grotto of Egeria was elsewhere in Rome; nevertheless, the passage shows the importance of highly textured ancient stone to the definition of the picturesque at the beginning of the nineteenth century.

27. Ian Jenkins and Kim Sloan, *Vases and Volcanoes: Sir William Hamilton and his Collection* (London: British Museum Press, 1996), 9–11, 223–40.

28. Marjorie Hope Nicholson has pointed out that in England, from the beginning of the common era to the seventeenth century, people were not interested in mountains at all; they were gloomy wastelands to be avoided and they were not celebrated if mentioned at all; they were generally described in terms of "distaste and revulsion." Over fifty years or so in the heart of the eighteenth century, there was a shift toward seeing mountains as places of glory, associated with the majesty of the creator. The first interest in such mountain glory was expressed in terms that we would now call sublime, and it was left to Gilpin to affirm an idea we now take for granted, that they could also be beautiful. See *Mountain Gloom and Mountain Glory: The Development of the Aesthetics of the Infinite* (Ithaca: Cornell University Press, 1956), 1–17.

29. William Gilpin, *Three Essays: On Picturesque Beauty; On Picturesque Travel; and On Sketching Landscape: To which is Added a Poem, On Landscape Painting* (London: Blamire in the Strand, 1794), 6–19.

30. Noble, *The Life and Works*, 159.

31. July 7, 1804, *Journals*, I, 36.

32. *The Complete Poetic Works of Alexander Pope*, ed. Henry W. Boynton (Boston: Houghton Mifflin Company, 1931), 32.

33. Weber, *William Kent*, 366–7.

34. Washington Irving, "The Author's Account of Himself," in *The Sketch Book*, CW, 8.

35. Nygren, "From View to Vision," , 44, 81, note 73.

36. Brigitte Bailey, "Irving's Landscapes: Aesthetics, Visual Work, and the Tourist's Estate," in *American Travel Literature, Gendered Aesthetics, and the Italian Tour, 1824–1862* (Edinburgh: University Press, 2018).

37. Washington Irving, *Bracebridge Hall*, in *Bracebridge Hall; Tales of a Traveller; The Alhambra*, ed. Andrew B. Myers (New York: Literary Classics of the United States, Inc., 1991), 8.

38. In the early nineteenth century, Americans would display a high degree of interest in geology and natural history broadly. Because the United States had so few historical associations, it was necessary to find a sense of identity and history in the land itself. One could argue that the tomes of Alexander Wilson and John James Audubon on America's birds were some of our first national "monuments."

39. Martin Sonnabend and John Whiteley, *Claude Lorrain: The Enchanted Landscape* (Oxford: Ashmolean Museum, 2011), 17.

40. Sonnabend and Whiteley, *Claude Lorrain*, 11–12.

41. See Lorraine's *Coast View*, 1633, discussed by Sonnabend and Whitely, 22–3.

42. Tim Barringer and Jennifer Raab, "An Inheritance in Print: Thomas Cole and the Aesthetics of Landscape," in *Picturesque and Sublime: Thomas Cole's Tran-Atlantic Inheritance*, ed. Tim Barringer et al. (Catskill, Thomas Cole National Historic Site in association with Yale University Press, 2018), 9–11.

43. Irving read voluminously in literature, travel literature, and history, but he got his aesthetic theory second hand.

44. John Bonehill and Stephen Daniels, eds. *Paul Sandby: Picturing Britain* (London: Royal Academy of Arts, 2009), 13–16.

45. Tim Barringer and Jennifer Raab, "An Inheritance in Print: Thomas Cole and the Aesthetics of Landscape," in *Picturesque and Sublime: Thomas Cole's Transatlantic Heritage*, ed. Tim Barringer et al. (Catskill: Thomas Cole National Historic Site, 2017), 17–18, 24–25, 88–93. Barringer and Raab emphasize that this new dramatic picturesque was the antithesis of the older, gentler Claudian picturesque; gentle undulating hills and a body of water in the middle distance framed by lush trees, which would now be classified as beautiful rather than picturesque. The distinction was lost on Washington Irving; he loved heightened variation, while speaking of the picturesque in Claudian terms. On the whole, Irving seems to have preferred the gentle paintings of Asher Durand to the dramatically picturesque portrayals of the Catskills by Thomas Cole. See my discussion of Irving and great trees in chapter 5.

46. I will discuss Irving and artists from 1815 onward in the final chapter.

47. Thomas Cole, "Essay on American Scenery," in *American Art: 1700–1960, Sources and Documents*, ed. John W. McCoubrey (Englewood Cliffs: Prentice Hall,

1965), 107. This use of towering elms can be seen in Cole's idealized pastoral Cole's *View on Catskill—Early Autumn* from 1836 to 1837.

48. Irving, *A Tour on the Prairies*, 70. Willows are streamside bushes that grow about 30 feet high. Cottonwoods and plane trees (American sycamores) have massive trunks and grow 100 feet high in moist settings; they tower like the tulip magnolia tree known as Major Andre's tree in "The Legend of Sleepy Hollow."

In 1866, the Hudson River School artist Worthington Whittredge traveled with a government expedition similar to that Irving joined in 1832; Irving traveled with the party of Commissioner Henry Ellsworth; Whittredge traveled west with General John Pope, who was inspecting Indian settlements after the Civil War. Whittredge became famous for painting cottonwoods along the Platte River, and his works portray scenes quite similar to Irving's description; the picturesque tree-clad promontory in Irving is often replaced by the Rocky Mountains in the distance, and sometimes he portrayed the kind of intimate space under a canopy of trees that Irving so appreciated. See *American Paradise*, 186–7.

49. Irving, *Tour*, XIV, 80.

50. *Tour*, VI, 30.

51. It's possible Irving saw prints or copies in well-to-do households of Philadelphia during social visits in 1803, and he would have known of Claude's civilized works and the wild Salvator Rosa through conversation with his Burrite friends even without personal reading about them, but it is highly unlikely he could have seen a Claude before his Grand Tour.

52. April 8, 1805, *Journals*, I, 289. The insight that these were two of Claude's best paintings probably came from a tourist guidebook. In his April 1 journal entry, he was guided in his artistic judgment by Laurence Stern's *A Sentimental Journey Through France and Italy*. See *Journals*, I, 271.

53. March 14, 1805, *Journals*, I, 239.

54. "The Author," in *Bracebridge Hall; Tales of a Traveller; The Alhambra*, 11.

55. Albert Boime, *The Magisterial Gaze: Manifest Destiny and American Landscape Painting, c. 1830–1865* (Washington and London: Smithsonian Institution Press, 1991), 35–55. The ruling class aspect of "the prospect" and the Grand Tour has also been fruitfully discussed in Brigitte Bailey, 1–30.

56. John Conron, *American Picturesque* (University Park: Pennsylvania State University Press, 2000), xxi.

57. "What can we reason but from what we know?" Alexander Pope, *An Essay on Man*, Epistle I.I.

As early as 500 BCE, the Milesian Greek philosophers tried to understand the unity of the cosmos in its diversity by positing an underlying substance that was capable of transformation. The most common speculation was that there was water or air beneath the surface of all things, manifesting in different forms according to regular patterns. Solid earth was a kind of frozen water. There must be an underlying substance, and it was only possible to discuss that mysterious unknown with the assistant of something we have already experienced. These speculations were very rudimentary, but they were rational. Shall we explain the unknown by another unknown? The same methodological question of knowing the unknown by means of the known was brought back into the foreground of discussion by John Locke, who was more methodic than the Milesians in observing the patterns by which the human mind processes sense data. Locke's insight was then popularized in the poetry of Pope, but it represents perhaps the oldest explanatory principle in Western history.

58. Stephen Ambrose, *Undaunted Courage: Meriwether Lewis, Thomas Jefferson, and the Opening of the American West* (New York: Touchstone Books, 1996), 236–7.

59. Jefferson had stated in 1771 that every gentleman should read Burke's *Philosophical Enquiry into the Origins of Our Ideas of the Beautiful and the Sublime*. See Nygren, "From View to Vision," 79, note 74. Meriweather Lewis was a gentleman educated in Virginia, and he was Thomas Jefferson's personal secretary from 1801 until the expedition. Lewis would have known Burke through conversations with Jefferson even if he did not read Burke himself.

60. April 7, 1805, *Journals*, I, 285.

61. Donald Ringe, *The Pictorial Mode: Space & Time in the Art of Bryant, Irving & Cooper* (Lexington: University of Kentucky Press, 1971), 24–5.

62. *Alhambra*, 725.

63. Irving mentions a fascination with racial mixture, Spanish and Moorish, at the beginning of *The Alhambra*. A combination of human and natural features in the south of Spain may have influenced Irving's choice to go west when he returned to America.

64. *Tour*, 107.

65. Peter Martin, *Pursuing Innocent Pleasures: The Gardening World of Alexander Pope* (Hamden, Connecticut: Archon Books, 1984), 8–9.

66. Nathalia Wright, "Introduction to Volume I," *Journals*, I, xxxi.

67. Letter to William Irving, *Letters: Volume I, 1802–1823*, 142.

68. Jonathan Wordsworth, *William Wordsworth and the Age of English Romanticism* (New Brunswick and London: Rutgers University Press, 1987), 60–77.

69. See William Kent's drawing of the first shell temple in Pope's garden, ca. 1725–30, published in Martin, 55.

70. April 3, 1805, *Journals*, I, 289.

71. Hedges, 40–1. Hedges mentions that Irving had read Patrick Brydone's *Tour Through Sicily and Malta*, and that he was carrying Ann Radcliff's *The Italian* with him on his trip. Both authors saw the "Italian landscape through the eyes of Lorrain, Poussin, and Rosa." Irving's remarks about Claudian light before he saw any paintings in Rome may be based on Radcliffe's or Brydone's description. His first reference to a Claude-like vista was found on the March 14 *Journal* entry he cited earlier, and the second was on March 25, a few days before arriving in Rome: "After leaving Capua, we found the road more diversified by hill & dale, and presenting the most lovely prospect of that gentle yet picturesque kind in which the pencil of Claude Lorrain has so much excelled. Everything was rich, luxuriant, & smiling at the reviving touch of Spring." The reference to pencil suggests he may have seen engravings of Claude's drawings before he saw any paintings. An oil copy of a Claude, *The*

Temple of Apollo by John Beale Bordley, was available to see in an upper-class home in Philadelphia from 1776 onward. See Nygren, "From View to Vision," 17.

72. March 27–30, 1805, *Journals*, I, 262–8.
73. Irving, "Memoir of Washington Allston," cited in Jones, 39.
74. May 25, 1815, *Letters I*, 393.
75. Andrew Hemingway, "Introduction," in *Transatlantic Romanticism*, 16.
76. Martin Sonnabend, *Claude Lorrain: The Enchanted Landscape* (Oxford: Ashmolean Museum, 2011), 15
77. William H. Gerdts, "The Paintings of Washington Allston," in *"A Man of Genius": The Art of Washington Allston (1779–1843)*, ed. William H. Gerdts and Theodore E. Stebbins, Jr (Boston: Museum of Fine Arts, 1979), 146–8.
78. Jones, *Washington Irving*, 40.
79. April 3, 1805, *Journals*, I, 276–7.
80. Dunlap, *The History of the Rise*, 153.
81. Gerdts, "The Paintings of Washington Allston," 11.
82. 'Introduction," *Astoria*, 179.
83. Gerdts, "The Paintings of Washington Allston," 43.
84. Irving returned to England in 1815, but he could not see his old friend immediately because he was consumed with family obligations, managing a bankruptcy and assessing his brother's health.
85. Pierre Rosenberg and Keith Christiansen, eds., *Poussin and Nature: Arcadian Visions* (New York: The Metropolitan Museum of Art), 189–99.
86. Gerdts, "The Paintings of Washington Allston," 75–128.
87. February 27, 1805, *Journals*, I, 219.
88. September 29, 1829, *Letters*, II, CW, 468.
89. Irving consistently describes sycamores, willows, and cottonwoods along rivers, poplars and sycamores at Battery Park, the tulip tree at Sleepy Hollow, dogwoods, elms, and chestnut trees, oak scrub forests out west, and constantly comments on the myrtles and other trees and bushes of the Mediterranean landscape. The proclivity to arboreal attentiveness may go back to Virgil, but Irving was certainly influenced by the Latin pastoral revival in early eighteenth-century England led by Alexander Pope and others, where Horace, Virgil, and Homer all found new translations into English as the restored monarchy entered its own classical age. However, Pope was also one of the early leaders of the trend toward naturalistic and landscaping that emphasized unity in great diversity. See John Dixon Hunt, *Figure*, 58–104.
90. Pierre Irving, *Life and Letters*, IV, 59.
91. Pierre Irving, *Life and Letters*, IV, 10–11.
92. August 16, 1803, *Journals*, I, 27.
93. Walter L. Nathan, "Thomas Cole and the Romantic Landscape," in *Romanticism in America*. Papers contributed to a Symposium held at the Baltimore Museum of Art, May 13–15, 1940, ed. George Boas (New York: Russell & Russell, 1961), 32. A helpful overview of the appeal for naturalistic, irregular but integrated gardens and estates, beginning with Addison in 1712, is found in Penelope Hobhouse, *Plants in Garden History: An Illustrated History of Plants and Their Influence on*

Garden Styles—from Ancient Egypt to the Present Day (London, Pavilion Bok, 1997), 190–6.

94. Mavis Batey, *Alexander Pope*, 24.

95. Cited in Sarah Rutherford, *Capability Brown and his Landscape Gardens* (London: National Trust Books, 2016), 22.

96. Batty Langley, *New Principles of Gardening* (London: Bettesworth and Batley, 1728), 3–4.

97. Rutherford, *Capability Brown*, 7.

98. Rutherford, *Capability Brown*, 20.

99. Rutherford, *Capability Brown*, 9.

100. See John Harris, *The Palladian Revival: Lord Burlington, His Villa and Garden at Chiswick* (New Haven and London: Yale University Press, 1994), 68–103.

101. Martin, 19–22. See the oil painting, *A View from Richmond Hill up the River*, by Antonio Joli, to gauge the success of the project, pictured on page 21.

102. Letter to Kate Irving, July 25, 1852, cited in Pierre Irving, *Life*, Vol. IV, 93.

103. Elizabeth de Feydeu, *From Marie Antoinette's Garden: An Eighteenth-Century Horticultural Album* (Paris: Flammarion, 2013), 13–27.

104. Jenkins and Sloan, *Vases and Volcanoes*, 17–22.

105. Hunt, *The Figure*, xiii. Horace Walpole had referred to poetry, painting, and landscape design as "the three graces."

Chapter 4

American Ovid, American Virgil, American Claude, and Pumpkin Smasher

Washington Irving was always crossing boundaries between the neoclassical and the romantic eras. From landscaping to his own understanding of the picturesque, he blurred early and late eighteenth-century conceptions, though he tended to rely more on early eighteen-century definitions of the picturesque, combined with Burke's understanding of the sublime. Another example of art at the boundary line of neoclassical and romantic eras—whether poetry or painting—is art or poetry based on or imitating the stories of Ovid and Virgil.[1]

Virgil was important to Irving. The original 1809 version of *A History of New York* was his own American version of Virgil's *Aeneid*. In the original version of *A History of New York*, Irving transferred Virgil's epic story of the founding of Rome to the shores of the Hudson: "In the joyous season of spring then, did these hardy adventurers depart on this eventful expedition, which only wanted another Virgil to rehearse it, to equal the oft sing story of the Eneid." The Dutch wandering by sea from Communipaw to Oyster Island, to Gibbet Island, through Buttermilk Channel and Hell Gate is likened to the storm-tossed wandering of Aeneas as he tried to fulfill his prophesied destiny of founding Rome.[2] The importance of Virgil for Irving is also seen in the fact that, when he was the U.S. ambassador in London in 1830, one of his priorities was to secure a good multilingual edition of Virgil's *Georgics* for the Library of Congress.[3]

Any artwork based on a story in Ovid's *Metamorphoses* must be classicizing in some sense; his collection was full of nostalgic stories of the old days when the gods populated the landscape, and wrought transformations that gave a kind of sacred history to that landscape. Nicolas Poussin painted many scenes from Ovid's stories such as *Echo and Narcissus, Apollo and Daphne Midas, Pan and Shepherds, Venus Anointing the Dead*

Adonis and Irving found such paintings an anchor for the soul, as indicated by his Christmas Eve meditation on the days when the gods were still with us.[4] However, many of Ovid's stories were profoundly elegiac and even tragic. Women were transformed into birds or trees to escape various levels of aggression, and these wistful stories often turned to heart-wrenching catastrophe.

The eighteenth-century English painter Richard Wilson displayed the power of Ovid's stories at this neoclassicalromantic cultural boundary line. Wilson was regarded as an English painter in the classical mode, but one whose work sometimes gripped the imaginations of emergingromantics; for this reason, he is sometimes called a proto romantic. When Wilson began his career in the 1740s, English landscape traditions barely existed;[5] Paul Sandby was about to go to Scotland and Wales for topographical studies, bringing back to England the first drawings and paintings of wild British vistas. Alexander Cozens began a series of drawings and etchings of Italy in a famous *Roman Sketchbook* in 1746.[6] The lords of great estates traveled on the Grant Tour of the continent and they brought back paintings by Claude Lorrain, Nicolas Poussin, and Gaspar Dughet, the seventeenth-century masters who all painted in Rome.[7] After traveling to Italy in 1750, Wilson developed his own style in the tradition of ideal art that would shortly be commended by Sir Joshua Reynolds at the Royal Academy of the Arts. Wilson followed the classicizing composition formulas of Claude Lorrain and the similar Gaspard Dughet to treat Italian and British landscapes, while adding touches of topological realism.[8] For example, discussing Wilson's painting *Llyn Peris and Dolbadarn Castle*, David Solkin notes,

> By classicizing a Welsh site, Wilson attested to the existence of a universal ideal underlying all of nature, no matter where one looks; according to most eighteenth century British aestheticians, it was the mimetic artists' duty to reveal this perfect order, for in doing so he demonstrated the providential plan pattern devised by an omniscient Creator.[9]

As Solkin puts it, "Though an actual return to perfection can never be achieved, the recovery of the Golden Age can be effected in the imagination, by means of art."[10] This description of Wilson's goals is an almost perfect description of Irving's own strategy in creating *A History of New York* and in conjuring up the sleepy villages of the Hudson River valley in "Rip Van Winkle" and "The Legend of Sleepy Hollow." While Irving would not have spoken so openly of a providential plan by a Creator, a similar assumption of a universal ideal behind nature—a stable order that was the basis for an enduring civilization—makes sense of his tendency to impose a Claudian lens on views of Italy and the American west alike.

We see sudden catastrophe and absolute pathos in Wilson's 1760 *Destruction of the Children of Niobe* (see figure 4.1) which portrays a scene from Ovid's *Metamorphoses*, Book VI.

It is the most brooding and turbulent of Wilson's works, and for this reason was appreciated by budding romantic artists when they saw it in person or in print.[11] Poussin had painted similar scenes of wailing over sudden catastrophes, such as *Landscape with a Man Killed by a Snake*, and *Landscape with Pyramus and Thisbe*.[12] The storm in the latter may have been an influence on Wilson's presentation of the turbulent stormy day in his *Destruction*.

Niobe was a very fertile and self-confident Queen, who had fourteen children, seven daughters and seven sons. Unfortunately, she insulted Latona, the mistress of Jupiter and mother of Apollo and Diana. Niobe discouraged the worship of the goddess, and she also insulted her for only having two children, compared to her own fourteen. Latona sent Apollo to avenge her, and he did so swiftly. He shot all seven sons in rapid sequence, and when the daughters were discovering and wailing over the bodies, he shot them too. Latona's hubris was swiftly punished. The abrupt transformation from prosperous abundance to absolute destitution was stark. She was transformed to stone and placed on a mountaintop, where the marble still weeps. The story

Figure 4.1 Richard Wilson, *The Destruction of the Children of Niobe*, 1760, Yale Center for British Art.

was famous and had a long history of artistic representation. Wilson's painting shows a sister grieving over the body of her brother, and Apollo taking aim from a rocky perch behind a towering tree that is in Claudian position center-left but curling into a more gnarly branch pattern toward the right, echoing the ridge of rocky outcrops that is the frame on the other side of the composition. Light breaks through very heavy clouds only to illuminate the pale body of the dead son. The only classical stability in this painting is the certainty that hubris shall be repaid by the gods. However great the arrogance of Niobe, one cannot but feel pity for the slain children, and the mother upon whom sudden calamity has fallen. The painting was highly acclaimed immediately, and it was widely available through prints by 1800.[13] Irving likely would have known it, as well as the original story from his reading of Ovid. Ovid's general tendency to tell a story to give an explanation and sense for a particular rock formation surely influenced Irving. He takes up the strategy comically in his account of how Saint Antony's Nose, a rock formation on the Hudson River got its name, and more tragically, how the Passaic Falls of New Jersey, came to be. Ovid truly provided excellent subject matter at the boundary line of classical and romantic art.

The theme of sudden catastrophe was not limited to Ovid, however; it was also found in the pastoral poetry of Virgil's *Georgics*, and the calamities at sea in his *Aeneid*. Virgil described the life of hardworking Italian farmers, and he was clear on the range of disasters that fell upon them as they struggle to wring an existence from the land once the Golden Age of Saturn had passed.

> The central thesis of the *Georgics* is that labor—sheer, ceaseless hard work—is the only barrier between the farmer and ruin. All too often it's a flimsy one. Storms strike, drought bakes the land, insects infest the granaries, weeds ensnarl the fields, disease fells flocks and herds wholesale, and nothing the farmer does—not hoeing with extra diligence, not saying prayers over and over again—can keep the random blows of nature from wrecking his enterprises. The last 150 lines of Book III show this bleak view: snakes threaten not just cattle but people too. Incurable infections kill the sheep; no life is safe.[14]

Poussin's painting about sudden death by snakebite need illustrated a theme from Virgil: "It was Jove who putting deadly venom in the hissing snake . . . so that, using their brains, men might gradually hammer out many skills."[15] However beneficial the process is in the long run, the immediate result is the terror and wailing of sudden death, often accompanied by storm, as in Wilson's *Niobe*. The theme of sudden calamities is common to both Ovid and Virgil—the most pastoral of literary sources. However, when you need an explanation for a feature of the landscape, Ovid is the inspiration to which you turn.

AMERICAN OVID—A FALSE START

Irving himself attempted a poem in Ovidian mode in 1806. *Passaic—A Tradition* offers a creation myth for the falls of the Passaic River in New Jersey, a popular tourist site that was more accessible to New Yorkers than Niagara Falls. I include it in entirety because it is important for understanding Irving's self-concept as an American Ovid, however flawed his first effort in such a direction may have been:

> In a wild tranquil vale fringed with forests of green/ Where nature had fashion'd a soft sylvan scene/ The retreat of the ring dove, the haunt of the deer/ Passaic in silence roll'd gentle and clear.
> No grandeur of prospect astonished the sight/ No abruptness sublime mingled awe with delight/ Here the wild flowret blossem'd the elm proudly waved/ And pure was the current the green bank that laved.
> But the spirit that rules o'er the thick tangled wood/ And deep in its gloom fix'd his murky abode/ who loved the rude scene that the whirlwind deforms/ And gloried in tempest and lightning and storms,
> All flushed from the tumult of battle he came/ Where the red men encountered the children of flame/ While the noise of the war whop still rung in his ears/ And the fresh bleeding scalp as a trophy he wears.
> So the sons of the forest in terror retire/ Pale savages chase them with thunder and fire/ In vain whirls the war club, in vain twangs the bow/By thunder and fire are his warriors laid low.
> From defeat and from carnage the fierce spirit came/ His breast was a tumult—his passions were flame/ Despair swells his heart, fury maddens his ire/ And black scowls his brow o'er his eyeballs of fire.
> With a glance of disgust he the landscape survey'd/ With its fragrant wild flowers, its wide waving shade/ Where Passaic meander'd through margins of green/So transparent its waters—its surface serene.
> He rived the green hills, the wild woods he laid low/ He turned the pure stream in rough channels to flow/ He rent the rude rock the steep precipice gave/ And hurl's down the chasm the thundering wave.
> A scene of strange ruin he scatter'd around/ Where cliffs piles on cliffs in rude majesty frown'd/ Where shades of thick horror embrown'd the dark wood/ And the rainbow and mist marked the turbulent flood.
> Countless moons have since rolled in the long lapse of time/ Cultivation has softened those features sublime/ the ax of the white men enlivened the shade/ and dispelled the deep gloom of the thicketed glade.
> Yet the stranger still gazes with wondering eye/ One rocks rudely torn and groves mounted on high/ Still loves on the cliff's dizzy border to roam/ where the torrent leaps headlong embosomed in foam.[16]

The reader may be grateful that Irving decided to take up fiction and essays rather than poetry. Nevertheless, *Passaic—A Tradition* is an important window into Irving's career for several reasons. The story tells how a beautiful, gently pastoral, Arcadian landscape, where a peaceful river calmly flowed among elm trees, became a sublime landscape dominated by a lofty chasm, crashing torrents, and strewn boulders and dark groves on high. First, we see very clearly sympathy for the Native Americans being forced off territory by superior firepower. The pale Anglo-American colonists were the savages in this poem. Irving turned to this theme again in Book I on *A History of New York*, in the mode of a very biting satire already discussed. The criticism of recent settlers in New Jersey found in this poem indicates that the satire of rationalizations for colonial abuse of Native Americans in the *History* did not only apply to Spanish Catholics in the distant past; they applied to Anglo-American behavior more recently as well. There was an ambiguity and irony in the description of "dispell'd gloom" of Eastern deciduous forests now turned to open farmland in the aftermath of battle. The land was now sunnier, but at a cost. The gloom was intensified for those who felt the loss; for anyone who had read the prior lines and senses the smoldering passion of the Spirit of the forest, the gloom was not at all dispelled. Given that the clearing of the woods led to more open sunny spaces, Irving might have said the cutting of trees enlightened or illumined the shade. If he were speaking as an Enlightenment advocate of the conquest of barbarian peoples, supporting the expansion into Native American territory, and the Puritan and Quaker task of turning the wilderness into a garden, that would seem a reasonable word choice. Instead, he opted for the more awkward phrase "enlivened the shade"; his use of the word "enlivened" was highly ironic because this enlivening came by way of an overwhelming slaughter. There were Anglo-American crops in fields experiencing new life, and the bustle of a new civilization emerging, but again, at a cost. Trees were felled and the "red man" was dead or in retreat. There was a lively task of establishing new farms and towns, but a shadow was cast. An angry and grieving Spirit of the forest, now limited to a much smaller patch of deep woods, haunted the falls created by the cataclysm of his own rage. The Anglo-American settlement went on in the light of these cleared spaces, but it did so in the shadow of a tragedy. Clearly, Irving was struggling to find the right words to convey his sympathy with the Native Americans who were slaughtered, and his ambiguity about the "enlivened" fields now available for agriculture. He was not entirely successful in his attempt, but we should remember that romantics loved mystery and darkness as much as the pure light of day, and they distrusted Enlightenment claims to clarity and reason—and so the destruction of a lush, shady forest and its replacement with open sunny farm fields would not necessarily be an improvement. The poem was written in the heart of Jefferson's two presidential terms, and Jefferson's policy of forcing Native Americans out of the woods to become Quaker-style farmers was surely the object of criticism.

Irving's ambiguity, however, and his struggle for words, stands in sharp contrast to Puritan preachers of civilizing enlightenment, who claim "the glad ray of knowledge shall burst upon those dark recesses where the wandering savage hold dominion," making the desert wilderness bloom like a garden in full sun, according to the frequently cited vision of an inhabited world in Isaiah 35. The average American in New England and elsewhere accepted the idea that Native Americans were "born for the shade," presumably the woodlands of the eastern deciduous forest that ranges to the Mississippi River, and that they could not withstand the light of cultivated civilization.[17] Such a notion was crafted before the Great Plains were discovered or seen as the ideal location for Indian removal. In the earliest period, Native Americans would keep on being displaced into the shade of the eastern forests such as those of Ohio, living in the primitive shade that suited them best.

There is a passage in Irving's *Traits of Indian Character* which would seem to echo this condescending and indeed genocidal language, but when understood in the context of his reading of Alexander Pope's *Essay on Man*, indicates the opposite of the usage described by Lubber.[18] In *Traits*, Irving contrasted the condition of Native Americans under present U.S. agricultural prosperity and their past natural way of life:

> Luxury spreads it ample board before their eyes, but they are excluded now from the banquet. Plenty revels over the fields, but they are starving in the midst of its abundance; the whole wilderness has blossomed into a garden, but they feel as reptiles that infest it.
>
> How different was their state while yet the undisputed Lords of the soil. Their wants were few, and the means of gratification within their reach. They saw everyone round them sharing the same lot, enduring the same hardships, feeling on the same aliments, arrayed in the same rude garments. No roof then rose, but was open to the homeless stranger, no smoke curled under the trees, but he was welcome to sit down and join the hunter in his repast. . . . Such were the Indians, while in the pride and energy of their primitive natures; they resemble those wild plants which thrive best in the shades of the forest, but which shrink from the hand of cultivation, and perish beneath the light of the sun.[19]

Irving's reference to Native Americans alienated in the sun was clearly not a celebration of the New England and Quaker farmer civilization that saw itself as turning the wilderness into a garden. The reference to "wild plants which thrive best in the shade" seems to be based on a passage in Pope's *Essay on Man*, a tour de force of post-Newtonian Deist-Catholic philosophical theology, regardless of how one assesses the poetry of it.

In *An Essay on Man*, everything in creation had a special place, and the small and great were equally created by God through the universal laws of physics; all creatures were equally adapted to particular habitats with unique features, such as the microscope-like eyes of a fly. Nothing in creation was better or worse than any other being, but each had a value and a place. This essay was not just a rehash of the medieval great chain of Being; it was a science-based philosophical theology that anticipated insights central to the theory of evolution, but described the plan as unfolding from the eternally organized mind of a good God. Pope's essay was not just a protest against cultural chauvinism, as was Goldsmith's "Citizen of the World." It was an assault on anthropocentrism itself, on the idea that humans were the center of the cosmos; it was also an attack on all forms of egocentrism.[20] The *Essay* also denied that reason and passion were opposed, but rather the self-interested needs of all creatures caused them to reach out to others and form communities. In such a world, reason and passion coexisted in a mutually beneficial relationship. The age-old fear of passion on the part of religious people and ancient philosophers must be dispensed with. Pope's *Essay* was full of rich and significant insights, and it was not simply a neoclassical string of trite couplets with a strong sense of symmetry. In Pope's cosmos, "all things work together for good" as stated by the Apostle Paul in Romans 8.

If some of his lines seem trite to the point of insensitivity—"Whatever is, is right!"—such a judgment must be tempered by the fact that Pope himself struggled with a lifelong spinal deformity ("This disease, which is my life").[21] Indeed, his inability to travel made it all the more urgent to make England a place worth living in; his friend Lady Montagu noted that his translation of Homer into the scenery of the Thames made English soil "classick ground," and the same could be said of his landscaping in conjunction with the neo-Palladian architectural revival.[22] This quest for classic ground in one's homeland made Pope very relevant to Irving and other Americans who needed more profound associations than mere wilderness in a landscape. Pope's grand cosmic vision of a good God designing a harmonious world that was graspable through Newton's physics was not just a glib vision insensitive to the suffering of the world—it was a statement of faith in the master designer, and it was also an assertion of his own dignity as one of the small, frail things of the world. Because the laws of nature were impartial to all, egocentrism was unnatural and incompatible with the divine structure of things. With such humility, he accepted his disease as part of God's plan; who was he to expect favoritism? However, because the same divine laws of nature generated everything in the universe; everything was equal in value. There was a place for even deformed beings in this majestic universe which showed partiality to none, but which gave life and eventually struggle and death to all. The assertion of the value of things in nature that people do not always value was central to a passage that influenced Irving's description of Native Americans.

Irving's remark about Indians as plants adapted to the shade makes sense in the light of Pope's worldview: in a world where all things are interwoven together, God pervades all, and expresses the divine self in every part: "Ask of thy mother earth why oaks are made taller or stronger than the weeds they shade."[23] Irving correctly paraphrased Pope's term "weeds" as "wild plants," for the use of the term "weeds" here did not have any clearly negative nuance in the context of an oak forest. A weed was any plant that grew up naturally by seeds in the soil without being planted by humans. The term generally referred to small herbaceous plants, but it could occasionally refer to trees such as elms or yews that just grew up naturally in certain areas without being planted. The term "weed" would only be negative in the context of agriculture, where native plants that grew up spontaneously would interfere with the crops.[24] The subject here was woodland herbs and there was no negative connotation to their spontaneous growth in the understory of a forest; however, for humans who were anthropocentric, plants in nature that did not serve human purposes would often be viewed as worthless or useless. Pope combated this idea, in defense of the small, sometimes belittled herbs, as well as in defense of his own existence. If some people would belittle "weeds" of the woods as useless, Pope was there to say they had a place in God's good, Newtonian world. Given that Pope has a major deformity that would lead many people to see him as useless, he no doubt identified with weeds that could easily be regarded as having no value. He was affirming the dignity of his own existence as well as all other beings in the cosmos, for all were equally generating by the laws of nature in the plan of Providence.

Irving and Pope both used the image of herbaceous plants that grew up in the shade of deciduous northern oak forests. As in Pope's universe, the herbs and wildflowers in the understory and the oaks that shade them had a unique place in the natural order. There was no good or bad, better or worse. The trees of the forest belonged there, and the plants in the understory were adapted to the shade; they too belonged. That is where they would thrive. When Irving compared Native Americans of the eastern United States to these shade-loving herbs, he was not saying they were not strong enough to survive, or that the new American civilization was more vigorous. He was saying, inspired by Pope, that Native Americans were adapted to a particular habitat. The Native Americans of the eastern United States were woodland peoples. Irving was not making a judgment about their failures; he was stating a fact. If you cut down the trees of the forest—if you destroyed the woodlands, turned it into farmland, and forced people into a lifestyle to which they were not adapted, they would obviously not thrive. In *Traits of Indian Character*, Irving maintained the same sympathy toward Native Americans that he did in *Passaic*, and both writings displayed a certain respect for the American farmers who were making the cleared, open fields so productive, while sustaining and expressing an awareness that the transformation of the woodlands to farmland came at a disturbingly high cost.

When Irving wrote Passaic in 1806, he had been in Europe for almost three years. He was feeling acutely the lack of historical associations in the United States, and he tried to fill that void by giving the falls of the Passaic a mythic history like the tragic stories in Ovid that account for how a specific grove or rock formation came to be. The northeasterner United States had no ancient ruins, but after the Forest Spirit was done, we would have ruins in the piles of rock strewn around the most famous waterfall of New Jersey, one that was much more accessible to New Yorkers than Niagara Falls.[25] His subtitle to the poem—"A Tradition"—is ironic because there could be no such legend or tradition. Native Americans had been near the falls for thousands of years, and they would not have told a local creation story based on a recent event. Only an American would do that, one for whom the falls were a newly discovered wonder. Feeling a lack of historical associations in the landscape, Irving simply made one up, albeit structured around the historical fact of Anglo-American aggression against Native Americans in the region. Now the United States would have a sublime monument to an historic event. As with Ovid, a wistfully tragic story was better than no story at all. If Irving showed this poem to any of his friends like Paulding, they would have recognized the problem of an implausibly recent creation account. We may consider the poem incoherent for this reason, but it was Irving's first trial run at making up a sacred history with gods or ghosts as a feature of the landscape. In this case they remained hidden in the woods even if they were no longer visiting us.

The brooding Indian Spirit of the forest anticipated Old Scratch in *The Devil and Tom Walker*. There a mysterious figure haunted the swamps that were the last retreat of Native Americans in Long Island. This is one way to create a world in which the gods still visit us—they linger with smoldering anger and entrap less than pure wayfarers in an act of judgment upon American civilization.[26] It is akin to the gods striking humans down for hybris in Ovid. Before Irving created Old Scratch, he would of course try his hand again at making up a history where a sense of history was needed in *A History of New York*, a piece based loosely on an outline of historical events, just as *Passaic* was based very loosely on the reality of regional Native American conquest and removal.

A similar ambiguity regarding the progress of civilization is found in Thomas Cole's 1835 work, *The Oxbow: View from Mt. Holyoke*, where wild and cultivated areas are juxtaposed in a panoramic vision where the wild side in the left foreground is presented with the turbulence of storm overhead, and the open fields and winding river with barely a few trees dotting distant landscape characterized by fine grids raise a question about the cost and relative barrenness of civilization. The storm over the wilderness portion evokes a sense of brooding similar to that of Irving's spirit that still dwells in the remaining shade at the top of the falls of the Passaic, and the sunny space of wide farmland is visually interesting only because of the winding river and oxbow loop that moves through an otherwise bland landscape. Elizabeth Mankin Kornhauser has pointed out that "the palette of pale green and yellow is distinctively muted"; there is a wide consensus among Cole scholars that this painting, with its juxtaposition of wilderness and civilization, expresses an environmentalist critique, and that it was thematically related to *The Course of Empire* series Cole was already working on.[27] The light of civilization was for both Cole and Irving an ironic light that was ambiguous at best.

AMERICAN VIRGIL, AMERICAN CLAUDE

Irving would portray a rather Ovidian and Virgilian vision of an abrupt shift from prosperity to sudden collapse in his vivid pictorial description of an October day in *A History of New York*, Book III, Chapter V of the 1809 version.[28] The entire chapter is a narrative intrusion by Diedrich Knickerbocker describing a walk on the Battery in the autumn of 1804; it is sandwiched between the end description of the Golden Age of Wouter Van Twiller and the first mention of the coming of barbarian hordes at the border—that is, Connecticut Yankees—in the next chapter. In the original version, autumn 1804 was notable because it was just before a remarkably cold winter where the leaders of the city allowed the wooden ramparts of the Battery, which has been very expensive to install, to be ripped apart to supply firewood to the poor. The seemingly random date therefore foreshadows impending destruction.[29] Knickerbocker thus began his meditation:

> The ground on which I trod was hallowed by recollections of the past, and, as I slowly wandered through the long alleys of poplars, which like so many birch brooms standing on end, diffused a melancholy and lugubrious shade, my imagination drew a contrast between the surrounding scenery, and what it was in the classic days of our forefathers. . . . For some time did I indulge in this pensive train of thought, contrasting in sober sadness, the present day, with the hallowed years behind the mountains; lamenting the melancholy progress of improvement. . . . I insensibly awakened to an enjoyment of the beauties around me.[30]

The passage that follows is Irving in one of his particularly sparking moments of the "pictorial mode" described by Donald Ringe. There were two phases of the same day, a crisp October day followed by the sudden appearance of a storm. The passages are very vivid and in fact constitute a verbal version of a pendant set. Pendants are pairs of paintings that are thematically related so as to emphasize relationship and contrast; it could be a person in youth and old age, as the city past and present was just invoked in Knickerbocker's imagination. A typical pendant set is *Landscape with a Storm* and *Landscape with a Calm*, a pair painted by Nicolas Poussin for one client in 1651.[31] While it is unlikely Irving would have seen those two paintings together in their intended relationship, he was aware of such traditions. Pendants initially arose in the seventeen and eighteenth centuries on the classical assumption of "symmetry as a principle inherent to beauty." At the Palais du Luxembourg, the first public art gallery in France, paintings in 1750 were grouped in "strategic pairs" and other "symmetrical groups based on stylistic comparisons," a Veronese next to a Poussin, and so on.[32] As Wendy Ikemoto explains,

> By the nineteenth century, "pendant" had assumed an additional inflexion: if it emerged in the late eighteenth century as a term identifying the parallelism or correspondence between pictures, through the next several decades it also came to signify contrast. Thus, if one pendant showed day, the other might show night. If one showed order, the other might show chaos. If one showed wilderness, the other might show an open plain. Pendants came more often than not to form counterparts, or complements, hanging in balanced opposition.[33]

Exactly such a pendant was created by Diedrich Knickerbocker as he provided a transition in his tale from the rise of the golden age to the fall of the Dutch colony, as he awakened to the beauty around him:

> It was one of those rich autumnal days which heaven particularly bestows upon the beauteous island of Mannahata and its vicinity—not a floating cloud obscured the azure firmament—the sun, rolling in glorious splendor through his ethereal course, seemed to expand his honest Dutch countenance into an unusual expression of benevolence as he smiled his evening salutation on the city, which he delights to visit with his most bounteous beams—the very winds seemed to hold their breathes in mute attention, lest they should ruffle the tranquility of the hour—and the waveless bosom of the bay presented a polished mirror, in which nature beheld herself and smiled!—The standard of our city, which like a choice handkerchief, is reserved for days of gala, hung motionless on the flagstaff, which forms the handle to a gigantic churn, and even the tremulous leaves of the poplar and the aspen, which, like the tongues of the immortal sex, are seldom still, now cease to vibrate to the breathe of heaven. . . . My own feeling sympathized in the contagious tranquility . . .
>
> In the midst of this soothing slumber of the soul, my attention was attracted to a black speck, peering above the western horizon, just in the rear of the Bergen

steeple—gradually it augments and overhangs the would-be cities of Jersey, Harsimus, and Hoboken. . . . Now it skirts along the shore of ancient Pavonia, spreading its wide shadows from the high settlements at Weehawk quite to the lazaretto and quarantine, erected by the sagacity of our police for the embarrassment of commerce—now it climbs the serene vault of heaven, cloud rolling over cloud, like successive billows, shrouding the orb of day, darkening the vast expanse, and bearing thunder and hail, and tempest in its bosom. The earth seems agitated at the confusion of the heavens—the late waveless mirror is lashed into furious waves that roll in hollow murmurs to the shore—the oyster boats that erst sported in the placid vicinity of Gibbet Island, now hurry affrightened to the land—the poplar writhes and twists and whistles in the blast—torrents of drenching rain and sounding hail deluge the battery walks . . . the late beauteous prospect presents one scene of anarchy and wild uproar, as though old chaos had resumed his reign, and was hurling back into one vast turmoil the conflicting elements of nature.[34]

Riding the crest of this pictorial pendant painted with words, Knickerbocker then interrupted his narrative intrusion with another intrusion: "Whether I fled from the fury of the storm, or remained at my post . . . I leave to the conjecture of the reader. It is possible he may be a little perplexed also, to know why I introduced this most tremendous and unheard-of tempest, to disturb the tranquility of my work."[35] The answer is that this pendant of a crisp still day that transforms into the stormy day foreshadows the impending end of the colony of Nieuw Nederlandt. The calm day and the stormy day portended nothing less than the rise and fall of nations, and even though it would take the reign of two more governors for the end to be enacted, in this panoramic pictorial narrative bridge, the suddenness of the storm that brings collapse echoed the structure of Ovid's tales of blessing followed by sudden woe.

However, Irving has done more than utilize the narrative structure of Ovid; he has also done for New York what Claude Lorrain did for Italy, namely, capture the sense of its light and skies. However, New York skies were not the same as Italian skies. Irving positioned himself as an American Claude Lorrain by capturing the glory of autumn in New York, and the changeableness of the weather—the atmosphere—the interplay of sun and cloud that was distinctive of New York City and the Hudson River valley.

The greatest display of Irving's atmospherics in pictorial mode in the *History* was found in his description of Peter Stuyvesant's journey up the Hudson River to fend off the invaders from Connecticut:

Wildness and savage majesty reigned on the borders of this mighty river—the hand of cultivation had not yet laid low the dark forests, and tamed the features of the landscape—nor had the frequent sail of commerce yet broken in on the profound and awful solitude of ages. Here and there might be seen a rude wigwam perched among the cliffs of the mountains, with its curling column of smoke mounting in the transparent atmosphere—but so loftily situated that the whoopings of savage children, gamboling on the margins of dizzy heights, fell almost as faintly on the ear, as do the notes of the lark, when lost in the azure vault of heaven. Now and then from the beetling brow of some rocky precipice, the wild deer would look down upon the splendid pageant as it passed below; and then tossing his branching antlers in the air, would bound away into the thickets of the forests.

Through such scenes did the stately vessel of Peter Stuyvesant pass. Now did they skirt the bases of the rocky heights of New Jersey, which sprang up like everlasting walls, reaching from the waves unto the heavens; and were fashioned, if tradition may be believed, in times long past, by the mighty spirit Manetho, to protect his favorite abodes from the unhallowed eyes of mortals.[36]

The different periods of the revolving day seemed each with cunning magic, to diffuse a different charm over the scene. Now would the jovial sun break gloriously from the east, blazing from the summits of the eastern hills and sparkling the landscape with a thousand dewy gems; while along the borders of the river were seen heavy masses of mist, which like midnight caitiffs, disturbed at his approach, made a sluggish retreat, rolling in sullen reluctance up the mountains. At such times all was brightness and light and gaiety—the atmosphere seemed of an indescribable pureness and transparency—the birds broke forth in wanton madrigals, and the freshening breezes wafted the vessel merrily on its course ...

But when the fairy hour of twilight spread its magic mists around, then did the face of nature assume a thousand fugitive charms, which to the worthy heart that seeks enjoyment in the glorious works of its maker, are inexpressibly captivating.[37] The mellow dubious light that prevailed, just served to tinge with illusive colors, the softened face of the scenery. The deceived but delighted eye sought vainly to discern in the broad masses of shade, the separating line between the land and the water, or to distinguish the fading objects that seemed sinking into chaos. Now did the busy fancy supply the feebleness of vision, producing with industrious craft a fairy creation of her own.[38]

Not only did Irving succeed as an American Claude, creating a distinctive sense of atmosphere for the Hudson River valley; he also offered a summary of the artist's task: By deceiving the delighted eye, the imagination of the artist was to make up what was lacking in the feebleness of vision.

The passage is eloquent enough, but, of course, Diedrich Knickerbocker must interrupt the panoramic mood he has just created with the dull, matter-of-fact announcement: "But all these fair and glorious scenes were lost upon the gallant Stuyvesant; nought occupied his gallant mind but thoughts of iron war, and proud anticipations of hardy deeds of arms."[39] Note that

Knickerbocker also disrupted the powerful mood of his verbal pendant of the calm day and the stormy day with a narrative intrusion about the role of the artist, just as he draws attention to the artist's ability to delight through deception here. In the intrusion to the October day, Knickerbocker drew very direct attention that he is an artist who had created a scene for a purpose; he was not precisely describing reality, even though the autumn day in New York is recognizably accurate for anyone who has experienced it. The trip up the Hudson with its varied description of cliffs and the sound of distant Native American children playing like larks in the distance would be picturesque travel; however, the extensive panoramic quality of the vista through so many places, moods, and times of day is so wide as to border on sublime, an overwhelming sequence of grandly picturesque settings. The earlier presentation of a day like a polished mirror on the Hudson giving way to the complete chaos of a severe storm is most certainly a sublime composition, not unlike Coles's juxtaposition of a storm in the mountains and a sunny but slightly desolate civilization in *The Oxbow*. Here we see a distinctive pattern in Irving. Irving was quite capable of creating sublime scenes. However, he did not trust the experience of the sublime and he almost always undermined it. In this case, the undermining intrusion could also be taken as an environment critique of Americans who were too busy with war or business to notice the beauty of the world around them.

THE SHATTERED PUMPKIN: SUBVERTING THE SUBLIME

Irving's incorporation, but subversion of, the sublime as a category was found in most of his mysterious tales. Though there would be the thrill of walking down overgrown country lanes in the dark with gnarly trees silhouetted in the moonlight, rocky crags, and pirate chains seeming to hang from trees, as we see in "The Money Diggers,"[40] Irving generally pulled back from true horror, softening fear with a comic element or a rational explanation. In *The Money Diggers*, the reader is amusingly aware that many of the effects of the stormy night are a product of Wolfert Webber's fevered imagination. In "The Legend of Sleepy Hollow," Irving showed himself again a master of mood in portraying the gently varied twilight terrain of Sleepy Hollow, even as he lampooned Ichabod Crane's voracious appetite for superstitious stories and his gullibility in "swallowing" Cotton "Mather's direful tales" whole:

> Then, as he wended his way, by swamp and stream and awful woodland to the farm house where he happened to be quartered, every sound of nature, at that witching hour, fluttered his excited imagination: the moan of the

whip-poor-will from the hillside, the boding cry of the tree toad, that harbinger of storm; the dreary hooting of the screech owl; or the sudden rustling in the thicket, or birds frightened from their roost. The fireflies, too, which sparkled most vividly in the darkest places, now and then startled him, as one of uncommon brightness would stream across his path; and if by chance, a huge blockhead of a beetle came winging his blundering flight against him, the poor varlet was ready to give up the ghost, with the idea he was struck by a witch's token.

And on such walks in winter:

What fearful shapes and shadows beset his path, amidst the dim and ghastly glare of a snowy night. . . . How often he was appalled by some shrub cover with snow, which, like a sheeted spectre beset his very path![41]

Here we see the folly of Ichabod, who was spooked by all sort of natural phenomena, for which simple, close observation would have easily provided a rational explanation.

There was only one truly sublime moment in "The Legend of Sleepy Hollow," the stalking of Ichabod by the mysterious rider, culminating in the rearing of the Headless Horseman against horizon. However, even this extraordinary moment was quickly and comically subverted by the chuckling of Brom Bones every time someone mentioned the pumpkin, and the news that Ichabod Crane appears to have moved to New York City and become a politician. There was a very strong hint that the Horseman was really Brom Bones, and that he succeeded in driving away an interloping suitor. Additionally, though Ichabod disappeared, it was quickly made apparent that he was safe, if humiliated. He made the best of the situation and became a lawyer in not too many years.

Another extended episode of the sublime, with accompanying subversion, was found in the three-part story of Dolph Heyliger. "The Haunted House" was a preface that set the scene for the telling of a ghost story, and *Dolph Heyliger* ended as a new campfire story, "The Storm Ship" was about to be told. The storm ship campfire tale ended midway through, and the story of Dolph was resumed and resolved. This pattern of segueing from one story to another in sets of tales, including a tale within a tale, seems inspired by Ovid's *Metamorphoses*. The technique is constant throughout that elegiac Latin classical work. Irving would take it up again in the series *The Money Diggers*, found at the end of *Tales of a Traveller*. What these series of tales have in common is that they are both collections by the late Diedrich Knickerbocker, embedded into works that are mostly ruminations by Geoffrey Crayon. Knickerbocker had told the reader directly that he was imitating Virgil in his own tale of the founding of New York; now, in these tales he was also imitating Ovid. Who says America cannot have a storied history of classics?

The sublime appeared at two prominent moments in *Dolph Heyliger*. First was when a mysterious ghost had entered the "bowerie" country house of Doctor Knipperhausen, which Dolph agreed to guard at night for the sake of a little adventure, and for a lack of a better job opportunity, since he was failing in his apprenticeship as a pharmacist, and he needed to stay in the doctor's good graces:

> Now the footsteps had ascended the staircase; they were slowly advancing along the passage, resounding through the silent and empty apartments. The very cricket had ceased its melancholy note, and nothing interrupted their awful distinctness. The door, which had been locked on the inside, slowly swung open, as if self-moved. The footstep entered the room; but no one was to be seen. They passed slowly and audibly across it, tramp—tramp—tramp! But whatever made the sound was invisible. Dolph rubbed his eyes and stared about him; he could see to every part of the dimly-lighted chamber; all was vacant; yet still he heard those mysterious footsteps, solemnly waking about the chamber. They ceased and all was dead silence. There was something more appalling in this invisible visitation, than there would have been in anything that addressed itself to the eyesight. It was awfully vague and indefinite.[42]

Irving explicitly invoked Burke on the horror of the sublime with this reference to darkness, obscurity, and indefiniteness. Nothing is more horrifying than a potential enemy in the dark that you know is out there, but you can in no way define.

The visitations recur each night, and there was a suspicion he may be dreaming, because the door was always locked just as he left it at bedtime. The whole story unfolded as a dreamscape that extended into waking hours. As evening progressed, the ghost took on visible form, wearing old Flemish clothing, boots and a broad hat; he was now an apparition, rather than an invisible menace, but he stared at Dolph for hours with a fish-like eye. Eventually, after nights of staring, the ghost led him outside to a well and a boat. When Dolph woke, he had a scant breakfast and wandered outside to reflect. There was a sloop going up the Hudson River to Albany. He decided to go on short notice, feeling led by the dream, and the commander had the appearance of the ghost. What followed was a trip up the Hudson River that showed Irving at his atmospheric best; it was a masterwork of nature writing in the pictorial mode. It recalled the panoramic trip of Peter Stuyvesant up the Hudson. However, the potentially picturesque travel turned to sublime horror as Dolph was swept off the sloop in a storm. His days of skipping school to go swimming served him well, for with all his strength, he at least made it to shore. Then he must stagger in the dark amid slippery banks, steep hills, precipices, and vipers that invited disaster with every step. Finally, he saw the light of a campfire, but noticed a dead body on the ground. Then he was shot at and realized he must step out of hiding.

It turns out that this was a friendly hunting party, a mix of Dutch Americans and Indian Americans, led by the landowner Antony Vander Heyden of Albany; the dead body turned out to be a deer. This great landowner decided to live off the land like an Indian to find true liberty. The entire scenario was ludicrous. Irving had returned to satire. Vander Heyden almost reads as a fusion of the James Fenimore Cooper, who was the heir of a great New York landowner, and Natty Bumpo, the frontiersman. The comic scenario is a spoof of Euro-American fantasies of owning the land but living with and as Native Americans. In such a fantasy, the Native Americans acknowledged the Dutch American aristocrat as the owner of the land, and gathered around his campfire like obedient hunting dogs. Irving was not likening the Native Americans to hunting dogs. He was mocking the colonial fantasy that would render them such, and the delusion that such a pleasantly hierarchical relationship could exist. What we see in this absurd scenario is that, however great Irving's descriptive powers, and however immense his capacity for conjuring sublime moments, he could not go very long without interrupting them with some sort of comic interlude or a narrative intrusion that disrupted the moment he had so skillfully created. What Knickerbocker did in his presentation of the sublime crisp and then stormy October day on the Battery in *A History of New York*, he has done again here. The sublime must be conjured up and then undermined. It happened again and again in the stories of the Knickerbocker. That shattered pumpkin at Sleepy Hollow is something to chuckle about.

Knickerbocker did the same thing in the following story of "The Ghost Ship," where he worked his magic with descriptions of uncanny experiences of the ship; people rowed toward it, and yet it remained always out of reach, or as you approached, it would disappear and when you turned around, it would be in the distance behind you. The imagery was vivid, and notable tension was sustained regarding this unknown ship. Then the narrator undermined it all with a footnote explaining how the Dutch were very anxious about ships that came only once a year from the old country. They brooded and dreamed on it incessantly, and this accounts for the superstitious stories of the ship. The Dolph Heyliger story resumed with Dolph joining Lord Anthony at his family home in Albany, where he recognized a portrait and remembers old family stories his mother told him; Dolph also met the woman of his dreams. Over the protests of the Sinbad of Albany, Dolph resolved to go home and build a future. He rejected the fantasy life of playing the lifelong adventurer with his aristocratic friend and his Native American hunting buddies, and he returned to New York. Dolph found his family's money in the well, perhaps the buried treasure of having cultural memories, a sense of family, and a community to belong to. Dolph wondered why the ghost could not just tell him the treasure was in the well, but it is clear Dolph had to go to Albany to find himself and his family identity. There was a moment of genuine transcendence on the way home. He shot at a bald eagle in the distance, and he skimmed its tail feathers; it soared tranquilly on, indifferent to his struggles and his infantile desire to shoot a bird just because he could. At this moment Dolph realized there was something greater than himself, and he returned home a new man. He became the son his mother always knew he could be. As for the ghost story, it turned out that this was a tale Dolph began to tell in his old age as a respected burgher when everyone loved him and held their side in laughter as he told stories of his old pranks. "No one ever had any doubts" about the hobgoblin parts of the story. This one line, of course, at the very end, raises questions about the whole story. What we know is that Dolph was a playful young man who did not fit into the expectations of the Anglo-American and German-Lutheran culture of his community in New York, and he needed to go to Albany to find himself and discover a path forward.

The other aspect of the story was the extreme idealization of life at Albany. The Dutch there had a warmth, ease, and capacity for enjoyment that Anglo-Americans lacked; however, the picture of a happy family with slaves was so exaggerated, it seems clear Irving was mocking this aspect of the fantasy of old Dutch New York. In this fantasy, slaves were so happy in their masters' households that they would come even when they were not called upon, and they would sit in the room gazing on them in sheer adoration as he told his adventure stories. Clearly, such behavior, if it ever happened, was a strategy of appeasement, and not sincere. Not even a ruling-class estate-owner with a notion that slaves could be part of a happy family could believe this extreme picture of complete adoration, and the broad grins as they would go off to repeat the story to their friends in the kitchen. Perhaps they were grinning in mockery, an image that was used in "The Legend of Sleepy Hollow," as awkward Ichabod Crane took the dance floor. The scenario here was so exaggerated as to be farcical. The fantasy was clearly delusional. Neither Washington Irving nor Diedrich Knickerbocker could stay away from satire for too long. The narrator was mocking the notion that slaves were happy and adoring of their masters, just as he mocked the fantasy that an aristocratic landowner could live the wild life of an Indian with Native American hunting buddies who happily acknowledged him as lord of the land and were as loyal to him as hunting dogs. Dolph grew up and rejected these fantasies, and he moved to New York, acquiring the old Dutch house in the bowery, happily wedding the distant kin Marie he met on the trip upstate. How he turned his life around and earned a living or came into his legacy, we will never know. We only know that when everything was falling apart in British New York, he needed to go home, and it made all the difference.

Irving's tendency to explain away the mysterious—thus subverting any sublime experience of true horror—is seen in Pierre Irving's description of one of Washington Irving's last dinners at Jacob Astor's mansion in the winter of 1848, an evening spent telling ghost stories. There was a story of two officers attending a corpse in the West Indies. The corpse rose and came to the one in the room at the time, and divulged a secret about a clandestine marriage in Ireland: "Mr. Irving suggested the solution that the man was not dead, and that this secret lay so heavily on his mind as to arouse him from his state of apparent death."[43] The corpse, truly just a man in a coma, simply had an important matter to resolve before he died, and he held onto life until it was off his chest. Irving the romantic storyteller remained a partial child of the Enlightenment until the end; in fact, this anecdote comes to us from the very year Irving was completing the authorized edition of his complete works. On the matter of subverting superstitions and the sublime moments that arose from the sense of mystery around them, Irving was consistent across his entire career.

Judith Haig has noted that Irving maintained a "compromise position between ingrained skepticism and emergent romantic faith." As she defines it, "the basic tenet of Romanticism is" that "imagination is a mode of penetrating to truth . . . Romantic literature" characteristically "takes one on a circuitous journey through alienation toward transcendent reintegration."[44] Irving's stories frequently leave us befuddled as to what actually happened. Was Brom Bones really the Headless Horseman? Did a ghost really show Dolph Heyliger where to find his fortune? Was Dirk Waldren really the person peering over the money digger's pit, mistaken by Wolfert Webber for the ghost of a pirate? Irving's mysterious tales almost always leave you with the possibility of a rational explanation, a pattern that also appears in the early Gothic novels of Anne Radcliffe.[45] There is no transcendent reintegration, though there are sometimes fairly happy endings. On Haig's reading, Irving's residual Enlightenment skepticism prevents him from being a full-blown romantic. However, if Melville may be praised for rejecting Emerson's naïve cosmic optimism, why may we not equally praise Irving for standing wryly aloof from grandiose promises of the power of imagination and mystery to fully integrate the self? Perhaps Irving's balancing act between Enlightenment skeptic and romantic dreamer should be regarded as a fruitful tension rather than a failure.

Over and over Irving has shown himself a nineteenth-century romantic who retained a heavy dose of eighteenth-century neoclassicism. Perhaps the most significant aspect of his classicizing romanticism is that—in supplying a sense of history and a sense of place through old stories reinvented imaginatively, and in rendering a distinctive Hudson River atmosphere, he successfully presented himself as an American Virgil, and even more centrally, an American Claude. Yet, he also remained partly an Enlightenment skeptic who would not allow you to be carried too long into any experience of the sublime.

NOTES

1. Tim Barringer and Jennifer Raab, "An Inheritance in Print: Thomas Cole and the Aesthetics of Landscape," in *Picturesque and Sublime: Thomas Cole's Transatlantic Inheritance*, edited by Tim Barringer, Gillian Forrester, Sophie Lynford, Jennifer Rabb, and Nicolas Robbins (Catskill: Thomas Cole National Historic Site in association with Yale University Press, 2018), 9–30.

2. *History*, Book II, Ch. III, 444.

3. Letter to Martin Van Buren, January 12, 1830, *Letters*, II, CW, 495.

4. Pierre Rosenberg and Keith Christiansen, *Poussin and Nature: Arcadian Visions* (New York: The Metropolitan Museum, 2007), 29–30, 57–8, 136–48.

5. The main artistic tradition in England was that portrait painting. While there were some successful English painters in the time of Elizabeth and James I, such as Nicolas Hilliard and Isaac Oliver, many greatest portrait painters, such as Hans Holbein, Rubens, and Van Dyke, were imported from the continent. See Mark Evans, *Renaissance Watercolors* (London: Victoria and Albert Publishing, 2020), 161–99.

6. Andrew Wilton, *The Art of Alexander and John Robert Cozens* (New Haven: Yale Center for British Art, 1980), 19–23.

7. David Hume argued that this tendency to run to Italy and France for paintings was undermining the emergence of English art. See "Of the Rise and Progress of the Arts and Sciences," 19.

8. David H. Solkin, *Richard Wilson: The Landscape of Reaction* (London: The Tate Gallery, 1982), 13–15.

9. Solkin, *Richard Wilson*, 216.

10. Solkin, *Richard Wilson*, 40.

11. It seems that Thomas Cole was so moved by Wilson's *Niobe* when he saw it in 1831 that he drew a sketch of it. He did almost no sketches of the art he saw on his Grand Tour, since he was afraid of losing his own style to too much imitation of masters, but this one apparently stood out. It is not certain this is the painting Cole sketched, but it seems unlikely that any of Wilson's more Claudian compositions would have moved him so. In any case, Wilson's 1760 painting rapidly became famous, was quickly put into print, and both Irving and Cole would have at least known of it through the print medium. See Elwood Parry III, *The Art of Thomas Cole: Ambition and Imagination,* The American Art Series (Newark: University of Delaware Press, 1988), 112–3. See also Tim Barringer et al., *Picturesque and Sublime: Thomas Cole's Tran-Atlantic Inheritance* (Catskill: New York, Thomas Cole National Historic Site, 2018), 90–1.

12. Rosenberg and Christiansen, 231–3, 264–5.

13. Tim Barringer, "Thomas Cole's Atlantic Crossings," in *Thomas Cole's Journey: Atlantic Crossings*, ed. Elizabeth Mankin Kornhauser and Tim Barringer (New York: The Metropolitan Museum of Art, 2018), 30–1. The painting was deeply moving to Thomas Cole when he saw it on his visit to England in 1829; it was one of the few works he copied in England.

14. Janet Lembke, *Virgil's Georgics: A New Verse Translation* (New Haven and London: Yale University Press, 2005), xvii.

15. Lembke, *Virgil's Georgics*, 7.

16. Washington Irving, *Miscellaneous Writings, 1803–1895*, Volume I, ed. Wayne R. Kime. The Complete Works of Washington Irving XXVIII (Boston: Twayne, 1981), 149–50.

17. Klaus Lubbers, *Born for the Shade: Stereotypes of Native Americans in the United States Literature and Visual Arts, 1776–1894*. Amsterdam Monographs in American Studies 3 (Amsterdam and Atlanta: Editions Rodolpi B.V., 19940. 30–9.

18. *Traits* was written in 1814 and revised for inclusion in *The Sketch Book*. The first draft was more harsh in its criticism of Anglo-American "extirpation of thousands," and the tone was softened for a more genteel readership, while maintaining the same main points. See Lubbers, *Born for the Shade*, 67.

19. *The Sketch Book*, LOA, 1004.

20. Pope, for example, pointed out that humans kill animals in huge numbers for food and even sport, yet they complain that God is not just when they have the slightest personal problem; God is just when they are killing hundreds of animals for sport, but unjust when allowing the hunter to suffer a wound. Pope lambasted this type of anthropocentric selfishness—and the logical inconsistency—throughout the essay.

21. For a brief discussion of the impact of Pope's spinal deformity on his classicizing poetry and his landscaping projects, see Mavis Batey, et al., *Arcadian Thames: The River Landscape from Hampton to Kew* (London: Barn Elms, 1994), 65. Because Pope translated the classics such as Homer, Vergil, and Horace into the contemporary mode of life on the Thames, he would be relevant to Irving and other early nineteenth-century Americans in romantic mode. For Pope's task—born of his disease as well as broader trends in the culture to remake England as a new Italy—was to make this small stretch of land along the river into a home. Though Pope's poetry was certainly neoclassical in form, he could perhaps in one way be regarded as a proto-romantic, in his all-pervasive drive—in both his poetry and in his landscaping—to create a strong sense of home. Perhaps that is one reason why Pope was the most widely read author in the United States along with Oliver Goldsmith in 1800. Citizens of the new republic needed that sense of home.

22. Peter Martin, *Pursuing Innocent Pleasures: The Gardening World of Alexander Pope* (Hamden, Connecticut: Archon Books, 1984, 27.

23. Alexander Pope, *An Essay on Man*, Epistle I. II.

24. *Oxford English Dictionary* online, ad. loc.

25. Before Lyell's *Geology* was published in 1830, where Lyell argued for gradual formation of the landscape by steady processes such as erosion over centuries, there was a tendency to explain mountains, rock formations, and erratic boulders by means of cataclysm, usually Noah's flood. Here a lesser cataclysm is postulated, but it is

in keeping with the Spirit of the age. Thomas Cole's drawing *Hunter Standing in a Cave: Rock and Waterfall*, shows a very small person in a large cave overwhelmed by giant rugged boulders and uprooted trees scattered by "floods from the mountains." It demonstrates that cataclysm theory could be quite good for the romantic imagination. See Howard Merritt, *To Walk with Nature: The Drawings of Thomas Cole* (Yonkers: The Hudson River Museum, 1981), 18.

26. I will try to offer a more extensive discussion of this complex figure in time for the 200th anniversary of *The Money Diggers*.

27. Elizabeth Mankin Kornhauser, "Manifesto for an American Sublime," in *Thomas Cole's Journey: Atlantic Crossings*, eds. Elizabeth Mankin Kornhauser and Tim Barringer (New York: Metropolitan Museum of Art, 2017), 78–83.

28. It is Book II, Ch. VI in the 1848 revision, due to the insertion of a chapter on the patroon Killian Ven Rennsallaer.

29. That paragraph criticizing the city for wasted money and showing perhaps not enough sympathy to the poor was removed in the 1848 edition.

30. *History* III.V, 488; III.VI, CW, 113.

31. Rosenberg and Christiansen, 260–3.

32. Wendy N.E. Ikemoto, *Antebellum American Pendant Paintings: New Ways of Looking*. Routledge Research in Art History (London and New York: Routledge Taylor and Francis Group, 2018), 6–8.

33. Ikemoto, *Antebellum American Pendant Paintings*, 9–10.

34. *History*, III.V, 489–91; *History* III.VI, CW, 114–5.

35. *History*, III.V, 491; *History* III.VI, CW, 115.

36. Here Irving has solved the problem with his earlier poem *Passaic: A Tradition.* If you are going to offer a Native American creation myth for a geological formation, similar to what Ovid did in his telling of ancient Greek myths, the event must be in distant history, not twenty years or a hundred years ago.

37. This seems to be the only place in the works of Irving where his narrator directs people from the contemplation of nature to the creator. Such conventional religious appeals were more common in other Knickerbocker writers, according to Ringe, and in Irving it occurs only in his earliest major work.

38. *History*, VI.III, 622–4.

39. VI.III, 625.

40. "The Adventure of the Black Fisherman," in *Bracebridge Hall; Tales of a Traveller; The Alhambra*, 700–3.

41. "The Legend of Sleepy Hollow," in *The Sketchbook*, CW, 277–8.

42. *Bracebridge Hall*, 320.

43. Pierre Irving, *Life*, 23.

44. Judith G. Haig, "Washington Irving and the Romance of Travel: Is there an Itinerary in *Tales of a Traveller*?" in *The Old and New World Romanticism of Washington Irving* (Westport, Connecticut: Greenwood Press, 1986), 67.

45. Marie Hendry, *SCF Venice Faculty Forum: Gothic and Horror*, October 31, 2019.

Chapter 5

Irving's Critique of American Culture in "The Legend of Sleepy Hollow"

"The Legend of Sleepy Hollow" is one of the most memorable works in Washington Irving's *Sketch Book*. Its status as a fully American work has sometimes been downplayed since Irving's use of German folktales was brought to light in the 1930s.[1] However, the exploration of American cultural life that Irving undertook was so thorough and so insightful, that this old question, with its attendant dismissiveness, needs to be put to rest. "Rip Van Winkle" is a German folktale that has been Americanized by way of reflection on the rapid pace of change in American culture since the American Revolution. As Donald Ringe points out, the quaint charm of the story's atmospherics sometimes leads readers to miss a more somber message:

> Rip Van Winkle's village has succumbed to the very onslaught, which in the form of Ichabod Crane, was turned away from Sleepy Hollow. . . ."Rip van Winkle" is a much more sober—and fundamentally more realistic tale, than "The Legend of Sleepy Hollow," for it admits that change is inevitable and can only be evaded—if at all, by paying a terrible price. . . . He has had to surrender the major part of his mature life and become an alien in the community of which he was once a valued part.[2]

"The Legend of Sleepy Hollow" is an equally penetrating analysis of what it means to be a culture without memories, and the kind of voracious, acquisitive appetite that emerges in the face of such emotional and intellectual hollowness. In such a reading, Ichabod Crane represents the new American emerging at the dawn of the American Republic, an American obsessed with "migration and improvement." Sleepy Hollow, on the other hand, represents a place where people can stand still long enough to have memories, and value community rather than mere mercantile exchange. The Headless

Horseman was a kind of protector of an anchored way of life from the predatory nature of the emerging American appetite for mobility and economic commodification.

Sleepy Hollow was, for the narrator Diedrich Knickerbocker, a place of memories, a sense of place, and a place of refuge from the constant bustle and change of the early Republic:

> In the bosom of one of those spacious coves which indent the easter shore of the Hudson, at that broad expanse of the River denominated by the ancient Dutch navigators the Tappaan Zee, and they always prudently shortened sail, and implored the protection of St. Nicolas when they crossed, there lies a small market town . . . by the name of Tarry Town. . . . Not far from this village, perhaps about two miles, there is a little valley, or rather lap of land among high hills, which is one of the quietest places in the whole world. A small brook glides through it, with just murmur enough to lull one to response, and the occasional whistle of a quail, or tapping of a woodpecker, is almost the only sound that ever breaks in upon the uniform tranquility. . . . From the listless repose of the place, and the peculiar character of its inhabitants, who are descendent from the original Dutch settlers, this sequestered glen has long been known by the name of Sleepy Hollow. . . . A drowsy, dreamy influence seems to hang over the land, and pervade the very atmosphere.[3]

Irving here displayed his skill in creating an atmospheric rendering of the Hudson River valley akin to the sense of mood, sky, and light that the seventeenth-century artist Claude Lorrain created for Italy. Lorrain created a defining sense of place for those touring Italy, and it became the lens through which tourists would be imagining the place even before they arrived; Irving has done the same for New York.[4] James Tuttleton rightly praised Irving for this "wizardry of style."[5]

However, the dreamy atmosphere and cozy sense of storied memory found at places like Sleepy Hollow was at risk due to an invasion of Connecticut Yankees. Donald Ringe points out that several New York writers—Washington Irving, James Fenimore Cooper, and James Paulding—all addressed the social implications of this invasion and consistently portrayed the gaunt wandering New England Yankee as restless, intrusive squatters and shrewd manipulators who would empty one's pockets.[6] Henry Adams, in his *History of the Administrations of Thomas Jefferson*, indicated that there was, indeed, such a westward migration as New England's barren soil and granite hills became more and more unusable; tensions emerged between the rival cultural values of New England Yankees and the landowners of the Mohawk River valley near Albany.[7] Irving's fiction addressed very real historical events and raised concerns about changes coming upon the early Republic:

To their more conservative neighbors, the Yankees' desire to move, change and improve posed a serious threat to the social order that New Yorkers were trying to establish and maintain. . . . To oppose the material desires they see in the Yankee desire for change, improvement and profit, the New York writers affirm a stable society that places its emphasis on order, tradition, and the family values that accompany social stability. Although the New York characters are not averse to amassing wealth, by and large, they seek their fortunes on the land. Once settled on the land, moreover, they tend to stay upon it. . . . The sense of permanence and social stability thus attained marks out the superiority of the New York characters.[8]

The historical realism of these literary portraits is confirmed by Richard Bushman: "In Connecticut, the most common economic ambition was the desire to produce an agricultural surplus for market."[9] This common Yankee value, derived from English Puritan values, stands in sharp contrast to the Dutch Van Tassel household; the Van Tassels shared their abundance with the community at harvest time rather than prioritizing profit and getting the surplus to market. The kind of communal values found in Sleepy Hollow, which revolved around the Van Tassel farm, are "impossible to be achieved by the restless Yankees."[10]

The centrality of the tension between stability and change, cultural memory, and perpetual mobility, is made clear in Irving's own words indicating why Americans need ghost stories in the first place:

Local tales and superstitions thrive best in these sheltered, long-settled retreats, but are trampled underfoot by the shifting throng that forms the population of most of our country places. Besides there is no encouragement for ghosts in most of our villages, for they have scarce had time to finish their first nap, and turn themselves in their graves, before their surviving friends have travelled away from the neighborhood, so that when they turn out of a night to walk the rounds, they have no acquaintance left to call upon. This is perhaps why we so seldom hear of ghosts except in our long-established Dutch communities.[11]

There are two things to note in this passage. First and foremost, Irving valued cultural memory and folk traditions in the face of the rapid changes overtaking both England and the United States during the Industrial Revolution and new market economies that accompanied the end of the Enlightenment. Most Americans had but one or two generations of memories, and Revolutionary War stories—in the face of the current pace of change—seemed like veritable "ancient history." However, the Dutch New Yorkers had a full 200 years of memories since Hendrick Hudson discovered the Hudson River valley. Thus, the Dutch New Yorkers, however susceptible they may be to Irving's lampooning and caricature in works such as Knickerbocker's *History*, represented the ideal of an ongoing community with real memories and a sense of place, something most Americans, whose essence was now found in the Connecticut Yankee, did not have.

The other point to note is that the migration patterns in early nineteenth-century America were as much rural as urban. There were, of course, more and more immigrants from Europe pouring into major U.S. cities with each passing decade; however, the more transforming migration in the early 1800s was as much an internal migration from the east to the west as stony New England soils were depleted and farmers needed desperately to move inland to find fertile lands.[12] The forthcoming opening of the Erie Canal in 1825 would only exacerbate the trend Irving commented on as early as 1809 in *The History of New York*. As New England farms faced new competition from grain coming in from Ohio, more and more farms and cottage industries in New England would fail in the new nationwide market economy; the changes forced more and moral rural migration.[13] Many Americans have tended to think of farmers as having a relatively settled—if difficult—life on one piece of land, in contrast to the ever-shifting bustle of urban life, but in the early 1800s this was simply not true. Thomas Jefferson's vision of America as a stable agrarian society began to collapse practically from the moment that he articulated the ideal.

The lack of ghosts, or storied memories and places hallowed by great poets and great deeds, was felt by many Americans in the early Republic, and it was exacerbated by the constant moving from place to place. The successful revolution was a new beginning, but too new for many who needed a sense of cultural continuity. A helpful example of this widespread struggle is seen in Thomas Cole's "Essay on American Scenery":

> I will now venture a few remarks on what has been considered a grand defect in American scenery—the want of associations, such as arise amid the scenes of the old world.
>
> We have many a spot as umbrageous as Vallambrosa, and as picturesque as the solitudes of Vaucluse; but Milton and Petrarch have not hallowed them by their footsteps and immortal verse. He who stands on Mont Albano and looks down on ancient Rome, has his mind peopled with the gigantic associations of the storied past; but he who stands on the mounds of the west, the most venerable remains of American antiquity, *may* experience the emotion of the sublime, but it is the sublimity of a shoreless ocean un-islanded by the recorded deeds of man.
>
> Yet American scenes are not destitute of historical and legendary associations—the great struggle for freedom has sanctified many a spot, and many a

mountain, stream and rock has its legend, worthy of a poets pen or the painters pencil, but American associations are not so much of the past as of the future.[14]

Cole would try to be bravely optimistic in imagining a new civilization where ploughs would glisten, tower and temple would rise, and "poets yet unborn shall sanctify the soul."[15]

However, P.T. Willis, in his contributing essay for the 1851 *Homebook of the Picturesque, or American Scenery*, to which Irving was also a contributor, would make clear what these thoughts of the future involved for most citizens of the Republic:

> The American often looks at a scene without inquiring into its antiquity. "Instead . . . he sits over the fire with his paper and pencil, and calculates what the population will be in 10 years, how far they will spread, what the value of the neighboring land will become, and whether the stock of some canal or railroad . . . will, in consequence, be a good investment. He looks upon all external objects as exponents of the future."[16]

Rural Americans without the means to invest would simply scramble from plot of land to plot of land, using up its fertility as they went along, ever looking for the next better opportunity. Prominent landholders in the east would invest in giant land companies, some of which ran afoul of government attempts to allot land. Whether rich or poor, almost everyone was on the move.[17]

An important passage from Chapter VII of Knickerbocker's *History of New York* corroborates this situation in American cultural life. In his portrait of the Connecticut Yankee, Irving notes the following qualities:

> The most prominent of these (peculiar habits) was a certain rambling propensity, with which, like the sons of Ismael, they seem to have been gifted by heaven, and which continually goads them on, to shift their residence from place to place, so that a Yankee farmer is in a constant state of migration; tarrying occasionally here and there, clearing lands for other people to enjoy, building houses for others to inhabit, and in a manner may be considered the wandering Arab of America.
>
> His first thought, on coming to the years of manhood, is to *settle* himself in the world—which means more nor less than to begin his rambles. To this end he takes unto himself a wife, some dashing county heiress . . .
>
> Having thus provided himself, like a true pedlar with a heavy knapsack . . . he literally sets out on peregrination. His whole family, household furniture and farming utensils are hoisted into a covered cart . . . which done, he shoulders his axe, takes staff in hand, whistles "yankee doodle" and trudges off into

the woods, as confident of the protection of providence . . . as a patriarch of yore . . .

But it is not the nature of this most indefatigable of speculators, to rest content with any state of sublunary enjoyment—*improvement* is his darling passion . . .

Being thus completely settled . . . He soon grows tired of a spot, where there is no longer any room for improvement—sells his farm, air castle, petticoat windows and all, reloads his cart, shoulders his axe, puts himself at the head of his family, and wanders away in search of new lands, again to fell trees—again to clear cornfields—again to build a shingle palace, and again to sell off and wander.[18]

This unflattering portrait of a Connecticut Yankee from the 1809 *History* found an almost exact parallel ten years later in Irving's description of Ichabod's Crane's aspiration after he visited the mansion of Old Baltus Van Tassel and formed his plan to court the buxom heiress Katrina:

As the enraptured Ichabod fancied all this, and as he rolled his great green eyes over the fat meadowlands . . . his heart yearned after the damsel who was to inherit these domains, and his imagination expanded with the idea, how they might readily be turned into cash, and the money invested in immense tracts of wild land, and shingle palaces in their wilderness. Nay, his busy fancy already realized his hopes, and presented to him the blooming Katrina, with a whole family of children, mounted on top of a wagon loaded with household trumpery, with pots and kettles dangling beneath, and he beheld himself bestriding a pacing mare, with a colt at her heels, setting out for Kentucky, Tennessee, or the Lord knows where.[19]

Now if one were to marry into the wealth and prosperity described in Irving's sumptuous picture of autumn harvest abundance on at estate of the Hudson River, the question arises as to why anyone would not want to stay and enjoy that prosperity. Ichabod only thought about how to turn this wealth into a transportable commodity, a tendency that was soon to dominate most of American culture. What are the possible reasons for such a fantasy? Perhaps as the New England intellectual that he fancied himself, he had no interest in personally managing a large farm, however successful. He did want vast lands in Kentucky, but this was perhaps to sell them at a profit, not to farm the land himself; Ichabod was, it seems, a proto-typical land speculator. Perhaps Ichabod knew he could not shake the stigma of being an outsider who merely managed to marry into a great family, and so he wished to move to a new place where he would already be known as a person of means. Perhaps also—by a stretch—if we were to see him as an astute economist, Ichabod might have anticipated that the New England household economy was to collapse within a generation, and insightfully saw that it was better to get out and make a profit from the land while it was still possible to do so. The Erie Canal was under construction since 1816, and Washington Irving at least foresaw that people such as Ichabod Crane were about to spread much further west than Sleepy Hollow. Irving, of course, attributed to Ichabod no such perceptive foresight, but only a restless acquisitiveness and a capacity to see persons, lands, and trees as commodities for exchange. Crane's ambition is summarized well by Frank Bergon's description of the true motive of western expansion: "What brought many of the early pioneers West was not a dream of adapting to the land and creating a new, distinct, society of equals, but rather the desire to transfer to the West society in the East, with one difference: they would be at the top of the heap."[20]

That Irving was consistently concerned about such land speculators with Yankee values of commodification is seen in his additions to *A History of New York* in the 1848 revision. He added a section on Oloffe Van Kortlandt. In the original version, there was a passing reference to the meager means of the original Dutch settlers. Van Kortlandt meant "without land" and so Knickerbocker joked that this must mean he was a wandering philosopher like Diogenes the Cynic, who was also without possessions.[21] Knickerbocker would create an ancient philosophical history of New York by all means, including deduction from the dubious meaning of words.[22] In Irving's revision, a new layer of meaning was added. Kortlandt (also known as Lackland) was a hustler who claimed he had "great landed estates somewhere in Terra Incognita. . . . He was the first great land speculator."[23] No doubt the great aristocratic patroons of New Netherlands had some land hunger of their own, but Irving's addition to *A History of New York* seems to reflect the conversion of many old family Dutch landowners in his own time to a more aggressive form of the dreaded Yankee values. A similar theme was explored in *The Money Diggers*, where the Dutch American Wolfert Webber was seduced by Yankee values and ended up as a landowner who rented out his property rather than working the land. Irving longed for the good old days when a tidy Dutch garden of cabbages was enough to assuage the hunger of the soul.[24]

As Irving wrote "Sleepy Hollow" in 1820, one of the biggest migrations—and land hustles—in American history was already underway. Andrew Jackson had ended both British and Native American military threats along the Mississippi by the end of 1815 with the Battle of Horseshoe Bend against Redstick Creeks, and with the Battle of New Orleans, which ended the fighting in the War of 1812. By 1817 General Jackson turned his sights toward the displacement of southeastern Native Americans and the seizure of West Florida from the Spanish (now Alabama and the Florida panhandle). Jackson invaded West Florida in 1818, and by 1819 it was a new American possession. Furthermore, although the federal government had just created a treaty with the

Creek Indian Federation restoring them to many traditional lands in Georgia and beyond, Jackson encouraged white settlers everywhere to rush in and take these Native American lands in flagrant disregard of the Federal Agreement formally encouraged by President Madison. The Senate and the president were neither capable of nor interested in defying Jackson's popular appeal, and so the great land rush to the southeastern United States was underway.[25]

In this ambitious new age, rapid expansion was accompanied by attempted "improvements," a concept that Irving associated with Yankees:

> Internal improvements, meaning roads and canals, were the complement to protection (from Indians). Immediately after the War of 1812, people eager to exploit the lands conquered from Tecumseh and the Creek nation began a new westward movement. Between 1810 and 1820 the population of the states and territories west of the Appalachians more than doubled. Four new states—Indiana (1816), Mississippi (1817), Illinois (1818), and Alabama (1819)—were admitted to the Union.[26]

Irving was not a writer of historical fiction who was concerned to meticulously recreate the conditions of the time described in his work. He followed a very loosely accurate historical outline and made up the details in *A History of New York*. Irving's fiction was designed to meet the needs of the present moment, not engage in precisely realistic historical retellings. Depending on whether Irving was thinking of his own time or Ichabod's, the "Lord knows where" of Ichabod's speculative could be anywhere from Indiana to Alabama and West Florida, as those territories were opening up for the taking just as Irving was writing. If Irving was consistent in projecting his story back in time thirty years[27] as indicated in the tale, Kentucky and Tennessee were the most likely candidates for immigration, though that territory tended to be claimed by Virginians who were just as land-hungry as Yankees. The Ohio River valley was desired by more than just Virginians, and Virginia gave up its claim to land north of the Ohio River as part of a compromise to get the Constitution ratified, just before the setting of the tale. Thomas Cole, for example, immigrated to the United States in 1818, and his family went almost immediately from Philadelphia across Pennsylvania to western Ohio by way of a mix of wagon, horse, and foot travel that was available along old Native American trails then functioning the Pennsylvania Road.[28] Western Pennsylvania, Ohio, or Indiana would be realistic options for the period Irving was describing, since they were a prime choice for westward migration from the birth of the Republic to the time these other southeastern states were opened up by Andrew Jackson's conquests.

However, "God knows where" sounds more remote than Kentucky and Tennessee. To go beyond those states before around 1790—even in fantasy—would indicate a desire to run as far from the East Coast as humanly possible, or an appetite as more fierce than any Virginian who claimed Illinois and Indiana regions as Virginia Territory during the Revolutionary War. Thomas Jefferson, in fact, as governor of Virginia, had sent George Rogers Clark on an expedition west during the Revolutionary War to claim this territory for Virginians. Jefferson tended to his own land hunger while leaving Virginia undefended and vulnerable to conquest by the British. Norfolk was destroyed and Richmond occupied as Jefferson fled.[29] Irving had lampooned such incompetence in the *History* and *Salgamundi*, where Thomas Jefferson was specifically targeted as a frail slender scholarly type in awkward red pants, always riding his horse rather than taking a carriage. Ichabod Crane may be the perfect conflation of a Connecticut Yankee and the land-hungry Virginian himself. On this reading, Irving might have been taking a jab at Jefferson in his image of Ichabod, and the new American would be a fusion of the undesirable qualities of Virginian and Yankee alike. Whatever the territory Ichabod desired, Irving's picture was shaped by the cultural energy of his own day. Ichabod Crane was in fact, not just a Connecticut Yankee; he was the prototype of the acquisitive American who was soon to rush headlong toward the Gulf and trans-Appalachian portions of the southeastern United States and Ohio River valley, without memory or value beyond that of future profits.

This new American was described primarily in terms of voracious appetite. Terry Thomson has written a helpful article describing Ichabod Crane as an agent of English hegemony over the Dutch New Yorkers; the "restless country" of Connecticut, in such a perspective, was an exporter of both intellectual and ecological appropriation of lands and peoples, its colonists bearing both ax and schoolbook. Ichabod was tall and lanky with a bottomless appetite. He was likened to a crane with a prodigious capacity for swallowing things whole; he was lean and gaunt like "the very genius of famine descending on the earth" described by Ovid. This one-man locust swarm was but a harbinger of things to come in America, and the clever Dutch farmers of Sleepy Hollow held this cultural famine momentarily at bay, temporarily maintaining a way of life where market days were "more social than commercial."[30] What is clear is that Irving saw this picture of the Connecticut Yankee as much more than a regional characteristic; Ichabod Crane is a character type that was to dominate American culture at the very moment a national market economy was emerging.[31]

To understand the seriousness of the picture emerging, it is helpful to turn to Ovid's own description of the genius of famine, which is found in the story of Erysichthon:

> This monarch scorned the gods, and brought no incense, /No offering to their altars, and one legend has it/ He once attacked a sacred grove of Ceres, / Violent

with steel against those ancient trees, Among which stood an oak centuries old, a grove in itself.[32]

Note that Irving describes Connecticut as exporting both schoolmasters and foresters. Ichabod Crane "was a native of Connecticut, a state which supplies the Union with both pioneers for the mind as well as for the forest, and sends forth yearly its legion of frontier woodmen and country schoolmasters." As Terry Thompson points out,

> These two groups, lumberjacks and teachers, are in reality colonizers, usurpers, for they overthrow the indigenous culture ahead of them as they spread out across the wilderness like an oil spill. First, the woodmen decimate the forests with their English broadaxes, reshaping the landscape to make way for what Knickerbocker calls "city innovation." . . . Then, in the wake of deforestation come the "authoritative" schoolmasters, furtive men like Ichabod.[33]

It is not a coincidence that Connecticut is associated with the felling of trees and the spirit of famine in a lanky schoolmaster. The Yankee ax was, of course, prominent in Irving's description of the restless Yankee in *A History of New York*, cited above.

The same connection between the felling of trees and the coming of the gauntly voracious specter of famine is drawn from Ovid. Erysichthon felled the sacred grove when the slaves resisted such irreverence, and he did not shrink from cutting down the great oak, even though it was the most beloved tree of Ceres. The oak was in fact inhabited by a nymph, and it bled when cut, crying out in death. The Dryads, in mourning for their dead sister, rushed to Ceres who commissioned famine to punish the tree-slayer; because famine and Ceres could never be together, a messenger was sent to the desolate place and even the messenger remained at a distance in relaying the divine command:

> She looked for famine/ And found her, in a stony field, her nails/ Digging the scanty grass, and her teeth gnawing/ The tundra moss. Her hair hung down all matted,/ Her face was ghostly pale, her eyes were hollow,/ Lips without color, the throat rough and scaly,/ The skin so tight the entrails could be seen,/ The hipbones bulging at the loins . . . /The breast seemed to dangle, held up barely by a spine like a stick-figure's, and her thinness made all her joints seem large
>
> Famine, whose task is always opposite/ To that of Ceres, none the less obeyed her,/ Flew through the air on the winds wings, and came/ To Erysichthon's palace, where the king,/ In the dead of night, was lying sunk in slumber./ She twined her skinny arms around him, filled him/ With what she was, breathed into his lips his throat,/ and planted hunger in his hollow veins,/Then, with her

duty done, fled from the land/ . . . And sleep, on peaceful wings, still hovering over Erysichthon, soothed him,/ But in his sleep he dreamed of food, his jaws closing on nothing, and his throat kept swallowing nothing,/His feast was empty air, and when he awakened he was ravenous.[34]

Irving describes the tall, lanky Ichabod Crane a person "whose frame was loosely hung together" like "the spirit of famine descending on the land" (see figure 5.1).

Irving also described Ichabod as a crane of "capacious swallow," a weathercock with a "spindle neck," and a grasshopper, implying a locust swarm, and a voracious anaconda with envious green eyes.[35]

A few Irving scholars are, perhaps, too quick to interpret characters in Irving's stories as manifestations of one or another dysfunction in Irving's psyche, such as an inability to grow up;[36] however, the severity of Irving's description of Ichabod Crane indicates a problem much more serious than failure to embrace adult responsibility. Rubin-Dorsky, for example, suggests that Irving and his two most famous characters, Rip Van Winkle and Ichabod Crane, are "overgrown versions of children, seeking to gratify boyish impulses for a carefree life devoid of adult male responsibility."[37] While the characterization is reasonable enough regarding Rip, it is not relevant to "Sleepy Hollow." First, though Ichabod was indeed "an ineffectual male," it is not true that Ichabod Crane was avoiding adult responsibility. Ichabod Crane was an itinerant teacher because Connecticut did not offer many other

Figure 5.1 Albert Pinkham Ryder, *The Race Track (Death on a Pale Horse)*, 1896, Cleveland Museum of Art.

options if you were not of the landed class.[38] Ichabod schemed to win the hand of an heiress, but this was not a failure to have an adult plan; he was simply aspiring beyond his station like many adults who wish to marry into money, and he was also intruding into a community that had a more stable set of values than the desire for land sales. Ichabod Crane was a ridiculous figure for many reasons, but refusing adult responsibility was not one of them. He became a lawyer and politician in New York City quickly enough after his marital prospects failed; he did not lack a work ethic, even if his loquaciousness would lend itself to the service of a political career that Irving enjoyed lampooning. At issue was the Yankee disposition to talk endlessly, voicing every possible opinion, and forcing yourself on others with schemes of "improvement," not avoiding work. Ichabod Crane, a failed land speculator turned lawyer and politician through persistence and hard work, was for Irving a harbinger of famine—both cultural and ecological destitution.

If any of Irving's characters might qualify as a "man-child," Bram Bones and Dolph Heyliger would be the strongest candidates. Even this assessment is overstated. Bram Bones was certainly mischievous; however, he settled into married life on a great old estate at a normative stage of life, and some of the pranks he played were designed to drive away the Connecticut Yankee who was threatening his dreams and his hometown. Bram Bones displayed a strategic commitment to normative adult goals—marrying the woman he had always loved and taking over the farm. He was not entirely an overgrown child; he was a young adult who knew how to enjoy himself as he worked toward his personal goals—a quality Irving surely appreciated—and he successfully protected Sleepy Hollow from an interloper. One might argue that his persona of childish playfulness led rivals to underestimate him, thus allowing him to outwit them. Dolph Heyliger likewise resolved his difficult transition to adult prosperity and, like Brom Bones, married the pretty, young Dutch woman. Lumping these characters together with Ichabod Crane seems unwarranted. Brom and Dolph both represent the older Dutch values that Irving wanted to affirm; they are the absolute opposite of what Ichabod Crane represented.

Rubin-Dorsky has followed the common scholarly trend of projecting Irving into his most famous characters. While it is surely true that Irving identified with Rip Wan Winkle's refusal to accommodate the all-consuming Puritan work ethic, the claim is more problematic regarding Ichabod Crane. Rubin-Dorsky, for example, claims that "Rip and Ichabod desire nothing but to live tranquil lives."[39] Such a claim is true enough of Rip, but utterly false regarding Ichabod Crane. Ichabod was a fundamentally restless soul, and he did not seek tranquility to resolve the restlessness. As the proto-typical Yankee, Ichabod sought more movement, not less, as an antidote to his itch, and he had an insatiable desire to devour. Ichabod represented almost everything that Irving rejected. Many of the characters in Irving's stories were displaced persons in one way or another, as Rubin-Dorsky rightly notes;[40] however, it is true of almost everyone, the good and the evil, the sympathetically portrayed and the not-so-sympathetically portrayed. Dislocation was a general feature of modern existence and reducing it to a mere projection of Irving himself is not sufficient. The fact that Irving, Crayon, and Ichabod were bachelors cannot outweigh the glaring difference of values in these refractorily analogous characters. Scholars need to move away from the psychologizing trend of interpretation to see Irving himself in characters and look more at the substance of the picture Irving was painting.

The problem of overly psychologized readings is seen in a valuable insight about "Rip Van Winkle" that is nevertheless problematic. Rubin-Dorsky suggests that this story "represented Irving's dream of returning to an American society that has finally made a place for him."[41] Irving was abroad for seventeen years, and Rip was asleep for twenty. There is probably some truth to the observation. However, when you see the text *primarily* as a projection of Irving's personal issues, larger matters are missed. "Rip Van Winkle" wrestles with the problem of rapid change in American culture, and perhaps the entire industrializing West. The passage of time and the taking over of Nicolas Vedder's Inn by Yankees represents the demolition of time-tested values in the face of rapacious acquisitiveness.[42] Perhaps at a secondary level, Rip's story also represents Irving's desire to return home from overseas, but it is not the primary substance of the story. Seeing personal psychological projection everywhere, as if it is the central storyline, leads us to miss more than it helps us to see.

Over a body of several works, Irving presented a consistent critique of the values of Anglo-American culture, including its Puritan/Yankee work ethic, its lack of ability to find enjoyment due to an excessive focus on material prosperity, and its proclivity toward "improvement." Irving loved the Dutch, the Spanish, French traders singing through the back woods, and African American storytellers, precisely because they offered an alternative to Yankee values; they knew how to enjoy life without the Yankee compulsiveness for endless labor and money-making. Characters like Rip Van Winkle, Bram Bones, and Dolph Heyliger, bore the values of the older and better Dutch civilization that was being rapidly replaced by aggressive New Englanders, and perhaps, land-hungry Virginians who were so like them even without the Puritan background.

One thing that is clear is just how prescient Washington Irving was in his cultural critique. Mercantile land-grabbing acquisitiveness remains an ongoing feature of American culture as developers take more and more wild and rural lands, all the way down to US 41 in southwest Florida, where pines and oaks continue to disappear by the day. Likewise, the attendant problem of lack of cultural memory haunts us still, as constitutional norms have been violated frequently in recent years, and people resist wearing medical masks during a pandemic just as they did in 1918. We Americans never seem to learn. The soullessness at the heart of a restless American culture today, indeed, goes back to the twin problems that Irving pointed out in *A History of New York* and "The Legend of Sleepy Hollow." Irving's concerns are as relevant and indeed more urgent than ever before as the once new American without memory or value continues to bring the genius of famine to the land, a metaphor that will be a reality soon enough if pollinators collapse due to pesticide use, habitat loss, and rapidly unfolding climate change. This story is as perceptive an analysis of American culture as has ever been written. The notion that this is not a truly American story because Irving has reworked a German folktale needs to be abandoned once and for all. The tale is thoroughly adapted to the realities of American culture.

GREAT TREES AS ANTIQUITIES

Washington Irving and Thomas Cole struggled profoundly with the lack of historical and poetic associations in the United States, and both arrived at the conclusion, and consolation, in 1835, that the great old trees in America's primordial forest should be regarded as our antiquities. The idea was first articulated explicitly in Irving's 1835 essay "Abbotsford" and attributed to Sir Walter Scott: Great logs from American forests were "like one of the giant obelisks which are now and then brought from Egypt, to shame the pygmy monuments of Europe; *and in fact these vast aboriginal trees that have sheltered the Indians before the intrusion of the white men are the monuments and antiquities of your country* (my emphasis)." William Owens has pointed out that this statement by Scott was not in Irving's *Journals* from the times he met Scott and may be a creation of Irving himself as he looked retrospectively back on his time from the vantage point of recently returning to America.[43]

Irving, in fact, seems to have had the core idea at an earlier stage than the writing of *Abbotsford*, for a giant tulip magnolia was designated as Major Andre's tree in 1820 "The Legend of Sleepy Hollow." The historical association from the Revolutionary War was linked to an even more primordial grand old tree, thus making this spot in Sleepy Hollow a place doubly hallowed:

> In the center of the road stood an enormous tulip tree which towered like a giant among all the other trees of the neighborhood, and formed a kind of landmark. Its limbs were gnarled, and fantastic, large enough to form trunks for ordinary trees, twisting down almost to earth, and rising again to the air. It was connected with the tragical story of the unfortunate Andre, who had been taken prisoner

hardby; and was universally known by the name of Major Andre's tree. The common people regarded it with a mixture of respect and superstition.[44]

The old growth tulip magnolia was a massive tree, very tall with a straight trunk and pendulous branches. It was hollowed out to make large canoes by Native Americans and early settlers, just as bald cypresses and longleaf pine were in the Southeast, and the immense size of the straight shaft made it valuable as timber;[45] the tulip tree may be in mind when Sir Walter Scott refers to trees as large as Egyptian obelisks. The first tulip trees were exported from North America to England by John Tradescant the Younger around 1650, along with sycamores and red maples, and they were widely planted on British estates.[46] Irving would have seen them in their more colossal form on home soil, and he would have also seen the extensive cutting of such tall straight trees for lumber, but Scott would likely have known what they were. Either one could have compared them to Egyptian obelisks, for the trunks are straight and monumental. It seems, in fact, likely that Irving and Scott did have a conversation about America's giant trees when they met in 1817, and that is why Irving attributes the notion to Scott in his later reminiscence; whether the idea that such trees are America's antiquities comes from Scott or Irving himself, the idea was operative when Irving wrote "Sleepy Hollow" in 1820. Given the reminiscence in "Abbotsford," we may reasonably infer that the insight indeed arose out of a conversation between the two, regardless of its absence in Irving's journals of their time together and regardless of which one made the point first.

The fact that they did have such a conversation is made more likely by the fact that a new edition of John Evelyn's *Sylva: A Discourse of Forest Trees and the Propagation of Timber* (first edition 1664) had just been published and reviewed in the *Quarterly Review* in March 1813. As the Napoleonic Wars concluded, the reforestation of Britain was a matter of national security as well as national heritage, since so many great trees had been felled to support the British Navy. As John Nisbet points out, "The *Quarterly Review* article of 1813 probably did as much to stimulate planting throughout Great Britain as the *Sylva* itself had previously done." Between 1800 and 1830, Sir Walter Scott did large-scale plantations of trees. He was already engaged in the project of naturalist restoration before this important reprint, but the article of 1813 gave new impetus.[47] At the end of the Napoleonic Wars in 1815, the celebration of which Irving witnessed just as he was arriving back in England, the planting of trees was a national emergency. Irving and Scott surely discussed the matter on Irving's visit to Abbotsford in 1817;[48] Irving's claim that he had such a discussion should be taken at face value, even if it is missing in his private journals. Both Washington Irving and Sir Walter Scott were part of the naturalistic landscaping movement begun by Alexander Pope and Lord Burlington a century before,[49] and now it was a cultural and ecological emergency, given the loss of cultural continuity during the destruction of the Napoleonic Wars and the emerging Industrial Age.

As Irving was writing "Abbotsford," Thomas Cole was making a similar point in his 1835 public lecture, "Essay on American Scenery," which was presented the same year Cole was painting *The Course of Empire*.

> The Forest scenery of the United States . . . being primitive . . . differs widely from the European. In the American forest, we find trees in every stage of vegetable life and decay—the slender sapling rises in the shadow of the lofty tree, and the giant in his prime stands by the hoary patriarch of the wood—on the ground lie prostrate decaying ranks that once waved their verdant heads in the sun and wind. These are circumstances productive of great variety and picturesqueness—green umbrageous masses—lofty and scathed trunks—contorted branches thrust athwart the sky—the mouldering dead below, shrouded in moss of every hue and texture, from richer combinations than can be found in the trimmed and planted grove.[50]

Indeed, "the hemlock, the sublime of trees . . . rises from the gloom of the forest like a dark and ivy-mantled tower."[51] Not only did American forests offer supremely picturesque texture and variety, but they also contained all the life stages contemplated in "The Course of Empire." The very towers and ruins that Cole painted in so many European landscapes, and which he presented went in the stages of a civilization he painted in his masterwork of 1835–1836, were found nearer at hand in America—towering adult trees at peak strength, older trees become hoary with storm-broken branches and lightning scars, and fallen giants decaying on the ground, all-in-one view together. As in Irving, these giants were America's antiquities, exactly parallel to the antique buildings and ruins in "The Consummation of Empire," "Destruction," and "Desolation," where a lone column stands in the foreground like a great hemlock whose top half has been removed by lightning. The stages of life seen in grand American trees, the peak growth, collapse, and decay so visible in one glance represented not only the precariousness of the individual life, but the rise and fall of civilizations, themes which were, of course, prominent in Irving's *Sketchbook* and *Alhambra* as well as Cole's masterpiece.

Washington Irving had also created a sense of historical time and place through the presence of great trees in a scene of Peter Stuyvesant relaxing in the park on the Battery after temporary success in nettle against the Swedes of New Jersey in the original version of *A History of New York*: "It would have done a heart good also to have seen the valiant Peter, seated among the old burghers and their wives of a Saturday afternoon, under the great trees that spread their shade over the Battery, watching the young men and women as they dance on the green. Here he would smoke his pipe, crack his joke, and forget the rugged toils of war in the sweet oblivious festivities of peace."[52] A painting of this scene from the 1809 version, *Dance on the Battery in the Presence of Peter Stuyvesant*, was made by Asher Durand in 1838; the trees appear to be ancient sycamores, with characteristic massive trunks and blotchy bark. When Irving revised the *History* in 1848, he made several changes. First, he added some remarks to the introductory "Account of the Author," expressing concern over changes and loss of cultural memory, in this case referring to Diedrich Knickerbockers stop at Albany:

> He found it, however, considerably altered, and was much concerned for the inroads and improvements which Yankees were making, and the consequent decline of good old Dutch manners. Indeed, he was informed that these intruders were making sad innovations in all parts of the state, where they had given great trouble and vexations to the regular Dutch settlers, but the introduction of turnpike gates and country schoolhouses. It is also said that Mr. Knickerbocker shook his head sorrowfully at noticing the gradual decay of the great Van der Heyden palace; but was highly indignant at finding that the ancient Dutch church, which stood in the middle of the street, had been pulled down since his last visit.[53]

This 1848 insertion of protest concerning cultural loss into a story from 1809 reads as a comment on changes Irving discovered in the United States after his seventeen-year sojourn abroad. When he returned to the United States in 1832, he was deeply concerned with how he would be received by Americans after so long away. It would not have been wise or gentlemanly to launch criticisms of an America with which he was not very familiar after such a long absence. However, by the time he was writing the authorized version of 1848, he was ready to make some remarks as part of his final statement and enduring legacy.

In this later version of the *History*, Irving also gave a little greater prominence to a grand old trees in southern Manhattan, such as great sycamores that were akin to the giant tulip tree of Sleepy Hollow, massive examples of which he had seen along rivers during his 1832 tour of the West. In this insertion into the original *History*, the scene was shifted from the time of Peter Van Stuyvesant to the first governor of the golden age, Wouter Van Twiller:

> It was a pleasing sight in those times to behold the honest burgher like a patriarch of yore, seated on a bench of his whitewashed house, under the shade of some gigantic sycamore or overhanging willow. Here he would smoke his pipe of a sultry afternoon, enjoying the soft southern breeze, and listening with silent

gratulation to the clucking of his hens, the cackling of the geese, and the sonorous grunting of his swine; that combination of farm yard melody, which may truly be said to have a silver sound, in as much as it conveys a certain assurance of profitable marketing.[54]

To be sure, the Dutch burghers were interest in making money, but the "marketing" mentioned here was the act of taking geese and pigs to market in a city that was little more than a village with a decidedly rural flavor, where the original willows and sycamores that grew streamside across the entire eastern United States were still present. "Marketing" here is part of the small-scale operation of a family farm, more akin to the market days of Tarry Town in "Sleepy Hollow"; this was not the kind of large-scale operation that came with the opening of a national market after the opening of the Erie Canal in 1825, an event which Irving has missed while he was abroad, and whose impact surely startled him when he returned to the United States in 1832. Indeed, after the canal was opened, cheap grain from the Midwest put a lot of small-scale family farms out of business, and people had to either move west or take up manufacturing on the soil which was at that point too depleted for farming.[55]

Irving's love of great trees—and their importance in contributing to a sense of place in a picturesque civilization—is seen in his response to a painting by Asher Durand, one of Thomas Cole's disciples and close friends. Irving gave a rave review of one of Asher Durand's vertical tree paintings in 1850 when he was sent to inspect it for his friend Governeur Kemble, who ran the foundry at Cold Spring near West Point (see figure 5.2):

> I have called with—to see Durand's picture, and we were both delighted with it. It is beautiful—beautiful. Such truth of detail with such breathe; such atmosphere, such harmony, such repose, such colouring. The group of trees in the foreground is admirable; the character of the trees so diversified and accurate; the texture of the bark; the peculiarities of their foliage. The whole picture had the effect on me of a delightful piece of music. I think it would be a charming addition to the *Kemble gallery*.[56]

Kemble did in fact buy Durand's 1850 painting *Early Morning Art Cold Spring*; the painting is a vertical composition with several tall trees in the foreground, including a giant beech with smooth gray bark just off center and a towering elm distinguished by its furrowed bark and distinctive V branch structure. A man stands alone in an almost Cathedral-like canopy of trees looking out across an inlet to a church steeple in the distance just below center, which is itself reflected in the water. A line from a William Cullen Bryant poem accompanied the painting: "O'er the still clear water

Figure 5.2 Asher Durand, *Early Morning at Cold Spring*, 1850, Montclair Museum of Art.

swells/ The music of the Sabbath bells."[57] Durand himself preferred to go to the woods on his Sundays for communion with nature rather than go to church.[58] The person in the painting perhaps liked to contemplate a picturesque steeple and gentle blue sky in the distance, listening to the bells ring in the distance sheltered by the protective canopy, but not actually attend services regularly, a sensibility Irving might have appreciated.[59] What is clear is that Durand captured the character of great old trees, and Irving responded with a sensitivity to the trees themselves as well as the picturesque sense of a homelike and secure civilization with a sense of history. The person in the painting was a bit of an outsider, as were many of Irving's characters, but he ultimately found a sense of home beneath a sacred canopy.

In general, Asher Durand was known for his tree portraits at a relatively close range compared to the wider distant vistas of Thomas Cole, and they formed a protective canopy for a stable community, perhaps almost a sacrament of God's grace, both symbolizing and bearing to us a higher sheltering presence. Both Durant and Cole valued great trees, though Cole frequently showed them in sublime settings, great hemlock trees, for example, along mount ridges and chasms, partly shattered by lightning and often about to topple. Asher Durand's paintings of a gentle civilization beneath the shelter of great trees are more akin to Cole's very Claudian Arcadia paintings. Cole also gave a prominent place to mature trees in his pastoral Catskill Creek series of painting, in which he utilized a Claudian formula or compositions, with tall, beautiful elms, oaks, and maples, framing the distant vista of the mountains, most famously in the elegant pastoral of 1836–1837, *View on the Catskill-Early Autumn*. In these paintings, Cole moved away from sublime wilderness and cultivated a sense of a home in a gently picturesque civilization. There was in fact an old Dutch farmhouse, the Van Vetchen house, in the line of view in the 1836 work, and this farmhouse was threatened by a railroad that went almost little to the doorstep and put the foundation of the building at risk.[60] Cole, Durand, and Irving were all disturbed by the widespread cutting of trees. Cole and Irving both saw it firsthand as new railroad tracks were built near their homes. Curiously, both Cole and Irving moved to property along the Hudson River valley around 1835–1836, and both lamented overly rapid "progress." In a letter to a patron, shortly after moving to Catskill, Cole complained,

> They are cutting down all the trees in the beautiful valley on which I have looked so long with a loving eye. This throws quite a gloom over my spring anticipations. Tell this to Durand—not that I want to give him pain, but that I want him to join me in maledictions on all dollar-godded utilitarians.[61]

Clearly, Thomas Cole expected Asher Durand to share his grief and outrage. Cole wrote a poem "The Lament of the Forest" in response to the cutting of a large swath of woods near Catskill Creek, and their mutual friend William Cullen Bryant had published a popular poem on a similar theme, "Woodman, Spare That Tree." Washington Irving, Thomas Cole, and Asher Durand would agree on one point above all others: Woe to the copper-hearted Yankees who fell such trees!

Indeed, one of Cole's last paintings in his Catskill Creek series stands as a protest against the cutting of trees. Alan Wallach has rightly called *River in the Catskills*, from 1843, an "antipastoral"[62] (see figure 5.3). The Claudian-framing trees in the foreground have been cut down, and you can see a line of mangled stumps. A lone viewer in a red jacket looks out over the distance,

Figure 5.3 Thomas Cole, *River in the Catskills*, 1843, Boston Museum of Fine Arts.
Source: Photograph © 2021 Museum of Fine Arts, Boston.

contemplating the changes. The golden light of late afternoon should not mislead. This is not a Claudian composition. Large zones of trees found in prior painting have been removed for farm fields, many more houses dot the landscape, and a train with its smoke runs on the opposite side of the creek, probably the first train in an American painting.

H. Daniel Peck has pointed out that this is the only Catskill painting where the mountains are not reflected in the river, an image typical of romantic painting—one expressive of the union of the human heart with cosmic depths of nature.[63] Likewise, when Washington Irving revised his works for posterity in 1848, especially in then new additions he made to *A History of New York*, he was surveying the changes of the past forty years, contemplating the Yankee America that was unrelentingly coming into being, and lamenting the loss of a more gently picturesque civilization that he, Thomas Cole, and Asher Durand longed for.

Both Cole and Irving addressed the rapid social, economic, and political changes of their time by affirming the value of a stable sense of place. Irving found an enchanted slower pace of life in the sleepy Dutch villages of the Hudson River in *The Sketch Book*, and the environs around Hell's Gate and Long Island Sound in *Bracebridge Hall* and *Tales of a Traveller*. Throughout these works, the stable sense of place was conveyed partly through the presence of native trees. H. Daniel Peck has recently pointed out the mild irony that Thomas Cole helped create a sense of national landscape through the portrayal of very specific local and regional sites, such as Catskill Creek, where he built a home, Kaaterskill Falls, and the White Mountains;[64] the same may be said of Irving. Both Cole and Irving created a sense of national identity, and yet both did so through the evocation of very specific local and regional places that would cultivate a sense of place.

NOTES

1. Henry A. Pochmann, "Washington Irving's Sources in 'The Sketchbook,'" *Studies in Philology* 27, no. 3 (July 1930), 477–507.
2. Donald A. Ringe, "New York and New England: Irving's Critique of American Society," *American Literature* 38, no. 4 (Jan 1967), 464–6.
3. *Sketch Book*, CW, 272–3.
4. Jeffrey Rubin-Dorsky, following William Hedges, has noted it is inconsistent to put a work by Diedrich Knickerbocker in a collection by Geoffrey Crayon: Knickerbocker "was almost always comic and irreverent, while Crayon is often sentimental and respectful." Rubin-Dorsky does allow that having "multifaceted" voices in a *Sketch Book* can still allow for a unified composition; see *Adrift*, 101. What has been missed is that Knickerbocker himself meditated on the rise and fall of nations—an aspect of Crayon's great theme of mutability, and that the richly atmospheric descriptions of the Hudson River valley in "Rip Van Winkle" and "Sleepy Hollow" are completely consistent with the richly pictorial descriptive ability that Knickerbocker developed in the *History*, especially in his descriptions of trips up the Hudson River, and autumn days on the Battery. The same pictorial descriptive skill is found in the inserted Knickerbocker tale of "Dolph Heyliger," who also journeyed up the Hudson River toward Albany.
5. Tuttleton, "Style and Fame," 17.
6. Ringe, "New York and New England," 456–9.
7. See Adams, Vol. I, Ch. I, "The World in 1800," 14.
8. Ringe, "New York and New England," 458–9.
9. Richard L. Bushman, *From Puritan to Yankee* (Cambridge: Harvard University Press, 1967), 25.
10. Ringe, "New York and New England," 459.
11. Washington Irving, *The Sketch Book of Geoffrey Crayon, Gent.*, ed. Haskell Springer, CW (Boston: Twayne Publishers, 1979), 289.
12. Aldo Leopold, one of the founders of modern ecology and land restoration, noted that the American soils had an initial "exuberance" when forests and prairies were first cleared for planting, but that such use is not sustainable and that rich soils will typically be depleted in a hundred years or so. *A Sand County Almanac: With Essays on Conservation* (Oxford University Press, 1949; deluxe reprint, 2001), 67.
13. The failure of the New England household economy in the early nineteenth century is discussed by Christine Stansell and Sean Willenz, "Cole's America," in

William Treuttner and Alan Wallach, eds. *Thomas Cole: Landscape into History* (New Haven, Yale University Press, 1994), 3–21.

14. Thomas Cole, "Essay on American Scenery," in *American Art: 1700–1960*, ed. John W. McCoubrey. Sources and Documents in the History of Art (Englewood Cliffs: Prentice Hall, 1965), 108.

15. Cole, "Essay," 109.

16. Willis's essay "On the Highland Terrace, Above West Point," cited in James T. Callow, *Kindred Spirits: Knickerbocker Writers and American Artists*. (Chapel Hill: University of North Carolina Press, 1967), 131.

17. Anthony J. C. Wallace, *Jefferson and the Indians: The Tragic Fate of the First Americans* (Cambridge and London: The Belknap Press of Harvard University Press, 1999), 21–49.

18. *History*, Book III, Ch. VIII. 498–500; CW, 121–2.

19. *Sketch Book*, CW, 279–80.

20. Frank Bergon, *Looking Far West* (New York: New American Library, 1978), 7, cited in Peter Antelyes, *Tales of Adventurous Enterprise: Washington Irving and the Poetics of Western Expansion* (New York: Columbia University Press, 1990), 39.

21. *History* II.III, 441–2.

22. "Thus, being totally denied the benefit of mythology and classical fable, I should have been completely at a loss to the early biography of my heroes, had not a gleam of light been thrown upon their origins from their names." II.III, 441.

23. *History* II.III, CW, 64.

24. The story also has a clever moral that sometimes people come to wealth in spite of their folly, a direct rebuttal of the old Puritan teaching, now carried on by meddlesome self-righteous Yankees, that wealth was the result of virtue.

25. Daniel Walker Howe, *What Hath God Wrought: The Transformation of America, 1815–1848* (Oxford University Press, 2007), 74–7, 96–107. Jefferson and Madison had had their eye on Florida for a long time. They originally wanted it more than Louisiana, and they were blindsided by the unexpected and fortuitous offer of Louisiana by Napoleon. They even tried to cheat Spain out of West Florida, claiming it was part of Louisiana, and met with Spanish objection. See Henry Adams, *History of the Administration of Thomas Jefferson*, diplomatic history 1803–1806. This avarice for Florida on the part of the Virginian dynasty suggests that Madison tacitly approved of Jackson's incursions into Florida, but Madison maintained a formal posture of supporting the treaty with the Creek Indians. It also gave him plausible deniability for purposes of diplomacy with Spain. The idea that Jackson was a rogue element who could not be controlled may well have been true, but it was also politically useful.

26. Morison, *The Oxford History*, 402.

27. *Sketch Book*, CW, 274.

28. Nancy Siegel, *Along the Juniata: Thomas Cole and the Dissemination of American Landscape Imagery* (Huntingdon, PA: Juniata College Museum of Art, 2003), 17–29.

29. Andrew Burstein and Nancy Eisenberg, *Madison and Jefferson* (New York: Random House, 2010), 76–82.

30. Terry W. Thompson, " 'Lively but Complicated': English Hegemony in 'The Legend of Sleepy Hollow," *Midwest Quarterly* 54, no. 2 (Winter 2013): 136–48.

31. Corroboration for this reading of "Sleepy Hollow" is found in Irving's own contributing essay on "The Catskill Mountains" in the mid-century *Homebook of the Picturesque, Or American Scenery, Art and Literature*, ed. William Cullen Bryant (New York: Putnam, 1937), 70–8. There Washington Irving teased more money-minded migrants with old tales about how certain Dutch burghers found gold in the Catskills, but every time they did so, there was a terrible shipwreck, and the gold was mysteriously lost at sea. These tales of uncanny events served as a warning to California gold digger types to go elsewhere and leave the Catskills alone. As in "The Legend of Sleepy Hollow" itself, the tall tales of mysterious happenings played a protective role for the region and its values.

32. Ovid, *Metamorphoses*, trans. Rolfe Humphries (Bloomington: Indiana University Press, 1955), 204.

33. Thompson, " 'Lively but Complicated,'" 140.

34. Ovid, *Metamorphoses*, 206–7.

35. *Sketch Book*, 274; Thompson, " 'Lively But Complicated,'" 139.

36. Another common concern, understandable enough in an age of gender studies, is to what extent Irving struggled with a sense of masculinity. Many such articles were listed in the Burstein bibliography. Such ruminations are not without basis in the texts at hand. However, in the face of such concerns, I would simply note that Irving had the stamina, in an age before trains, to travel all over Europe and the American west, and he did so cheerfully. The regime of travel he undertook for over thirty years was rigorous at a level twenty-first century people cannot even comprehend. He was a person of immense vigor. The fact that he had self-doubts on many issues, like where his next book contract was coming from and whether he was up to the task, should not lead us to ignore his immense strength and his boundless cheerfulness in the face of travel difficulties, and the full range of life's obstacles. This is a man who succeeded as the first American author who earned a living by writing, and he made a major contribution to rebuilding the U.S. relationship with England after two major wars. Debating his masculinity while ignoring his wide range of life achievements seems counterproductive. The question about gender identity is a legitimate one, but it becomes unhelpful if it leads one to ignore almost everything else a person did. In the case of Irving studies, the personal psychological aspect in Irving's work had been given too much attention. We need to see Irving first in his own context, and then we can more accurately assess him in terms of late twentieth-century and early twenty-first-century interests. Given the number of close friends Irving had who were artists, and given the way that art shaped his pictorial mode of description, art history is a significant part of the historical context that made him who he was, and it is in this light that I see him. Understanding the artistic and landscaping traditions that shaped his pictorial vision seems more illuminating than perpetual debates about why he remained a bachelor.

37. Rubin-Dorsky, *Adrift in the Old World*, 51.

38. Bushman, *From Puritan to Yankee*, 83–103.

39. Rubin-Dorsky, *Adrift in the Old World: The Psychological Pilgrimage of Washington Irving* (Chicago and London: University of Chicago Press, 1988), 102.

40. Rubin-Dorsky, 106.

41. Rubin-Dorsky, 110.

42. Ringe, "New York and New England," 455.

43. William Owen, "Reevaluating Scott: Washington Irving's 'Abbotsford," in *The Old and New World Romanticism of Washington Irving*, ed. Stanley Brodwin (Westport, Connecticut: Greenwood Press, 1986), 73.

44. *Complete Works*, Vol. VIII, 291.

45. Elbert Little, *National Audubon Society Field Guide to North American Trees: Eastern Region* (New York: AlfredA. Knopf, 1980), 436–7.

46. Stephen A. Spongberg, *A Reunion of Trees: The Discovery of Exotic Plants and Their Introduction into North American and Europeans Landscapes* (Cambridge and London: Harvard University Press, 1990), 12. North American trees were considered exotic in England and France, and they functioned as status symbols on upper-class estates in both countries, from about 1600 to 1820. Eventually, interest and status shifted to Asian and southern Pacific discoveries, and North American trees lost their novelty. However, grand American trees were almost as prominent in the upper-class English imagination as the American aborigines themselves during the period of Irving's storytelling productivity. When Irving referred to American trees such as magnolias, chestnuts, and sycamores (buttonwood) in the stories of Dietrich Knickerbocker, the English audience knew what he was talking about.

47. John Evelyn, *Sylva: A Discourse of Forest Trees and the Propagation of Timber*, ed. John Nisbet (Teddington, Middlesex: The Echo Library, 2009), 47–50.

48. Sir Walter Scott wrote a review of another "Sylva," Steuart's *Planter's Guide* in *Quarterly Review* 37 (1828): 311: "The ancient English poets, Chaucer and Spenser in particular, never luxuriate more than when they get into a forest; by the accuracy with which they describe particular trees, and from their noticing the characters of the difference, and the various effects of light and darkness upon the walks and glades of the forest, it is evident they regarded woodland not merely associated with their favourite sports, but as having in itself beauties which they could appreciate." Cited at www.spenserians.cath.vt.edu. This description of Spenser's vivid skill in portraying accurate details of trees in a forest and the effects of shade could easily have been written in a review of Irving's American stories by Diedrich Knickerbocker; see, for example, the early evening walk of Black Sam and Wolfert Webber to the haunted house of the red-capped pirate in "The Adventure of the Black Fisherman," in *Tales of a Traveller*, 700–1. Irving did not get his attentiveness to trees from Sir Walter Scott; he displayed it much earlier in his journals, and he also had the example of Addison. Nevertheless, Scott and Irving were clearly kindred spirits on the matter, and one can imagine them discussing trees in Spenser during Irving's decisive visit to Abbotsford in 1817. Indeed, it is notable that the very skill Scott saw in Spenser manifested most vividly in Irving's naturalistic descriptions in "Sleepy Hollow" just two years after the life-altering visit with Scott.

49. Discussed in the last section of the previous chapter.

50. Thomas Cole, Essay on American Scenery," in *American Art, 1700–1960: Sources and Documents*. Ed. John W. McCoubrey. Sources and Documents in the History of Art Series (Englewood, NJ: Prentice Hall, Inc., 1965), 106.

51. "Essay," 107.

52. *History*, VII.1, 674. The elegance of this passage has been lost in the 1848 revision, now as VII.II, where an expanded account of the city's festivals includes the governor's investment in fiddles, and the role of trumpeter Anthony Van Corlear provides a more elaborate picture of a happy day.

53. *History*, "Account of the Author," CW, 12.

54. *History*, III.II, CW, 99.

55. Christine Stansell and Sean Wilentz, "Cole's America: And Introduction," in Treuttner and Wallach, 4–10.

56. Pierre Irving, *The Life and Letters of Washington Irving*, Vol. IV (London: Richard Bentley, 1864), 51.

57. David Lawall, *Asher Durand: A Documentary Catalogue of the Narrative and Landscape Paintings* (New York and London: Garland Publishing, Inc., 1978), 79–80.

58. John Durand, *The Life and Times of Asher Durand* (Hendersonville, NY: Black Dome Press, 2007), 39–40, 145–6.

59. Irving converted to Anglican Christianity in 1850, inspired by a print of *Christus Consolator* by Ari Schaefer discovered on Broadway. Given the timing of Irving's conversion, and his enthusiastic response to Asher Durand's painting, it is possible that Irving heard the call of those distant church bells and decided to return to active fellowship in a Christian community.

60. H. Daniel Peck, *Thomas Cole's Refrain: The Paintings of Catskill Creek* (Catskill: Thomas Cole National Historic Site, 2019), 84–8, 129–31.

61. March 26, 1836, Noble, 217.

62. Alan Wallach, "Thomas Cole's *River in the Catskills* as Antipastoral," *Art Bulletin* 84, no. 2 (June 2002): 334–6. H. Daniel peck has more recently drawn attention to the significance of this seminal article by Wallach; Peck, *Thomas Cole's Refrain*, 121–9.

63. Peck, *Thomas Cole's Refrain*, 129.

64. Peck, *Thomas Cole's Refrain*, 5–14.

Chapter 6

World Citizenship on Frontiers Near and Far

Washington Irving had been trained in an ethic of world citizenship as a young man, inspired by Diogenes and other ancient Cynics, in the writing of Oliver Goldsmith. He was also influenced by Alexander Pope's teaching that all creatures were equally generated by the laws of nature, and thus there was no room for anthropocentrism or any form of partiality. Irving embodied this Enlightenment ethic by way of satire in his early years, lampooning notorious cases of chauvinism—or what we may call "cultural egocentrism." In *A History of New York*, the colonial desire to conquer, displace, and convert Native Americans met his ire, as did the Puritan trial and execution of witches, and the Calvinist harassment of Quakers in the early colonial period. Most famously, Connecticut Yankees such as Ichabod Crane were also acute violators of world citizenship by their constant meddling in other people's lives and their aggressive push into old Dutch American territory. Irving was a person of genial and diplomatic temperament; when he launched into an open critique of someone, it was because the violations of the ideal of world citizenship were severe.

Yet, Irving also had another mode of arguing for world citizenship in his sympathetic portrayal of a wide range of marginalized characters, some of whom were of Dutch descent, such as Dolph Heyliger, but many of whom were of varying ethnicities. Though his narrator Dietrich Knickerbocker could occasionally make condescending and, indeed, racist remarks, the overall picture he painted of African Americans in colonial America and the early Republic was quite sympathetic. Irving was not generally inclined to racist caricature, and when he did resort to images that today could seem belittling, such as an African American storyteller crooning away like a raven on the mantel of the fireplace, it is generally with great admiration for the skill of the old, raspy-voiced person. Frequently, these marginalized characters were the bearers of values Irving wished to support, such as a sense of local history through storytelling. As his stories became more contemporary, freed slaves entered the picture, and they too were portrayed with sympathy and, in fact, an affirmation of friendship, as when Dietrich Knickerbocker buried the scattered bones of his old childhood friend Pompey in "The Haunted House."

Interpreters in the tradition of Albert Boime's style of social analysis might say, first, the Pompey burial episode was one of those stories where African Americans needed to be taken care of by patronizing European Americans. As such the story would stroke the egos of the mostly Anglo-European American audience, reassuring them how kind they were to blacks. Second, such an interpreter might say, the burial is too little, too late. White Americans kept black Americans in slavery for years; then when slavery ended, they left them to struggle on small subsistence farms where they could barely eke out a living. Now stopping by to help after someone was already dead would simply not suffice. The story of Knickerbocker's kindness would serve only to ease "white guilt," by presenting a kindly Euro-American who took care of an African American friend. It may well be that the story functioned in such a way for some of Irving's readers, and one may fairly say Irving knew his audience. To such an interpreter I would say, first, Knickerbocker was a Dutch American, and Irving may have intended his kindness to stand in pointed contrast with normative Yankee, Anglo-American behavior. Furthermore, Irving was a romantic for whom such scenes of pathos would tug at the heart. One may criticize Irving for being a sentimentalist, but there is no reason for thinking the feelings conjured up by the image of a person gathering the scattered bones of a beloved childhood friend were anything but authentic. Irving was a person of boundless sensitivity. It is more likely that the story functioned for him as a kind of invitation to empathy. Irving was gently pointing out to his readers that America had left African Americans in a difficult situation: first slavery, then the poverty of subsistence farming and meager day labor. Perhaps, Anglo-Americans should take better care to include vulnerable minority populations in a community based on respect and kindness, and with provision of some form of economic opportunity, so that people would no longer be neglected like Pompey in death. There is no denying that a mere burial would be too little, too late, yet it remains true that the burial of the dead has long been classified as one of the seven great works of mercy, and a significant gesture of respect in any generation, in comparison with leaving bones scattered to be perpetually plowed over and dragged around by animals.[1]

In *The Legend of Sleepy Hollow*, African Americans made two major appearances. The first was the appearance of a domestic servant at the schoolhouse—most likely a slave around 1790—to invite Ichabod Crane to the quilting party: "A kind of buzzing stillness reigned through out the school room. It was suddenly interrupted by the appearance of a negro in tow cloth jacket and trousers, a round crowned fragment of a hat, like the cap of Mercury, and mounted on the back of a wild, ragged half broken colt."[2] With a playfulness akin to Knickerbocker's likening of the crossing of the Hudson Bay from New Jersey to the journey of Aeneas in the founding of Rome, this ragtag servant was presented as Mercury, the swift messenger of the gods. The appearance of the African American man was abrupt indeed, for up until now the story had been a duel of Dutch versus English cultures, with only a distant memory of an Indian chief, a German doctor, and a Hessian soldier in the remote background. Into the world of Anglo-European rivalries, the black servant appeared like a jack-in-the-box springing open. The scene was, in fact, the springing of a trap for Ichabod. The narrator noted that the African American servant made his announcement with the typical pomposity of a slave sent on an important task. Whether the pomposity on the part of the African American man was real, merely perceived, or even feigned is unclear, for it is possible—even likely—that he was in on the secret that Ichabod was being lured to the party to be jilted. Perhaps the messenger of the gods had seen such ambitious Yankees fall again and again to the trickery of Brom Bones, and he knew all too well the predetermined fate of the schoolmaster. With an insider's knowledge, it would be hard for anyone to resist a little grandiosity of gesture as one lured an unwitting and even more pompous know-it-all to his destiny. The messenger of the gods played his role, the trap was laid, and he disappeared from whence he came.

Irving's use of an African American man to announce the dance was fitting enough, for this was a night in which all Ichabod's hopes and fears would be summed up. For a Connecticut Yankee who was superstitiously afraid of wilderness, witches, and all darkness, who better to push the button at the anxious edge of hope and fear than an African American man who, though a slave, was less marginalized in this community than Ichabod himself? Irving had a way of finding Americans' vulnerable spots, our anxiety pressure points, like an acupuncturist today who finds a tender knot in the muscle, and then bears down directly with a firmly jabbing thumb to stimulate healing blood circulation.

The dance itself featured an African American fiddler: "The musician was an old grey headed negro, who had been the itinerant orchestra of the neighborhood for more than half a century. His instrument was as old and battered as himself."[3] There was a larger group of African Americans around the margins of the scene, watching him closely, admiring—Ichabod thought—his skill in dancing:

> Ichabod prided himself as much on his dancing skills as upon his vocal powers. Not a limb, not a fiber about him was idle, and to have seen his loosely hung frame in full motion, and chattering about the room, you would have thought

that Saint Vitus himself, that blessed patron of the dance, was figuring before you in person. He was the admiration of all the negroes, who, having gathered, of all ages and sizes, from the farm and the neighborhood, stood forming a pyramid of shining black faced at every door and window, gazing at the scene, rolling their white eyeballs, and showing grinning rows of ivory from ear to ear. How could the flogger of urchins be otherwise than animated and joyous; the lady of his heart was his partner in the dance, and smiling graciously in reply to all his amorous oglings, while Brom Bones, sorely smitten with love and jealousy, sat brooding in one corner.[4]

This passage is clearly dominated by the subjectivity of Ichabod's fevered imagination as he believed he was about to fulfill all his dreams.[5] He imagined that Brom Bones was brooding jealously in the corner, when in reality Brom was more likely to be watching for the right moment to play his ordained role in this episode of "Pride Cometh Before a Fall." Ichabod also imagined that the gathered African Americans admired his dancing skills as he clacked like a rattling skeleton.

The African Americans of the town, perhaps a mix of slave and free, were indeed watching him, but they were gathered round to watch his fate unfold. Knickerbocker spared no vividness in describing their eyes and teeth so white in the darkness, and he used the stereotype of the wide grinning negro, so their faces clustered around the doors and windows in the fire-lit darkness took on a specter-like quality. Note that this striking and highly stereotypical image is two layers of storytelling removed from Irving himself. First, there is the Knickerbocker, who reveled in the mildly outrageous as a means of holding a listener's attention (not unlike Irving himself), and then there was Ichabod's fantasy itself. Like Wolfert Webber's vision of the pirate at the money pit in *The Money Diggers*, this was clearly a picture of what Ichabod saw in the fever of the moment, not necessarily what was there. Ichabod was happy in the moment, because he did not realize that, if they were grinning at all, they were laughing at him, not with him. However, the specter-like images—perhaps created in his own unconscious mind—were a premonition of the alienation that he was not quite able to anticipate in the deluded pleasure of the moment. Nevertheless, Ichabod's fall came soon enough, and Katrina Van Tassel dispatched him after the dance with the same abruptness as the slave who had invited him to the party. The slaves and freed blacks of Sleepy Hollow were in on the plot; they remained members of the community, as Ichabod's status as outsider was bluntly enacted, causing him to flee the scene. The striking image was so clearly a product of Ichabod's titillated and frenzied imagination, that one wonders if Irving was not mocking him, and by extension all Yankees and Euro-Americans, who saw African Americans in such a flagrantly caricatured way. As in the early chapters of *A*

History of New York, Irving was again defending an ethic of world citizenship by lampooning its most flagrant violators.

One interesting feature of the scene is that the African Americans, except for the old fiddler himself, were all standing at the edges, around but apparently outside the room. That is why they gathered eagerly at all doors and windows. These African Americans were all accepted members of the community, and they were welcome to come to the dance and enjoy the music—and the spectacle of Ichabod's fall from glory—at a slight distance. Irving, or perhaps the Knickerbocker who would bury his old friend Pompey's scattered bones, was here acknowledging an element of marginalization in the African American experience, even in a Dutch community he wanted to idealize as much as possible.

A similar scene of marginalization is found in a famous fiddling scene by Long Island genre painter William Sidney Mount. Mount painted scenes of fiddling and country dances, including a couple of portraits of African American fiddlers. Mount himself was a fiddler and was moved by the power of music to bind people together in a community. *The Power of Music*, painted in 1847, displayed a sharply geometric composition of perpendicularly intersecting rectangles (see figure 6.1).

The most prominent was the broad flat barn door and floorboard which created a clear marker of space inside the barn and outside the barn; inside, two of Mount's Anglo-American neighbors gathered to listen to his nephew play the fiddle. On the outside, a slightly tired but relaxed and seemingly pleased African American leaned against the barn door, listening to the music. He held a black top hat and beside him against the barn door were a jug and an ax. Slavery had ended a generation earlier, with manumissions picking up pace since 1800. Henry Adams says the figure is identifiable as Robin Mills, and that he was the descendant of slaves on the local Mills farm, but he may or may not have experienced slavery directly. At this point in American history, he was a free day-laborer in the community, taking a moment of rest. Some viewers might have projected stereotypical laziness onto him, but that does not seem to be Mount's intention. The gentle smile of satisfaction suggests true pleasure in the middle of a day's work.[6] The day-laborer was separate from the neighbors inside, and yet he experienced the music that was not limited by the barn door. The scene is quite like Irving's barn dance scene in that the African Americans were positioned just outside the door, listening, and in Irving's case also looking in. Here, Robin Mills gazed in downward in seemingly peaceful contemplation.

Deborah Johnson has pointed out that Mount had deep admiration for an old black fiddler, Anthony Hannibal Clapp, "a master of the violin, at whose knee Mount sat as a youngster." In view of this historical connection, it is likely that the older African American man was listening with satisfaction

Figure 6.1. William Sidney Mount, *The Power of Music*, 1847, Cleveland Museum of Art.

because he in fact taught Mount's nephew how to play the fiddle. He was not a lazy African American skipping work; he was a family friend who had the pride of a teacher taking pleasure in a student's accomplishment.[7] Despite the gap between the inner and out space of the barn door, there is a sense that the distance between Anglo and African American people was being partially bridge by the power of music, and that indeed seems the point of the work's title. On Johnson's reading, the man reclining against the door was a skilled musician, like the negro fiddler in Irving's story who had been playing barn-dances for fifty years and was known and loved in the community. Like the woman in Mount's *Eel-Speering*, the prominent African figure was an indicator of relationship, and a sense of being an accepted member of a community. Perhaps the African American in *The Power of Music* was a conflation of Robin Mills and Anthony Clapp, just as the monumental heroic African American woman in Mount's *Eel-Spearing at Setauket* seemed to be a conflation of the female slave that raised Mount and the African American man who taught him fishing. The main figure in this painting has stopped by to listen; the neighbors in the barn did not see him for the moment, but they would also not be surprised to find him there. Who, after all, could resist the power of music? There is no sense that he was delinquent or that they would be angry if they noticed him. The main figure was just a member of the local community in Long Island passing by and stopping for a moment. He was separate, and yet an organic part of the community. This picture of gradual integration into New York communities as slavery was ending in New York is consistent with the overall portrait Washington Irving portrayed of black storytellers, musicians, and fishermen in New York. What is most important is that they were there, part of a real community, even if partly marginalized. Indeed, in Irving's "Sleepy Hollow," some of the most striking stereotypes of blacks were a product of Ichabod's delusional imagination, fed by his anxieties over status. When Irving portrayed African Americans without this element of fever shaping the picture, they were ordinary members of a community. As slaves, freed slaves, or immediate descendants of slaves, they were poor, such as Black Sam who lived in a shack by the river in *The Money Diggers*; however, they were there, and there to stay. Black Sam was beloved by the children of the neighborhood just as Rip Van Winkle was. For Washington Irving, being loved by children was not a failing, and African American storytellers were especially beloved. There was, in Irving, no fantasy of sending African Americans to Africa, the Caribbean, or the far western plains, as was common among Anglo-Americans from Thomas Jefferson to Abraham Lincoln. The African Americans in Irving's stories were just folks—fold who were there, who belonged there, and who had valued skills such as fiddle-playing, storytelling, fishing, farming, and, most crucially—a talent for surviving the vagaries of the weather, no matter how severe the storm.[8]

Another aspect of Irving's advocacy of world citizenship is found in his abiding interest in "half-breeds." Near the beginning of *A Tour on the Prairies*, Irving remarked, "I had been taught to look upon half-breeds with distrust, as an uncertain and faithless race."[9] It was implied but never directly stated that Irving has found this caricature to be false; in fact, the entire work stands as a rebuttal to this commonplace Anglo-American attitude. Irving made his argument not by preaching at people, but by simply portraying his experience. Irving did not tell Americans this distrust of "half-breeds" was misguided; he simply showed them, in keeping with his own gently diplomatic temperament.

Given the number of ways Irving was himself a boundary-crosser, a person torn between worlds, it is not surprising he would have a fascination with and sympathy for such mixed-race persons. The interest went all the way back to his 1809 *A History of New York*, where Irving seemed to identify with Dirk Schuiler (also known as Skulker) a kind of prototype modern who didn't quite belong anywhere. He was a kind of hanger on to the garrison; who seemed to belong to nobody, and in a manner to be self-outlawed. One of those vagabond cosmopolites as if they had no right or business in it, and who infest the skirts of society, like poachers or interlopers. Every garrison and country village has one or more scapegoats of this kind, whose existence is without motive, who comes from Lord knows where. Who lives the Lord knows how, and seems to be made for no other earthly purpose but to keep up the ancient and honorable order of idleness. This vagrant philosopher[10] was supposed to have some Indian blood in his veins, which was manifested by a certain Indian complexion and cast of countenance; but more especially by his propensities and habits.[11]

There are a few things to note. First, he is "supposed" to have Indian blood. No one knew for sure. He was a marginal figure. He had a Dutch name and may well have been a mixed-race person, but this too may have been an assumption on the part of the community because he didn't fit in. He was a liminal figure, and he may also have taken up Native American dress simple as an expression of his marginality. Second, given that Washington Irving spent his life resisting Puritan sternness and inability to enjoy life, "maintaining the ancient and honorable order of idleness" was reason enough for being. On this matter, Dirk anticipated Rip Van Winkle, and one senses in the Knickerbocker a hint of admiration for the cosmopolitan skulker. One of the benefits of being of two worlds was that some unique survival skills unfolded: "He played the perfect jack-of-both-sides—that is to say, he made a prize of everything that came within his reach, robbed both parties."[12] The ability to play both sides, of course, might be considered a crucial skill in the art of diplomacy that Irving would later formally take up.

Most telling passage by the Knickerbocker is when he noted that such a marginal and mixed character might be half devil:

> He was generally equipped in half Indian dress, with belt, leggings and moccasons. His hair hung in straight gallows locks, about his ears, and added not a little to his shirking demeanor. It is an old remark that persons of Indian mixture are half civilized, half savage, and half devil, a third half being expressly provided for their particular convenience. It is for similar reasons, and probably with equal truth, that the back-wood-men of Kentucky are styled half man, half horse and half alligator, by the settlers of the Mississippi, and held accordingly in equal respect and abhorrence.

Here we see Irving the child of the Enlightenment lampooning superstition. Irving enjoyed fantastical tales, but he did not believe that mixed-culture people were devils any more than he believed New England witches should have been burned. Knickerbocker's voice was always a complex voice, but once again, as in *History*, Book I, chauvinistic folly was glaringly pointed out. People who said mixed-race or uncategorizable people were troublemakers utilized the mathematical nonsense that such persons have a third-half from the devil. Such an irrational claim was clearly for their own chauvinistic "convenience" in ostracizing that which they did not understand. If one wanted to say such things about Dutch-Native American half-breeds, one should equally say such things of marginal Anglo-Americans, such as frontier people in Kentucky. Both claims were nonsense, but if one must indulge, then one must indulge the "logic" with fairness and consistency. There is here perhaps a hint of Irving's claim in the early poem "Passaic" that aggressive Anglo-Americans were more aptly labeled savages than the Native Americans they marginalized. When Irving told tales of the devil, he did so partly for the vividness of the imagery, while simultaneously poking into the hidden anxieties at the heart of American culture. This was true in his later description of the devil sitting on rocks mid-river near Hells Gate in Knickerbocker's East River-Long Island stories and it was especially true in his presentation of Old Scratch, a dark, seemingly mixed-race black Indian who was the sum of all Anglo-American fears in "The Devil and Tom Walker."

Irving's fascination with mixed-race people returned in full force while he was in the south of Spain studying the history of the Spanish conquest of the Moors. In his "Preface to the Revised Edition" of *The Alhambra*:[13]

> It was my endeavor scrupulously to depict its half Spanish half Oriental character; its mixture of the poetic, and the grotesque; to revive the traces of grace and beauty fast fading from its wall; to record the regal and chivalrous traditions concerning those who trod its courts, and the curious and superstitions of the motley race now burrowing among its ruins.[14]

One aspect of the romantic temperament was the savoring of pathos, bittersweet tales of a lost cause, and people who behaved chivalrously even in the face of impossible odds. In *The Alhambra*, the chivalry of the Moorish princes was highlighted. Irving treated them more sympathetically than the Spanish conquistadors. While such empathy is understandable as part of the romantic temperament, it was nevertheless rare for an Anglo-American to display such pronounced sympathy for Muslims. Stanley Williams pointed out that travel within Spain was so difficult in the early nineteenth century that almost no one did it until mid-century; Irving was indeed a groundbreaker. Partly there was the anti-Catholic bias of most Anglo-Americans, poverty worse than found in France or Italy, as well as was the sheer difficulty of roads in Spain, especially in the South.[15] Irving was intrepid in his ambition to see new sites, and his inquisitiveness and good humor were almost without limit as he came to empathize with a marginalized people.

> Such were our minor preparations for the journey, but above all we laid in an ample stock of good humor and a genuine disposition to be pleased; determining to travel in true contrabandista style; taking things as we found them, rough or smooth, and mingling with all classes and kinds in a kind of vagabond companionship.[16]

The other thing to note is Irving's love of intercultural mingling, and his use of the word "motley." For Irving, "motley" was a term of endearment, and it expressed his love of diversity, finding beauty in a high degree of texture and variation, as was consistent with the traditions of picturesque art and travel. Two striking examples are found in *Astoria*:

> S' Louis, which is situated on the right back of the Mississippi River, a few miles below the mouth of the Missouri, was, at that time a frontier settlement and the last fitting out place for the Indian trade of the South West. It possessed a motley population, composed of the Creole descendants of the original French colonists; keen traders from the Atlantic states; the backwoodsmen of Kentucky and Tennessee; the Indians and half breeds of the prairies; together with a singular aquatic race that has grown up from the navigation of the rivers, the "boatmen of the Mississippi," who possessed habits, manners, and almost a language peculiarly their own and strongly technical. They at that time were extremely numerous, and conducted the chief commerce of the Ohio and the Mississippi, as the voyageurs did of the Canadian waters; but like them, their consequence and characteristics are rapidly vanishing before the all-pervading intrusion of steamboats.[17]

While Irving particularly lamented the decline of the boatsmen of the Missouri in the face of emerging technology, this entire picture of a motley assemblage of diverse peoples in one place was romanticized as almost a golden age of cultural diversity. He would have a similar response when he went to New Orleans on the way back from his trip to the prairies.[18] Irving was a cosmopolitan lover of cultural and racial mixture, and nothing attracted him less than the monolithic hegemony of Yankee "improvement" that was on the horizon.

In *Astoria*, Irving also used the term motley to describe a beautifully diverse landscape:

> The party continued their voyage with delightful May weather. The prairies bordering on the river were gaily painted with innumerable flowers, exhibiting the motley confusion of colors of a Turkey carpet. The beautiful islands, also, on which they occasionally halted, presented the appearance of mingled grove and garden. The trees were often covered with clambering grape vines

in blossom, which perfumed the air. Between the stately groves were grassy lawns and glades covered studded with flowers, or interspersed with rose bushes in full bloom. These Islands were often the resort of the buffalo, the elk, and the antelope, who made innumerable paths among the trees and thickets, which had the effect of mazy walks and alleys and alleys of parks and shrubberies.[19]

The first thing to note here is that Irving was not imposing a civilized fantasy of parkland onto the wilderness. Fire-dependent ecosystems, such as southeastern U.S. pine forests, oak and hickory ridgetop groves through the Midwest, and savannahs almost everywhere all have a park-like appearance that is naturally occurring. In the continental United States, fire caused by lightning strikes, or—at that time—also by Native American burning, cleared away underbrush and released nutrients that fed a high diversity of wildflowers and grasses.[20] Irving's picture was ecologically accurate, and many explorers and pioneers were astonished to find that in so many such spots, the wilderness looked like a park. This effect was the result of regular fire, not a European colonial fantasy. It did, however, make it easier for Americans of Anglo-European descent to feel at home in such locations.

The other important point is that Irving was reveling in the picturesque beauty of a highly varied and richly textured landscape, but the landscape was not limited to terrain, wildlife, or wildflowers. For Irving, picturesque beauty was also found in human civilizations that allow for mixture and interaction. The Dutch culture of the Hudson valley was like a community naturally adapted to its environment. The Yankees were villains because they single-mindedly stamped out the diversity of such niche populations in the name of their own invasive monoculture, violating the ethic of world citizenship. The Yankees were akin to what we might now metaphorically call an "invasive species," albeit formally a distinctive cultural type within the human species. Irving on the other hand celebrated diversity wherever he found it, in the mixed Catholic-Moorish culture of southern Spain and in the motley mix of St. Louis, New Orleans, and the western frontier. For Irving, picturesque beauty was not just an aesthetic for upper-class travelers who wanted to prove that they were cosmopolitan sophisticates. It was an aesthetic combined with an ethic of world citizenship, and in Irving the ethic and the aesthetic were bound together by an almost boundless capacity for empathy, for sympathy with those marginalized as other. He himself knew what was to be a person of mixed standing. Irving opted for empathy, and lived his life as a celebration, not only with a capacity for enjoyment, but with a heartfelt warmth of interest in diverse peoples and places. He loved the places, and he loved the people; he even loved the bats, "those equivocal birds" who could not quite make up their minds as to whether they were in fact birds or mammals.[21] Indeed,

Figure 6.2 George Caleb Bingham, *Fur Traders Descending the Missouri*, 1845, **Metropolitan Museum of Art.** *Source*: Image copyright © The Metropolitan Museum of Art. Art Resource, NY.

Charles Ellsworth described Irving as a genial and caring person, "the kindly impulse of whose nature is to love every living thing."[22]

One can see a similar nostalgia for days of the boatsmen, old French traders, and empathy for mixed-race persons in an elegant and provocative painting by Caleb George Bingham, *Fur Traders Descending the Missouri* (see figure 6.2).

In this picture, an old French trader plies his oar on a crystal river at the back of a canoe on a sunlit but still misty morning. The trader's cargo is in the middle of the canoe, and the trader's ruddy, black-haired, mixed-race son reclines happily in the center. The son looks almost directly at the viewer with a sweet and gentle smile as he rests his head on his forearm, leaning on the crate. In the front of the canoe is a black animal tied to the canoe; it looks at first glance like a large black cat, but on closer examination it turns out to be a bear cub.[23] In the middle background is an island in the river with willows and other trees, its reflection darkening the water slightly with a dull green shadow. There is a ridge of morning clouds lit by soft morning sunlight and pale blue sky made slightly hazy by the mist. It is a moment of absolute calm on the river, a special moment of morning stillness and one can almost hear the trader's paddle lapping the water in the silence. The bear is in full sunlight and its blackness stands out against the smoothly crystalline unbroken river. The stillness is the absolute antithesis of the bustle of American life as understood by both Bingham and Irving.

The image is romantic in the sense of longing for simpler days of old, but classicizing in composition, in terms of balanced harmony.[24] The child has the kind of black, floppy bangs Irving attributed to Dirk Schuiler. The boy is a "half-breed," and he is a happy one. Unlike Irving's Dirk, this child has found his place in the world, at least as long as the river way of life would remain sustainable. Of course, Irving told us it was already disappearing when he wrote *Astoria* in 1836, and it was certainly almost a thing of the past by the time Bingham painted in 1843. Nevertheless, the boy in the painting has a certain charm, and one cannot but wish him well. The relaxed life on the river is also soothing. The French trader is taking care of his son by including him in his life. The bear at the front of the boat raises more questions. Is it a pet? Will it be sold at the market down the river? Is it tied only so a beloved pet will not jump out of the boat, or is it merely a captive waiting to be sold? A black creature tied going down the river seems to address the issue of slavery in the only way possible for one who wanted to sell paintings in a time of heightening social tension, that is, indirectly. The difficulty in determining whether it is a cat or bear may be parallel to the experience of the mixed-race child, who would probably have received stares in town, and the inevitable question, "What are you?" It is an elegant painting that raises fascinating questions about nineteenth-century America; all three figures are viewed sympathetically, and there is an affirmation by Bingham of the value of cultural diversity on the frontier.[25] In general, the French were more tolerant of intermarriage and racial mixing than the English were. Bingham seems to have sided with the French, displaying a sympathy for the mixed-race family, as well as for the bear. In his *Tour of the Prairies*, Irving would show a similar favor for French tolerance and profound empathy for people of diverse ethnicity, including mixed-race peoples. Irving frequently expressed empathy for many animals as well, and sometimes those animals seem to function as cyphers for human beings who were having similar experiences, such as a wild horse captured and broken to be put to civilized use.

Irving's capacity for empathy and love of picturesque variation in both natural and human communities is seen quite vividly in *A Tour on the Prairies*. When he returned to the United States after seventeen years abroad, he was feted publicly at a dinner, acknowledged by New York mayor Philip Hone as a true "citizen of the world." After seeing family and friends briefly, he embarked on a "rediscover the Hudson Valley tour." On the way to Albany, he met Charles Ellsworth, recently appointed commissioner of Indian Affairs out west, and he invited Irving on a mission to see what was happening out there. This was a golden opportunity, born of chance and his personal charm when meeting strangers. They would go to St Louis, then to Fort Gibson at the edge of Arkansas and then loop west into Osage Territory now known as Oklahoma. Irving had gone from living in the Alhambra to being a diplomat in London the last two years, and he jumped immediately at this chance to go as far west as possible. Though it was indeed a chance to establish himself as a writer on the theme of the American frontier, Stanley Williams was correct to emphasize that such a trip was the fruition of a long-standing interest in the west, born partly of adventure stories he heard as a child, and even more notably born of a trip to Montreal in 1803.[26]

Irving's realism and skepticism about federal government policy in the aftermath of President Jackson's Indian Removal policy and the sweeping nature of other migrations were noted in his account of an interaction with a group of Osage warriors. The most aggressive Native Americans in the region—from the standpoint of the American delegation—were the Pawnees. Ellsworth solemnly declared that the "father at Washington" had sent him to bring peace to the land. The Osage should not attack the Pawnees anymore, because the authorities in Washington would protect them from their enemies and establish a "universal peace." The Osage group apparently saw through this pretentious claim. How, in any case, would a few government agents protect the Osage from incursions by other tribes? The Osage Indians conferred among themselves in their native tongue, and the mixed-race interpreter Beatte went and spoke to them on behalf of Ellsworth. They told him that since universal peace was coming, they had better hurry up and steal as many horses as they could while it was still possible. Irving was a guest of Ellsworth, and he would not openly criticize the man who had given him such a unique opportunity to see the American West. However, he did report this incident, and one can sense his knowing wink.[27]

Irving's adventure was full of interesting characters, but the two most prominent were a very energetic French creole named Antoine, but nicknamed Toney to distinguish him from another Antoine. He was petit and energetic, barely able to control his excitement, and constantly bragging in endless chatter about his exploits. He was quite lovable, if annoyingly amusing, and Irving's *Tour* made him famous. Irving stated he was a Gil Blas of the American frontier, and so the picturesque in this case merged into the picaresque. Toney was played off as a foil against the taciturn half-breed Beatte, who was "Stoic" to a fault, and extremely reliable. While Toney was bouncing around the camp, rushing headlong to the hunt and often startling the potential dinner through his eruptive enthusiasm, Beatte would go off in silence, do the job, and quietly return to drop off an elk or antelope at the mess-cook's tent. If Toney was the star of Irving's show, the half-breed

Beatte was the hero. His consistent knowledgeability of the terrain, and his wisdom in handling many difficult situations were constantly admired by Irving. The viewpoint that Irving was once taught, that one cannot trust half-breeds, was formally rebutted in his presentation of Beatte.

Again, while Irving would not too harshly criticize members of his party, on whose protection and kindness he had depended for survival on the journey, he did report a few concerning incidents that occurred, a message for those with ears to hear. There were incidents of excess in relation to the environment that Irving did not always explicitly judge, but he presented them as part of the record, as a matter of his diplomatic mode. In his most direct criticism of his hosts, he reported that the rangers were "heedless"; when they had a large supply of meat, rather than jerking it and packing it for the future, they would leave what they didn't need in the immediate moment lying to waste on the ground; this lack of strategy risked starvation for the group at a later time, and it amounted to an unnecessary and pointless slaughter of so many deer, elk, and buffalo.[28] Once in October they were caught in a storm, and to warm themselves and dry their clothes, they cut down an entire grove of trees—something relatively scarce along the riversides in the vast prairie and scrub wilderness—leaving behind a ravaged wasteland as they moved on the next day. In contrast to this excess, when Beatte slipped away to go hunting based on a tip from his Osage friends, he would come back with four buffalo to feed the group, not more than needed, whereas the Anglo-American explorers would kill a much larger number of buffalo unnecessarily just to feast on the succulent fatty hump meat that was regarded as a delicacy. In terms of adaptation to an environment, and respectful use of nature, Native Americans and half-breeds were far wiser than Anglo-American rangers and settlers. Irving did not say this directly; he simply showed it.

Another important example is documented in Irving's description of the group's tendency to feast on honey trees; on some occasions they did not cut down simply one or two trees to get the honey, but they would cut down an excessive number. In his first reference to honey trees, Irving simply noted that when you see a felled oak tree, pillaged for the honey in its hollow spaces, with flakes of beeswax strewn around, it indicated you were near a temporary camp of rangers or settlers.[29]

Irving noted that honeybees were not native to America, and they were known to go west with the settlers, often in advance as a kind of harbinger of ecological and cultural change. Where the honeybees increased, the buffalo decreased. Nevertheless, the Native Americans loved to feast on the unexpected "ambrosial . . . luxury" now discovered in the hollows of old trees. When Irving went with a group of rangers to fell one tree, he displayed his characteristic empathy for the dazed and confused bees who now found themselves homeless, while making a moralizing analogy regarding the collapse of civilizations.

> After proceeding some distance, we came to an open glade on the skirts of the forest. Here our leader halted, and then advanced quietly to a low bush, on the top of which I perceived a piece of honeycomb. This I found was the bait or lure for the wild bees. Several were humming about it, and diving into its cells. When they had laden themselves with honey, they would rise in the air, and dart off in a straight line, almost with the velocity of a bullet. The hunters watched attentively the course they took, and then set off in the same direction, stumbling along over twisted roots and fallen trees, with their eyes turned up to the sky. In this way they traced the honey laden bees to their hive, in the hollow trunk of a blasted oak, where, after buzzing about for a moment, they entered a hole about sixty feet from the ground.[30]
>
> Two of the bee hunters now plied their axes vigorously at the foot of the tree, to level it with the ground. The mere spectators and amateurs, in the meantime, drew off to a cautious distance, to be out of the way of the falling of the tree and the vengeance of its inmates. The jarring blows of the ax seemed to have no effect in alarming or disturbing this most industrious community. They continued to ply at their usual occupations, some arriving fully freighted into port, others sallying forth on new, like so many merchantmen in a money-making metropolis, little suspicious of impending bankruptcy and downfall. Even a loud crack which announced the disrupture of the trunk, failed to divert their attention from the intense pursuit of gain; at length down came the tree with a tremendous crash, bursting open from end to end, and displaying all the hoarded treasures of the commonwealth.[31]

Irving's theme here is the same as that of *The Sketch Book*, the mutability of all things and the rise and fall of empires, the theme so dear to romantics, whether that empire was Rome, a great bee colony, mercantile capitals such as London and New York, or the Native Americans who went about their lives oblivious to the fact that their entire way of life was about to change forever. Curiously, when Irving was writing such passages in *A Tour on the Prairies* in 1835, Thomas Cole was back in New York painting his epic series *The Course of Empire* on precisely the same theme: All empires were subject to the same universal laws of history. In fact, the U.S. economy itself would crash in 1837 due to Andrew Jackson's war with the Federal Bank. Irving's description of a great crash was not a little precocious.

While Irving drew the most direct attention to the parallel with mercantile civilizations and their capacity for sudden, catastrophic collapse, his subsequent remarks return us to an awareness of the experience of those whose lives were being torn asunder by such momentous changes:

One of the hunters immediately ran up with a wisp of lighted hay as a defense against the bees. The latter however, made no attack and sought no revenge; they seemed stupefied by the catastrophe and unsuspicious of its cause . . .

It is difficult to describe the bewilderment and confusion of the bees of the bankrupt hive who had been absent at the time of the catastrophe, and who arrived from time to time, with full cargoes from abroad. At first they wheeled about in the air, in the place where the fallen tree has once reared its head, astonished at finding it all a vacuum. At length, as if comprehending their disaster, they settled down in clusters on a dry branch of a neighboring tree. Whence they seemed content to contemplate the prostrate ruin, and to buzz forth doleful lamentations over the downfall of their republic.[32]

The group then returned to camp that evening and discovered that their fellow travelers had felled not one or two, but at least twenty such grand old trees.

Here one sees that Irving had an empathy for the smallest of creatures. One also cannot help but think that the stupor of the bees who come home to nothing was also analogous to the experience of Native Americans who came home to their village after a short trip and found it in ruins, or had been forced to move west and now recollected their abandoned villages in North Carolina or Georgia now overrun by a new civilization. Central to the passage is a sense of stupefied loss and disorientation in the face of rapid change. Irving himself felt such loss as Yankee values replaced the more communally oriented Dutch villages in New York, and he knew that Native Americans were experiencing such disorientation as he was writing. The description of the disoriented lamentation of the bees was surely an invitation to empathize with the situation of Native Americans as well, and anyone else in America who was experiencing dislocation and cultural loss.

The parallels Irving sometimes drew between animal experience and human experience also make sense in view of Alexander Pope's philosophical theology in *An Essay on Man*: the laws of physics had equally generated all life forms. Not only could humans understand and empathize with foreign cultures as citizens of the world, but human beings could also understand and empathize with the experience of animals; we are not so different after all, since all share a common maker through a common cosmic process. It is not so hard to understand the stupor of the bees at the felled tree; think what it would be like to come home one evening and find that your house had burned to the ground and all that remained was a charred lot? Such devastation is what the bees experienced, and it is what the Native Americans experienced as well. It is not so hard to understand them and care for them. Though Irving did not want to openly criticize Ellsworth or Jackson directly so shortly after his return to the United States, he did present this pitiful picture of what it must be like to suddenly lose one's home and one's community and be dispersed so abruptly into isolating fragments drifting across the prairies.

Irving was impressed with the Native Americans who lived wild and free—seeing them almost as proto-typical Americans who loved liberty, and he described them as living out precisely the ancient values of Diogenes the Cynic:

> Such is the glorious independence of man in a savage state. This youth (a young Osage), with his rifle, his blanket, and his horse, was ready at a moment's warning to rove the world; he carried all his worldly effects with him, and in the absence of artificial wants possessed the great secret of person freedom. We of society are slaves, not so much to others but ourselves; our superfluities are the chains that bind us, impeding every movement of our body, and thwarting every impulse of our souls.[33]

Note that Irving had made a similar compassion of Native Americans with ancient Cynic and Stoic philosophers in his 1809 *History*, Book I, and he noted that if they were ancient Greeks, they would be regarded as the wisest of sages. Irving was consistent and his core values were stable across the prime years of his writing career from 1804 in his *Journals* to 1835 when he completed the *Tour*.

Irving was not quite as impressed by the Native Americans who had learned to scavenge around ranger and missionary outposts.[34] At one point, he comments that the missionaries had disrupted their way of life unhelpfully, though some missionaries who focused on agriculture rather than religious dogma at least did a little good. On this point, Irving seems to have been a Cynic who perceived the attempt to convert people to one's own religion an act of cultural chauvinism, and thus a violation of world citizenship. He then described the Osage as very dignified, worthy of being portrayed in sculpture, and he again likened them to the ancient Greek philosophers whose radical independence formed his own ideal. He noted that Osage warriors appeared as Stoic philosophers, but they were not truly Stoic (see figure 6.3).

They were taciturn and solemn in the presence of the white men, but when they were at home in their camps they relaxed and became much more playful around the campfire in the evenings. The problem with Irving's association of Native Americans with these ancient philosophers is not one of respect or intention. He respected and admired them, and he himself tried to live as a wandering citizen of the world. The problem, as Martha Nussbaum has pointed out, with the Stoic and Cynic philosophies is that they taught such fierce independence from all material circumstance that one could be happy in any condition. Such transcendence of personal circumstance was indeed the point of these philosophies. Like Buddhists, they taught that one can

Figure 6.3 George Catlin, *Osage Warrior, Tal-Lee*, 1834, Smithsonian Institution.
Source: Smithsonian American Art Museum, Washington, DC / Art Resource, NY.

control one's happiness by attitude and mental fortitude, not by the wavering circumstances of time and fortune, the vagaries of wealth and property that ebb and flow. The problem with these philosophies, according to Nusbaum, is that they taught that any person could be free and happy without a material base of stability. No matter what happened, a person could be ok. On the frontier, projection of these philosophical ideals onto Native Americans could easily become a kind of unconscious means of denying the full impact of what was happening, as more and more Native Americans were displaced. Such philosophies could function as a means of convincing oneself that the Native Americans would be fine even if you took all their land, and then forced them into a way of life that was alien to them, in a home that was no longer home.

Irving himself had suggested in *Traits of Indian Character* that the Indians of the eastern deciduous forests were highly adapted to the shade of the forest, and they would not flourish if forced into the full sun of open agricultural fields. Therefore, Irving was not necessarily using these philosophical themes to deny reality, even if his readers might do so. Irving understood the importance of a sense of home as much as anyone. If you destroyed the homes of Native Americans, they would be at a loss, just like the bees coming home to the felled tree, and just like any human thrown into poverty by an economic crash. Though some may criticize Irving for not addressing the Indian removal policy crisis firmly enough, he was clearly there to see for himself what was happening, and he protested the tendency of white settlers to always jump to the worse conclusions about Indians, knowing well the catastrophically violent outcomes of such bias. He also presented several poignant images, such as the breaking of a wild horse or a blind dog wandering the camp; such images functioned as an invitation to empathy toward the situation of Native Americans and anyone else who was staggering through the world with their vision of that world shattered.

There is an old caricature of Irving that he was an insecure sycophant who wanted nothing other than to be liked and make money. Stanley Williams took up this old criticism and applied it to Irving especially after his return to the United States. Irving ceased to spend his time with artists, as he had in England, and began to spend almost all his time with venture capitalists.[35] In other words, when Irving returned to the United States, he virtually abandoned all his prior values, or, more severely, showed what his values truly were, money and public approval. On such a reading of Irving's character, he would be constitutionally incapable of courage or of rendering any meaningful critique of American civilization. In addition to the unforgiveable sin of being a sentimentalist inclined to reverie, Irving also committed the unforgivable sin of wanting to make enough money to finance a home upon his return. He sold his soul to John Jacob Astor no less than Tom Walker lost his soul in a deal with the devil.

Such a caricature of Irving really needs to be dismissed. Irving did have something to say about American culture, including the migrations and dislocations out west. He chose to make his statements diplomatically rather than abrasively. In an America that is still rife with white supremacy 200 years after Irving criticized Anglo-American Yankee monoculture in "The Legend of Sleepy Hollow," it was surely not cowardly or spineless for Irving to advocate consistently for the value of multicultural coexistence in New York and on the American frontier. In Washington Irving's ideal republic, hunters, trappers, newly American explorers, Native Americans, half-breeds, creoles, and African Americans "of every hue" could all coexist.[36] *A Tour on the Prairies* ended with the group hungry and worn out, almost at risk of starvation before they made it back to the fort. They happened upon a homestead run by a mixed-race couple, a "white man" and a "good-humored negress." The husband happened to be away. Irving commented on the gracious hospitality, the hearty food, and the uniqueness of the cooking vessels (the "corpulent cauldron" used to cook beef and turnips); he made no other remark about a relationship that would have been to so many Americans radically taboo, but which was possible on the outer limits of the frontier.[37] The mixed-race, black-white couple was simply there, and the African American wife was robustly generous and kind in providing such a feast for weary travelers. This manner of acceptance was in keeping with Irving's presentation of African Americans going all the way back to Dutch New York in his 1809 *History*.

Irving did not abandon his values when he returned to the American Republic in 1832. He was the same citizen of the world he always was, schooled on the tolerance and love of cultural diversity found in Oliver Goldsmith, and given philosophical grounding by Alexander Pope in his reverence for all things great and small that were equally generated by God's laws of physics. Irving was a lover of picturesque travel in 1832 just as he was on his Grand Tour, and his love of the picturesque was not merely an aspiring upper-class aesthetic taste. For Irving, the picturesque aesthetic expressed an ethic of world citizenship, where respect for cultural and natural diversity was the moral norm that he would articulate with nearly perpetual warmth and occasional biting satire. The fact that he was a diplomat with a truly diplomatic temperament should not be taken as implying he was incapable of analyzing or criticizing his home culture. He in fact did so with a genial combination of wit, humor, and transparent appeals for empathy, ranging in modes of literature from burlesque to romantic storytelling to travel literature. Washington Irving was the United States' first great advocate of a truly pluralistic American society. This was no small feat in the first third of the nineteenth century. Unfortunately, many scholars have not noticed his extraordinary vision, because they have accepted the assessment of Stanley Williams too quickly, and in doing so they have assumed that Irving was incapable of saying anything of substance. It is time to abandon this almost century-old bias and engage Washington Irving anew.

NOTES

1. For a similar "invitation to empathy," see my discussion of the bee tree below.

2. Washington Irving, *The Sketch Book of Geoffrey Grayon, Gent.* edited by Haskell Springer. The Complete Works of Washington Irving, Volume VIII (Boston: Twayne Publishers, 1978), 284.

3. *The Sketch Book*, 287–8.

4. *The Sketch Book*, 288.

5. For characters, such as Ichabod and Wolfert Webber, imagination had its problematic side, as it gave free rein to greed. Irving was not a romantic who saw all acts of imagination as liberating to the soul. For Irving, imagination could enchant with sacred memories, or lead down a delusional path of folly.

6. Henry Adams, *What's American about American Art? A Gallery Tour in the Cleveland Museum of Art* (New York: Hudson Hills Press, 2008), 60–1.

7. Johnson, *William Sidney Mount*, 58–62.

8. Black Sam has an ability to survive harrowing nighttime storms even at the dangerous channel of Hells Gate.

9. *Tour*, III, 17

10. Dirk is portrayed as a wandering Cynic philosopher: "He would lay in the sun and enjoy all the luxurious indolence of that swinish philosopher Diogenes.... Such was this Dirk Schuiler," his philosophy manifest "from the total indifference he showed to the world or its concerns" (*History* VI.II, 618). This indifference was the chief ideal of both Stoic and Cynic philosopher in the Hellenistic world.

11. *History*, VI. II, 617.

12. *History*, VI. II, 618.

13. The 1851 version of the text is printed in the Library of America edition, albeit without the scholarly annotation of the Complete Works.

14. *The Alhambra*, 723.

15. Stanley Williams, *The Spanish Background of American Literature*, Vol. I (New Haven: Yale University Press, 1955), 58–9.

16. *The Alhambra*, 730.

17. *Astoria*, 287.

18. Williams, Vol. II, 43.

19. *Astoria*, 326.

20. Elie Whitney, D. Bruce Means, and Anne Rudloe, *Priceless Florida: Natural Ecosystems and Native Species* (Sarasota: Pineapple Press, 2004), 33–64.

21. *Tour*, Ch. III, 14.

22. Williams, Vol. II, 38.

23. Nennette Luarca-Shoaf, et al. *Navigating the West: George Caleb Bingham and the River* (New Haven and London: Yale University Press, 2011), 102–8.

24. Luarca-Shoaf, *Navigating the West*, 142. See also Barbara Novak, *American Painting of the Nineteenth Century: Realism, Idealism and the American Experience*, 3rd edition (Oxford and New York: Oxford University Press, 2007), 125–30.

25. The classicizing form of this painting, the shimmer of still water and mist, the mixed quality of the boy and the "bear-cat," and the issues of liminality and marginalization explored, make Bingham's work here a kind of precursor of Magic Realism in American art. For an excellent discussion of this mid-twentieth-century movement, see the catalogue accompanying the recent show at the Georgia Museum of Art:

Jeffery Richmond-Moll, Philip Eliasoph, and William U. Eiland, *Extra Ordinary: Magic, Mystery, and Imagination in American Realism* (Athens: Georgia Museum of Art, 2021).

26. Williams, Vol. II, 72.
27. *Tour*, XXVI, 163–5.
28. *Tour*, XXXIV, 220.
29. *Tour*, VIII, 43.
30. The great oak was sixty feet tall after being blasted by lightning. Before the giant had been topped by a storm, it probably stood ninety feet tall. Such blasted trees, whether giant oaks or hemlocks, were prominent anthropomorphic "characters" in the paintings of Thomas Cole, especially in the late 1820s, before he went to Europe.
31. *Tour*, IX, 48–9.
32. *Tour*, IX, 49–50.
33. *Tour*, V, 28.
34. *Tour*, III, 16.
35. Williams, Vol. II, 54–60, 74–82. Williams did go on to note that Irving gave patronage to several American artists upon his return, thus implying he was not entirely abandoning his prior values.
36. *Tour*, III, 14. There is sometimes a tone of aristocratic condescension toward the rough and tumble quality of the "rabble" in a few such passages, but, even so, this old Federalist who wanted to be a gentleman farmer accepted the level of diversity throughout America. The overall tone of his references, taken together, is one of celebration. Irving did not have to poetic skill of a Walt Whitman, but he had a share of that energetic embrace of variety extraordinary for a person of Irving's generation and social class.
37. *Tour*, XXXV, 230.

Bibliography

Abrams, M. H. *The Mirror and the Lamp: Romantic Theory and the Critical Tradition*. New York and London, Oxford University Press, 1953.

Adams, Henry. *What's American about American Art? A Gallery Tour in the Cleveland Museum of Art*. New York: Hudson Hills Press, 2008.

Adams, Henry. *History of the United States of America during the Administrations of James Madison*. New York: Literary Classics of the United States, 1986.

———. *History of the United States of America during the Administrations of Thomas Jefferson*. New York: Literary Classics of the United States, Inc., 1986.

Alderman, Ralph, ed. *Critical Essays on Washington Irving*. Boston: G.K. Hall & Co., 1990.

Ambrose, Stephen E. *Undaunted Courage: Meriwether Lewis, Thomas Jefferson, and the Opening of the American West*. New York: Touchstone Books, 1996.

Avery Kevin J. "A Historiography of the Hudson River School," in *American Paradise: The World of the Hudson River School*. New York: The Metropolitan Museum of Art, 1987.

Bailey, Brigitte. *American Travel Literature, Gendered Aesthetics, and the Italian Tour, 1824–1862*. Edinburgh Critical Studies in Atlantic Literatures and Cultures. Edinburgh: University Press, 2018.

Barringer, Tim. "The Englishness of Thomas Cole," in *The Cultured Canvas: New Perspectives on American Landscape Painting*, edited by Nancy Siegel, 1–52. Durham: university of New Hampshire Press, 2011.

Barringer, Tim, and Gillian Forrester, Sophie Lynford, Jennifer Raab, and Nicholas Robbins. *Picturesque and Sublime: Thomas Cole's Trans-Atlantic Inheritance*. Catskill, NY: Thomas Cole National Historic Site, in association with Yale University Press, 2018.

Batey, Mavis. *Alexander Pope: The Poet and the Landscape*. London: Barn Elms Publishing, 1999.

Batey, Mavis, Henrietta Buttery, David Lambert, and Kim Wilkie. *Arcadian Thames: The River Landscape from Hampton to Kew*. London: Barn Elms Publishing, 1994.

Boas, George, ed. *Romanticism in America*. Papers Contributed to a Symposium Held at the Baltimore Museum of Art, May 13–15, 1940. New York: Russell and Russell, 1961.

Boime, Albert. *The Art of Exclusion: Representing Blacks in the Nineteenth Century*. Washington: Smithsonian Institution Press, 1990.

———. *The Magisterial Gaze: Manifest Destiny and American Landscape Painting, c. 1830–1865*. Washington and London: Smithsonian Institution Press, 1991.

Bonehill, John, and Stephen Daniels. *Paul Sandby: Picturing Britain*. London: Royal Academy of Arts, 2009.

Brewer, John. *The Pleasures of the Imagination: English Culture in the Eighteenth Century*. New York: Farrar, Strauss, and Giroux, 1997.

Brodwin, Stanley, ed. *The Old and New World Romanticism of Washington Irving*. Prepared under the auspices of Hofstra University. Westport, Connecticut: Greenwood Press, 1986.

Burke, Edmund. *On Taste; On the Sublime and the Beautiful; Reflections on the French Revolution; A Letter to a Noble Lord*. Harvard Classics 24. Edited by Charles W. Eliot. New York: P.F. Collier and Son, 1909.

Burstein, Andrew. *The Original Knickerbocker: The Life of Washington Irving*. New York: Basic Books, 2007.

Burstein, Andrew, and Nancy Isenberg. *Madison and Jefferson*. New York: Random House, 2010.

Bushman, Richard L. *From Puritan to Yankee: Character and Social Order in Connecticut, 1690–1765*. Cambridge: Harvard University Press, 1967.

Callow, James. *Kindred Spirits: Knickerbocker Writers and American Artists*. Durham: The University of North Carolina Press, 1967.

Caroselli, Susan L. *Guido Reni, 1575–1642*. Los Angeles: The Los Angeles County Museum of Art, 1988.

Conron, John. *American Picturesque*. University Park: Pennsylvania State University Press, 2000.

Dunlap, William. *The History of the Rise and Progress of the Arts of Design in the United States*, Vol. II. New York: George P. Scott and Co., 1934.

Durand, John. *The Life and Times of Asher Durand*. Introduction by Linda S. Ferber. Hendersonville, NY: Black Dome Press, 2007.

Ellsworth, Henry Leavitt. *Washington Irving on the Prairie: Or a Narrative Tour of the Southwest in the Year 1832*, ed. Stanley T. Williams and Barbara D. Simison. New York: American Book Company, 1837.

Emerson, Ralph Waldo. *Emerson: Essays and Lectures*, edited by Joel Porte. Library of America. New York: Literary Classics of the United States, Inc., 1983.

Evans, Mark. *Renaissance Watercolors: From Dürer to Van Dyck*. London: Victoria and Albert Museum, 2020.

Evelyn, John. *Sylva: A Discourse of Forest Trees and the Propagation of Timber*, Vol. I. Edited by John Nisbet. Middlesex: Echo Library, 2009. Original 1664.

Carol Fabricant, "The Aesthetics and Politics of Landscape in the Eighteenth Century," in *Studies in Eighteenth-Century British Art and Aesthetics*, edited by Ralph Cohen. Berkeley: University of California Press, 1985.

Gerdts, William H. and Theodore E. Stebbins, Jr. *"A man of Genius": The Art of Washington Allston (1779–1843)*. Boston: Museum of Fine Arts, 1979.

Giles, Paul. *Transatlantic Insurrections: British Culture and the Formation of American Literature, 1730–1860*. Philadelphia: University of Pennsylvania Press, 2001.

Gleig, George Robert. *The Life of Sir Walter Scott: Reprinted with Corrections and Additions from the Quarterly Review*. Edinburgh: A & C. Black, 1871.

Harris, John. *The Palladian Revival: Lord Burlington, His Villa and Garden at Chiswick*. New Haven and London: Yale University Press, 1994.

Hebel, Udo J. *The Construction and Contestation of American Cultures and Identities in the Early National Period*. American Studies 78. Heidelberg: Universitätsverlag, 1999.

Hemingway, Andrew, and Alan Wallach, ed. *Transatlantic Romanticism: British and American Art and Literature, 1790–1860*. Amherst and Boston: University of Massachusetts Press, 2015.

Howarth, David. *Lord Arundel and his Circle*. New Haven and London: Yale University Press, 1985.

Howe, Daniel Walker. *What Hath God Wrought: The Transformation of America, 1815–1848*. New York: Oxford University Press, 2007.

Hume, David. *An Enquiry into the Principles of Morals*, edited by Tom L. Beauchamp. Oxford Philosophical Texts. Oxford and New York: Oxford University Press, 1998.

———. *More Works by David Hume*. London: Forgotten Books, 2008.

Hunt, John Dixon. *The Figure in the Landscape: Poetry, Painting and Gardening during the Eighteenth Century*. Baltimore and London: John Hopkins University Press, 1976.

———. *Gardens and the Picturesque: Studies in the History of Landscape Architecture*. Cambridge and London: MIT Press, 1992.

Hunt, John Dixon, and Peter Willis, eds. *The Genius of the Place: The English Landscape Garden, 1620–1820*. New York and San Francisco: Harper and Row, 1975.

Huth, Hans. *Nature and the American: Three Centuries of Changing Attitudes*. Berkeley: University of California Press, 1957.

Ikemoto, Wendy N. E. *Antebellum American Pendant Paintings: New Ways of Looking*. Routledge Research in Art History. London and New York: Routledge Taylor and Francis Group, 2018.

Irving, Pierre. *The Life and Letters of Washington Irving*, Volume IV. London: Richard Bentley, 1864.

Irving, Washington. *A History of New York*. Edited by Michael L. Black and Nancy B. Black. The Complete Works of Washington Irving (hereafter CW), Volume VII. Boston, Twayne Publishers, 1984.

———. *A Tour on the Prairies*. Edited by James Playsted Wood. New York: Pantheon Books, 1967.

———. *Bracebridge Hall, Tales of a Traveller, The Alhambra*. Edited by Andrew B. Myers. Library of America 52. New York, Literary Classics of the United States, 1991.

———. *The Crayon Miscellany.* Edited by Dahlia Kirby Terrell. CW, XXII. Boston: Twayne Publishers, 1979.

———. *History, Tales, and Sketches.* New York: Literary Classics of the United States, Inc., 1983.

———. *Letters: Volume 1: 1802–1823.* Edited by Ralph M. Alderman, Herbert L. Kleinfeld, and Jenifer S. Banks. CW, Volume XXIII. Boston: Twayne Publishers, 1978.

———. *Letters, Volume II: 1823–1838.* Edited by Ralph Alderman, Herbert Kleinfeld and Jenifer Banks. CW, Volume XXIV. Boston, Twayne Publishers, 1979.

———. *Oliver Goldsmith: A Biography; Biography of the Late Margaret Miller Davidson.* Edited by Elsie Lee West. CW, Volume XVII. Boston: Twayne Publishers, 1978.

———. *The Sketch Book of Geoffrey Crayon, Gent.* Edited by Haskell Springer. CW, Volume VIII. Boston: Twayne Publishers, 1978.

Jefferson, Thomas. *Notes on the State of Virginia,* in *Thomas Jefferson: Writings.* Edited by Merrill D. Peterson. Library of America 17. New York, Literary Classics of the United States, Inc., 1984, 2011.

Jenkins, Ian, and Kim Sloan. *Vases and Volcanoes: Sir William Hamilton and His Collection.* London: British Museum Press, 1996.

Johnson, Deborah. ed. *William Sidney Mount: Painter of American Life.* New York: American Federation of Arts, 1998.

Jones, Brian Jay. *Washington Irving: An American Original.* New York: Arcade Publishing, 2008.

Kasson, Joy. *Artistic Voyagers: Europe and the American Imagination in the Works of Irving, Allston, Cole, Cooper, and Hawthorne.* Contributions in American Studies 60. Westport, Connecticut: Greenwood Press, 1983.

Kushner, Marilyn S. and Alejandro Anreus, Marion Grzesiak, and Virginia Wageman, eds. *Three Hundred Year of American Painting: The Montclair Art Museum Collection.* New York: Hudson Hills Press, 1989.

Laertius, Diogenes. *Lives of Eminent Philosophers,* Vol. II, trans. R. D. Hicks. Loeb Classics. Cambridge and London: Harvard University Press, 1931, 2005.

Langley, Batty. *New Principles of Gardening.* London: Bettesworth and Batley, 1728.

Lawall, David B. *Asher Durand: A Documentary Catalogue of the Narrative and Landscape Paintings.* New York & London: Garland Publishing, Inc., 1978.

Leslie, Charles Robert. *Memoirs of the Life of John Constable: Composed Chiefly of his Letters.* Landmarks in Art History. Ithaca: Cornell University Press, 1980, 1951.

———. *Autobiographical Recollections, Volume II,* edited by Tom Taylor. London: John Murray, 1860. Scholar Select Reprint.

Luarca-Shoaf, Nenette, ed. *Navigating the West: George Caleb Bingham and the River.* New Haven and London: Yale University Press, 2014.

Lubbers, Klause. *Born for the Shade: Stereotypes of the Native American in United States Literature and the Visual Arts, 1776–1894.* Amsterdam Monographs in American Studies 3. Amsterdam and Atlanta: Editions Rodopi B.V., 1994.

Lueck, Beth L. *American Writers and the Picturesque Tour: The Search for a National Identity, 1790–1860.* Garland Studies in 19th Century America 7. New York and London: Garland Publishing, Inc., 1997.

Mack, Maynard. *The Garden and the City: Retirement and Politics in the Later Poetry of Pope, 1731–1743.* Toronto and Buffalo: University of Toronto Press, 1969.

Mann, Barbara Alice. *George Washington's War on Native America.* Native America Yesterday and Today. Westport, Connecticut: Praeger, 2005.

Martin, Peter. *Pursuing Innocent Pleasures: The Gardening World of Alexander Pope.* Hamden: Archon Books, 1984.

Mattheissen, F. O. *American Renaissance: Art and Expression in the Age of Emerson and Whitman.* New York and London: Oxford University Press, 1941.

Merritt, Howard S. *To Walk with Nature: The Drawings of Thomas Cole.* Yonkers: The Hudson River Museum, 1981.

Miller, David, ed. *American Iconology: New Approaches to Nineteenth Century Art and Literature.* New Haven and London: Yale University Press, 1993.

de Montaigne, Michel. *The Complete Works: Essays, Travel Journal, Letters*, trans. Donald M. Frame. Everyman's Library. New York: Alfred A. Knopf, 1976.

Morison, Samuel Eliot. *The Oxford History of the American People.* New York: Oxford University Press, 1965.

Moore, Robert J, Jr. *Native Americans, A Portrait: The Art and Travels of Charles Bird King, George Catlin, and Karl Bodmer.* New York: Stewart, Tabori, and Chang, 1997.

Nuesner, Jacob, ed. *World Religions in America*, 4th ed., Louisville: Westminster John Knox Press, 2009.

Novak, Barbara. *American Painting of the Nineteenth Century: Realism, Idealism and the American Experience*, 3rd ed. Oxford and New York: Oxford University Press, 2007.

———. *Nature and Culture: American Landscape and Painting, 1825–1875*, 3rd ed. Oxford and New York: Oxford University Press, 2007.

Nussbaum, Martha. *The Cosmopolitan Tradition: A Noble but Flawed Ideal.* Cambridge and London: The Belknap Press of Harvard University Press, 2019.

———. *Cultivating Humanity.* Cambridge: Harvard University Press, 1997.

Nygren, Edward J. *Views and Visions: American Landscape before 1830.* Washington, D.C.: The Corcoran Gallery of Art, 1986.

Parry, Elwood C. III. *The Art of Thomas Cole: Ambition and Imagination.* The American Art Series. Newark: University of Delaware Press, 1988.

———. "Thomas Cole's Early Career: 1818–1829," in *Views and Visions: American Landscape before 1830*, edited by Edward J. Nygren. Washington, DC: Corcoran Gallery of Art, 1986.

Peck, H. Daniel. *Thomas Cole's Refrain: The Paintings of Catskill Creek.* Ithaca, Cornell University Press, 2019.

Pochmann, Henry A., "Irving's German Sources in 'The Sketch Book," *Studies in Philology* 27, no. 3 (July 1930): 477–507.

Prosperetti, Leopoldine. *Landscape and Philosophy in the Art of Jan Bruegel the Elder (1568–1625)*. New York and London: Routledge, Taylor & Francis Group, 2016; Ashgate, 2009.

Ringe, Donald A., "New York and New England: Irving's Criticism of American Society," *American Literature* 38, no. 4 (Jan. 1967): 455–67.

———. *The Pictorial Mode: Space and Time in the Art of Bryant, Irving and Cooper*. Lexington: University of Kentucky Press, 1971.

Remini, Robert V. *Andrew Jackson and his Indian Wars*. New York: Viking Penguin, 2001.

Rosenberg, Pierre, and Keith Christiansen, eds., *Poussin and Nature: Arcadian Visions*. New York: The Metropolitan Museum of Art, 2008.

Rosenthal, Michael. *Constable: The Painter and his Landscape*. New Haven and London: Yale University Press, 1983.

Rubin-Dorsky, Jeffery. *Adrift in the Old World: The Psychological Pilgrimage of Washington Irving*. Chicago and London: University of Chicago Press, 1988.

Ruland, Richard, and Malcom Bradbury. *From Puritanism to Postmodernism: A History of American Literature*. New York: Viking, 1991.

Rutherford, Sarah. *Capability Brown and His Landscape Gardens*. London: National Trust books, 2016.

Saranski, Rüdiger. *Romanticism: A German Affair*. Translated by Robert E. Goodwin. Evanston, Northwestern University Press, 2014 (original German Verlag, 2007).

Sarna, Jonathan D. *American Judaism: A History*. New Haven and London: Yale University Press, 2004.

Seigel, Nancy. *Along the Juniata: Thomas Cole and the Dissemination of American Landscape Imagery*. Huntingdon, PA: Juniata College Museum of Art, 2003.

Shaftesbury, Earl of, Anthony Ashley Cooper. *Characteristics of Men, Manners, Opinions, Times*. Edited by Lawrence E. Klein. Cambridge Texts in the History of Philosophy. Cambridge: University Press, 1999.

Slaughter, Thomas P. *The Natures of John and William Bartram*. New York: Alfred A. Knopf, 1996.

Smith, Huston. *The World's Religions: Our Great Wisdom Traditions*. New York and San Francisco: HarperSanFrancisco, 1991.

Solkin, David H. *Richard Wilson: The Landscape of Reaction*. London: The Tate Gallery, 1982.

Sonnabend, Martin, and John Whiteley. *Claude Lorrain: The Enchanted Landscape*. Oxford: Ashmolean Museum, 2011.

Spongberg, Stephen A. *A Reunion of Trees: The Discovery of Exotic Plants and Their Introduction into North American and European Landscapes*. Cambridge and London: Harvard University Press, 1990.

Stuart, David O. *American Emperor: Aaron Burr's Challenge to Jefferson's America*. New York: Simon and Schuster, 2011.

Sutton, Peter C. *The Age of Rubens*. Boston: Museum of Fine Arts, 1993.

Treuttner, William H. *The Natural Man Observed: A Study of Catlin's Indian Gallery*. Washington, DC: Smithsonian Institution Press, 1979.

———. *The West as America: Reinterpreting Images of the Frontier, 1820–1920.* Washington and London: Smithsonian Institution Press, 1991.

Thompson, Terry. "'Lively But Complicated': English Hegemony in 'The Legend of Sleepy Hollow.'" *Midwest Quarterly* 54, no. 2 (Winter 2013): 136–48.

Tuttleton, James W. *A Fine Silver Thread: Essays on American Writing and Criticism.* Chicago: Ivan R. Dee, 1998.

Verhoogt, Robert. *Art in Reproduction: Nineteenth Century Prints after Lawrence Alma-Tadema, Joseph Israels and Ary Sheffer.* Amsterdam: Amsterdam University Press, 2007.

Virgil. *The Eclogues of Virgil: Bilingual Edition*, trans. David Ferry. New York: Farrar, Straus and Gireaux, 1999.

Virgil. *Virgil's Georgics: A New Verse Translation*, trans. Janet Lembke. New Haven and London: Yale University Press, 2005.

Wallace, Anthony J. C. *Jefferson and the Indians: The Tragic Fate of the First Americans.* Cambridge: Belknap Press of Harvard University Press, 1999.

Wallach, Alan, "Thomas Cole and the Aristocracy," in *Reading American Art*, edited by Marianne Doezema and Elizabeth Milroy, 79–108. New Haven and London: Yale University Press, 1998.

———. "Thomas Cole and Transatlantic Romanticism," in *Transatlantic Romanticism: British and American Art and Literature, 1790–1860*, edited by Andrew Hemingway and Alan Wallach. Amhurst and Boston: University of Massachusetts Press, 2015.

———. "Thomas Cole: Landscape and the Course of Empire," in *Thomas Cole: Landscape into History*, edited by William H. Treuttner and Alan Wallach, 23–112. New Haven and London: Yale University Press, 1994:

———. "Thomas Cole's *River in the Catskills* as Antipastoral." *Art Bulletin* LXXXIV, no. 2 (June 2002): 334–50.

———. "What's in a Name? Interpreting Thomas Cole's *Course of Empire*." Beecher Lecture. 24 November 2019. Thomas Cole National Historic Site.

Weber, Susan, ed. *William Kent: Designing Georgian Britain.* New Haven and London: Yale University Press, 2014.

West, Michael. *Transcendental Wordplay: America's Romantic Punsters and the Search for the Language of Nature.* Athens: Ohio University Press, 2000.

Williams, Stanley T. The Life of Washington Irving. Vol. I–II. New York: Oxford University Press, 1935.

Williams, Stanley T. *The Spanish Background of American Literature.* Vol. I. New Haven, Yale University Press, 1955.

Wolf, Bryan Jay. *Romantic Revision: Culture and Consciousness in Nineteenth Century American Painting and Literature.* Chicago and London: University of Chicago Press, 1982.

Wordsworth, Jonathon, Michel C. Jaye, and Robert Woof. *William Wordsworth and the Age of English Romanticism.* New Brunswick and London: Rutgers University Press, 1987.

Wordsworth, William. *The Prelude, with Selected Poems and Sonnets*, edited by Carlos Baker. New York: Holt, Rinehart and Winston, Inc., 1954.

Index

Addison, Joseph, 10, 22–23
aesthetics: Irving's subversion of the sublime, 113–19; of association, 68–73; of the beautiful, 65–67; of the picturesque, 65, 79–81; of the sublime, 65–66, 79–80
African Americans, representations of, 49–55, 149–55, 169
Alison, Archibald, 67–68
Allston, Washington, 3, 84–87
archeology, British, 68–71

Bingham, George Caleb, 160–61
Boime, Albert, 50–52, 150–51
Burke, Edmund, 65–69

Cole, Thomas, xi, 10–11, 76, 81, 108, 126–27, 136–38, 142–44
Cynic philosophy, 16–20, 25, 55, 166–68

Durand, Asher, 140–42

Emerson, Ralph Waldo, 44–45

folk traditions, 9, 11, 15

gardening and landscaping, 18th-century English, 89–91

Gilpin, William, 68, 70–71, 75
Goldsmith, Oliver, 5, 16, 24
Grand Tour, 69–70, 72, 78, 82

A History of New York, 42–58, 127–29, 138–40, 155–57
Hudson River, 110–13, 124
Hume, David, 9–10

Irving, Washington: abroad, 3–5, 82–86; diplomatic temperament of, 25–26, 155; and ecology, 131–33, 138–40, 163–65; gardening and landscaping, 7, 87–89; politics of, 15, 19; religion, attitude toward, 13, 15, 37–45, 56–58n2, 82–83, 141

Jefferson, Thomas, and Native Americans, 19, 47–48; land hunger, 131

"The Legend of Sleepy Hollow," 7–8, 123, 128–29, 133–36, 150–53
Locke, John, empiricist influence on literature, 6–9, 64–65
Lorraine, Claude, 73–79, 83, 100, 111, 123

mixed-race peoples, attitudes toward, 155–63

Mount, William Sidney, 50–51, 153–55
Native Americans, 19, 44, 46–49, 103–8, 162–68

Ovid, 83, 99, 102, 131–33; Ovidian mode, 103–5, 109–11

pendants, 110–11
Pope, Alexander, 5, 70–71, 81–83, 89, 95n57, 105–7, 165

Quakers, 56–58

Radcliffe, Ann, 64, 96n72, 118

"Rip Van Winkle", 8, 11–12, 123, 133–35
romanticism, 2, 9, 13–14, 84
Rubin-Dorsky, Jeffrey, 4–5, 133–35

Scott, Sir Walter, 3, 22, 88, 136–37

A Tour on the Prairies, 155–69

Virgil, 99, 109

Williams, Stanley, 5–6, 162, 168
Wilson, Richard, 100–102

Yankees, 124–36, 159

About the Author

J. Woodrow McCree was raised in central and southern Illinois, where he first appreciated woods and country lanes. His academic interests arose through the influence of a farming family that would read history books during the long Midwestern winters. He studied English literature at Augustana College in Rock Island, Illinois, and from there went on to get an MA in English and American Literature at the University of Illinois at Champaign-Urbana. At the University of Illinois, he also completed an MA in Philosophy, focusing on ethics and philosophy of religion. He went on to do a PhD in the History of Ancient Christianity at Union Theological Seminary in the city of New York.

Dr. McCree has taught philosophy and religion at community colleges and state colleges in New Jersey, Ohio, and Florida. In the last decade at the State College of Florida, Manatee-Sarasota, his research has taken an interdisciplinary turn, with interests ranging from native plant landscaping to support wildlife, to the Hudson River School of painting, aesthetic theory in eighteenth-century England, the intersection of romantic art and literature, and the history of naturalistic landscaping. He recently presented on Washington Irving at the American Literature Association with the Washington Irving Society, and on Thomas Cole at the American Academy of Religion Southeastern Regional Conference.

www.ingramcontent.com/pod-product-compliance
Lightning Source LLC
Chambersburg PA
CBHW061715300426
44115CB00014B/2697